10.95

UNCERTAIN GREATNESS

UNCERTAIN GREATNESS

Henry Kissinger and
American Foreign Policy

ROGER MORRIS

1817

HARPER & ROW, PUBLISHERS
NEW YORK, HAGERSTOWN, SAN FRANCISCO
LONDON

For Peter, Ethan, and Dylan

That your foreign policy should be far better,
and your country's true greatness, its example,
no longer in doubt

Brief passages of this book have appeared in substantially different form in *The New York Times*, the *New Republic*, the Columbia Journalism *Review*, the *Progressive*, and the *Washington Monthly*, and acknowledgment is given those publications.

FIRST EDITION

Designed by Sidney Feinberg

Library of Congress Cataloging in Publication Data

Morris, Roger.
  Uncertain greatness.
  Includes index.
  1. United States—Foreign relations—1969–1974.
2. United States—Foreign relations—1974–1977.
3. Kissinger, Henry Alfred. 4. Statesmen—United States
—Biography. I. Title.
E855.M67 1977   327.73   75-30339
ISBN 0–06–013097–0

77 78 79 80 10 9 8 7 6 5 4 3 2 1

Contents

58040

Contents

Acknowledgments

Defending the Vietnam war in the late 1960s, McGeorge Bundy reportedly told a college audience that former officials who had seen the making of foreign policy at the higher levels held a loaded gun at the head of the President of the United States. Those witnesses, he argued, should not reveal what they really knew from their inside view of men and events. It was a matter of honor as well as national security.

As so much else presumed by Bundy and men like him—most especially Henry Kissinger—the point is wrong, the analogy twisted. That figurative gun in foreign policy is always in the hands of those in power, whatever their politics, from the bureaucracy to the senior officialdom of the establishment, to the President himself. It is loaded with ignorance, incompetence, hypocrisy and deceit. And the heads under its barrel belong to the rest of us—mostly that relatively less affluent, less educated, less well-connected majority of Americans whose sons do the dying and whose pocketbooks do the paying that are the true costs of foreign policy.

This book is an effort to begin unloading that gun. It makes no pretense to be either a comprehensive record of American foreign policy during 1969–1976 or a conventional biography. It does not probe a number of important issues and events—most notably, perhaps, the international economic problems Kissinger himself so long ignored. That larger history, and the deserved biography, will have to await the distant opening (if ever) of official memories and archives. Meanwhile, I have tried no more nor less than to give some analysis of and insight into the man and the main thrust of his diplomacy at home and abroad, to explain in intensely human terms why and how much of it happened as it did, and so to draw a unique portrait of the making of U.S. foreign policy—all with a relevance that reaches well beyond Henry Kissinger and the régimes he served.

The book draws on my own experience in the State Department and White House from 1966 to 1970 and as a Senate aide from 1970 to 1972, with the obvious limits and advantages of an intense personal involvement. The narrative depends too on the eyewitness accounts of several other people who saw Henry Kissinger and his policies from the inside. Some are still in government; some have left and hope to return; some have just come back with the new Carter Administration; all requested anonymity. So I must pay several debts with this one general acknowledgment, and hope that some day soon the puckered little conventions of career and foreign policy will afford human beings to say openly what they know and feel, without forfeiting their rung on the ladder.

In the freer air of published sources, I have admired and profited very much from the remarkable investigative journalism of Tad Szulc, Laurence Stern, and Seymour Hersh; from John Newhouse's *Cold Dawn*, a skillful evocation of the SALT negotiations; and especially from *Nightmare*, by J. Anthony Lukas, by far the best book among so many on the generic beast of Watergate. Not least I must thank the several Congressional investigators, fortunately braver and more imaginative than their employers, who for a fleeting moment in 1974–1975 managed to excavate some squalid relics of the foreign policy record for all of us to see, if we would.

I owe special gratitude to Kitty Benedict, my editor at Harper & Row, whose patience, tolerance of some tortuous delays and uncertainties, and sheer skill and encouragement were all extraordinary. And to James Fox, also of Harper & Row, whose help with the final editing was truly remarkable in stamina as well as wisdom.

Most of all, I want to thank again all those who loved and supported me through this book, and they, of course, know who they are.

ROGER MORRIS

Tesuque, New Mexico

Prologue

It is Moscow, the spring of 1972.

At midnight, Friday, May 26, the leaders of the United States and the Soviet Union come to the gold and green hall of St. Vladimir in the Kremlin to sign the first SALT agreement limiting nuclear arms. The climax of months of negotiations and a frantic last day of bargaining, the treaty is historic. It is due largely to the statesmanship of two Americans, who now stand characteristically ill at ease amid the social small talk of the two delegations before the signing ceremony begins. For both men, the occasion is a personal and political triumph. Photographers record their smiles. Yet the moment is also full of irony, much of it tragic and unseen.

Henry Alfred Kissinger will be forty-nine the next day. A refugee from Nazi Germany, he is becoming the most powerful and celebrated public servant in modern American history. He has risen dutifully and carefully, as Harvard professor, Pentagon consultant, and adviser to Nelson Rockefeller, through the establishment that has run America's foreign policy. But he is among and not of that élite; privately, he disdains many of its members and much of its diplomacy.

He is brilliant, ambitious, publicly charming, privately petty, consistently successful, and ever anxious about his prospects. For all practical purposes, he is now the sole executor of U.S. foreign policy, its achievements and its disgraces, though relatively few of the latter are yet known or understood by an enthralled press and public watching his performance. "The main point stems from the fact that I've always acted alone," he will later analyze his acclaim for an interviewer. "Americans admire that enormously. Americans admire the cowboy leading the caravan alone astride his horse . . ."

Ahead is a Nobel Prize, tenure as Secretary of State, and a popularity which will eclipse that of the two presidents he serves. But he will never be more powerful, or more relevant, than he is this night in the Kremlin.

He has earned a place in history with the détente he has negotiated in Moscow and Peking by seizing the foreign and domestic opportunities for the United States to come to terms at last with the Russian and Chinese revolutions. Significant as it is, however, that grand settlement is a belated recognition of an era that has already ended. Neither his genius nor his politics match the world that is emerging. America's greatest diplomat, he serves at a moment when his diplomacy is becoming an anachronism.

Richard Milhous Nixon, thirty-seventh President of the United States, is now fifty-nine. He won office in 1968 by a narrow margin. Until this spring, his administration has been without conspicuous accomplishment or wide public support. He has run behind in presidential campaign polls over the past year, and he believes that he must now take extraordinary steps, both at home and abroad, to retrieve the situation. After a quarter of a century's political career erected on shrill anticommunism, he has come to Moscow in part to gain reelection.

He is intelligent, bigoted, and reclusive, a nearly characterless President who presides over a foreign policy of enlightened initiative and sophistication, of ignorance and impulsive savagery. He is fresh from a dramatic trip to Peking in February that, to the approval of most Americans, has moderated over two decades of ominous hostility with the world's largest country—a hostility Nixon himself had nurtured and exploited in seeking national office. After these summit meetings, he will never again trail in the polls on the way to a sweeping reelection. And he will never again travel abroad without fatal public doubt about the integrity of his leadership.

When the agreement has been signed, champagne arrives. The ritual toasts are made. Nixon acknowledges his Soviet hosts, then finds Kissinger's eyes across the hall. He silently raises his glass in a private, personal tribute. Kissinger returns the gesture, smiling broadly.

To his staff, Kissinger has often referred to Nixon early in the administration as "my drunken friend," and jokes about him contemptuously. To others, he will later say with equal earnestness that Nixon is "genuinely heroic." His words express conviction as well as his customary ingratiation toward the audience of the moment. Kissinger sees in the President a fearful and beguiling mixture of weakness and decisiveness. It is the lack of such decisiveness, believe men close to him, that Kissinger doubts most in himself. In a sense Kissinger is the vacillating politician, Nixon the brooding intellectual now given the power to act. The paradox haunts both men and the government they conduct. It also eludes most observers, who prefer, for their own reasons, to see each man in his preconceived role.

"I don't trust Henry, but I can use him," Nixon confided to one of Kissinger's rivals at the outset of the administration. Among the handful of men who shield him from the hostile press and politics he feels all around him in Washington, Nixon sees Kissinger as an outsider to be watched, a man with his own alien constituency, yet perhaps the one figure who can save the régime from its many enemies.

Later, in the spring of 1975, his presidency and reputation shattered in scandal, Nixon will telephone his former adviser as public criticism of Kissinger mounts after the fall of South Vietnam. Aptly, Kissinger is then meeting with President Ford and cannot take the call. "Tell Henry to stay in there," the familiar voice says to an astonished Kissinger aide. "He's a great man and the country needs him." Kissinger, when told of the call, is visibly moved.

The relationship between the two men is complex, contradictory, and momentous. In its impact on world politics and American government, their collaboration may be the most important event of the century. Their mutual respect and suspicion, honesty and deception, have shaped decisions of enormous human cost. From the beginning, aides to both men were anxious to cite differences between them, but no one is able to document major distinctions in their approach to policy. "I'll never know where one ended and the other began," admits an official closest to their decisions. "Our Ludendorff and Hindenberg," another aide calls them, with a sense of their ultimate aloofness and the vast life-and-death power they dispose. Yet the relationship seems without genuine precedent. Its fascinating psychology will be largely lost to history in the secrecy of their encounters and the self-serving distortions of each man's public memory.

Together, they have carried out—and been caught in—a revolution in the making of foreign policy. They replaced an administration of worse misrule in foreign affairs than even its critics suspected. From widely different vantage points, they see more clearly than any of their Democratic counterparts the careerism and conventions that have rendered American diplomacy not just impotent but often tragicomic. They share a bitter scorn of bureaucracy. They distrust the abilities and motives of most of the other senior officials with whom they govern. They have fastened an unprecedented White House control—Kissinger's control—over the many provinces of decisionmaking in foreign relations. And by a combination of intellectual superiority, evasion, compromise, and plain lying, they have made it work.

On several fronts they have broken through the customary inertia and mediocrity of bureaucratic government. They are ideological and pragmatic. They can be more reactionary than their critics on the right, more accommodating than the left. They preempt much of their opposition in American politics by simply accomplishing most of the actions their Democratic predecessors advocated but could never realize. They have often moved, as they orchestrated the negotiations that brought them to the Kremlin, with an audacity and skill beyond parallel in recent American history. When they wish, their will is now total, dangerously beyond restraint in a submissive executive and hesitant Congress.

But it has been a revolution without larger purpose. It will leave no lasting reform. To remedy arbitrary and disorderly government, to avoid mistakes, they have believed in and established only themselves. Their system has substituted the flawed judgment and passion of two men for the wider if ponderous bargaining of bureaucratic ambitions. With disarming humor, Kissinger more than once in 1969 assured critics of the Vietnam war, "We will not repeat the same old mistakes." (A pause for effect.) "We will make our own"—it will be an unintended prophecy, for Indochina and elsewhere.

Obscured by the headline diplomacy in Moscow and Peking is another world of blunder and neglect. By the spring of 1972, the record already includes a calculated disregard of enormous human catastrophe in South Asia, a feckless indifference to international economic issues, and an affinity for tyrannical régimes that will have its reckoning for U.S. interests on every continent.

Then there is Vietnam. Both men took office promising peace. It is still more than four years away. Of all the trusts to be broken by this government, none will be more costly in sheer human anguish. Before it is over, the poisonous boundaries of the war will have spread throughout Indochina. More Americans and Asians will have been killed or wounded, more devastation wrought, under the policy of Henry Kissinger and Richard Nixon than during the previous administration supposedly driven from office by the war. Now the final negotiations have begun here in Moscow. There will be many more months of needless carnage.

In the end, as figures in a Greek drama, their own will seems to thwart their purpose. Though they feel an unconcealed disgust for the foreign policy bureaucracy and establishment élite, they share the traditional contempt of both for authentic public knowledge and participation in international relations. The means of their government—its secrecy, its expediency, its ruthlessness—will eventually corrupt and nearly destroy the very concept of national security they are both so intent to preserve. They will have wrenched American foreign policy out of its past at the price of essential public trust in its future. All this as well belongs to these two men who stand smiling proudly at one another in St. Vladimir's Hall.

Their moment of triumph is brief. The toasts are soon over. The delegations leave the hall, Nixon to his bed in the Kremlin apartment, Kissinger to give a dazzling and triumphant news conference to his admirers in the press in the tawdry nightclub of a Moscow hotel. As he talks to reporters it is already past midnight, now Saturday, May 27, his birthday. This same night in Washington—"on or about May 27," in the words of the House Judiciary Committee's report on impeachment—the plumbers attempt their first break-in at the Democratic Party Headquarters in the Watergate Apartments. They will try again.

And so these men will pass another, very different historic midnight two years later. As Nixon resigns the presidency in disgrace, he telephones Kissinger again and again, long into the early morning hours. Their talk is maudlin, and poignant.

Wistful, already detached, Kissinger says to an assistant after one of the calls, "History will treat him better." That too is ironic.

Though he survives in office for two more years, Kissinger must also look beyond the moment to a longer view. Behind the semblance of his success, building as relentlessly as the evidence that has destroyed Nixon, are the forces of a different world—new limits on American power to deal with the most dangerous crises abroad, and a corrosive new cynicism toward leadership in foreign policy at home. For Henry Kissinger, as for the country he has led from one era to another, greatness is still uncertain.

I

---◆---

"By People Who Are Expert at It" —Foreign Policy, 1968

There would be a sense of the meeting as climactic, a turning point. Yet at the time there was no audible drama in their talk. These men were suitably casual in their manner of making great decisions about America and the world. Though they sat in the White House with Lyndon B. Johnson and spoke of war and terrible human suffering, reality was sealed off by their trite, lifeless vernacular: "capabilities," "objectives," "our chips," "giveaway." It was a matter, too, of culture and style. They spoke with the cool, deliberate detachment of men who believe that the banishment of feeling renders them wise and, more important, credible to other men.

They were indeed known as the "Wise Men" by a press and President given to ready labels. Among them were famous figures of America's rise to world responsibility, names still ringed with the aura of great events. They included General of the Army Omar Bradley, former Secretary of State Dean Acheson, General Matthew Ridgway who commanded U.S. troops in Korea, Arthur Dean, negotiator of the Korean War settlement, and Robert Murphy, the professional diplomat who had been political adviser to the American high command in Europe during World War II. From a later period came Henry Cabot Lodge, former senator, U.S. representative in the United Nations, and ambassador to South Vietnam; General Maxwell Taylor, World War II hero, former army chief of staff, chairman of the joint chiefs, and another ambassador in Saigon; former Treasury

Secretary and Under Secretary of State Douglas Dillon; McGeorge Bundy, who had been Special Assistant for National Security to both Presidents Kennedy and Johnson; Cyrus Vance, once a Deputy Secretary of Defense; and George Ball, lately an Under Secretary of State.

The average age of the group was nearly seventy. Their combined experience at the highest levels of policy spanned three decades and the administrations of five presidents. They represented continuity with a past in which American might had grown, swiftly, undefeated, unquestioned, from the provincial isolationist country of the Depression to the economic and military superpower of the 1960s. They were an élite of attained rank as well as class—men like Bradley and Taylor whom the army lifted from obscure origins in Missouri joined with an Acheson, a Lodge, and a Dillon, representatives of the social and financial élite who came to government from the patrician families and private schools, the old law firms and banking houses of the East. More important than their varied origins or the predictable shades of personality and mind, they were all members, now the most senior members, of the foreign policy establishment—the 100 or so officials and ex-officials, patrons and protégés, who had dominated American foreign policy for the last quarter-century. Their disagreements confined to tactics, they shared a common view of the basic interests and purposes of the United States in international affairs, and an unquestioned acceptance of the propriety, to most of them the sheer necessity, of men like themselves, solid and dependable men, making decisions on these fateful matters. As Acheson put it with characteristic elegance and authority in his farewell remarks to the State Department in 1953, national security is "a problem which must be dealt with wisely and justly and quietly by people who are expert at it."

They had made, after all, so many decisions in foreign policy—or were generally presumed to have made them. They had spent so many years in that secret realm of interdepartmental meetings, of urgent cables, of intelligence operations and reports, of calls to the White House. Each was accustomed to the intimate talks with men who ruled elsewhere, and, always, they were aware of the presence of history. Surely, they knew how to cope with the troublesome and seemingly bewildering perils and irritations that pressed upon the nation from abroad. Not least, they had learned how to deal as well with the uninitiated presidents, the politicians who came and went and needed their help, and in whose name the decisions were announced to the waiting world. It was all familiar to these men. Their special province was not something, they and many others believed, that anyone could be trusted to understand: only they were equipped to deal with the mysteries and mystique of foreign policy.

Experience was their ultimate certification, and the source of their own certainty. In that sense, they were all men who had played by the rules, had been well rewarded, and took the game for granted. Now the rules had summoned them from private life, from the comfortable "retirement" of business, to another secret meeting, another decision to be reached, discussed in discreet, manly tones. They were known officially as the "Senior Advisory Group" of the President of the United States. Today Lyndon Johnson had invited them to lunch at the White House to consider the war in Vietnam, where developments were not going as well as expected.

Only four months earlier, as often in the past, the group had given its weighty reassurance to the administration's involvement in Southeast Asia. "The really smart people out there know we're on the right track," Johnson summed up for a puzzled Indian diplomat after his November 1967 meeting with the "Wise Men." Now, suddenly, everything had changed.

Through February and early March 1968, the Tet offensive had shattered the remaining façade of Washington's war policy. On February 2 an anxious President, unknowingly armed with reports deliberately falsified for bureaucratic self-protection by both the military and the CIA, called White House reporters into the Cabinet Room to pronounce the attack "a complete failure." Scarcely three weeks later, he entered the same room to receive a request from his military commanders for more than 200,000 additional U.S. troops in the field. Tet had been "a very near thing," reported the chairman of the joint chiefs, General Earle Wheeler, after a hurried visit to Saigon in late February. The reinforcements were necessary, he told the President, "to regain the initiative."

Unstated but starkly implicit in the troop request was the larger reality the administration had long struggled to deny to itself as well as to the public: that the war could be neither won nor controlled at some politically acceptable margin of human and material sacrifice. Amid all the figures cascading over the Vietnam policy, the endless

Pentagon counts, the vague, strained calculus of White House and Treasury economists, the government would somehow never bring itself to add up the single, comprehensive cost of the war, its insidious toll of inflation as well as the waste of thousands of lives and billions in national wealth. But from tortured budgetary and manpower decisions of 1967, the White House would know well enough the reckoning of these further troop commitments in 1968. To send 200,000 additional men would mean at least a partial call-up of reserves and, unavoidably, some wartime controls over the economy. The Tet reinforcements now drew Johnson, a President who wanted desperately to be remembered for his domestic achievements, into the lengthening shadows of national mobilization.

The issue had been settled during Tet by the Viet Cong sappers who briefly occupied the U.S. Embassy in Saigon in full view of American television. Over a few savage hours, the Viet Cong's demonstration of strength destroyed the apathy and naïveté that had provided the balance of American public consent to a growing commitment of U.S. troops in Vietnam. The intervention in America's electoral politics was decisive. Ten thousand miles away, in New Hampshire, a Johnson campaign aide and a British reporter watched workers leave a factory on a February evening before the state's presidential primary. "There they go," the politician said ruefully, "all our voters . . . straight home to television." By mid-March, Senator Eugene McCarthy had nearly defeated Johnson in New Hampshire, and Senator Robert Kennedy had joined the presidential race. All this evidence of disarray in U.S. policy, save perhaps the details of the Pentagon maneuvering on the troop request, was dramatically apparent as the "Wise Men" gathered the last week in March to advise the President. It was less evident, to them or to the country, that Vietnam was in fact only the most conspicuous failure of the administration in foreign affairs.

So vast was the carnage it brought, so huge the public repudiation it eventually provoked, so widespread the wreckage of ideals and reputations, that the Vietnam war would seem to many, in 1968 and afterward, an unparalleled calamity of American policy, a single tragic intersection of men and mistakes. Yet if the sheer magnitude of the disaster seemed unique, perhaps even accidental, the flaws it exposed in government were not. The intellectual shallowness, the consuming personal ambitions, the bureaucratic arrogance and inertia, the fatal weaknesses of presidential leadership: all had become pervasive in the making of U.S. foreign policy. The consequences outside Vietnam, however, the dangers and the absurdities inherent in American policies around the world, were still largely hidden, invisible behind the official secrecy and indifferent monitoring of Congress and press that had long masked the war. But in 1968, American diplomacy in most of the rest of the world had found its way into many another quagmire, unaided by the Viet Cong.

The summer before Tet had provided unusually apt and serious examples of this wider disarray. In June 1967, the Six-Day War in the Middle East and a US-Soviet summit meeting at Glassboro, New Jersey, momentarily blotted out Washington's preoccupation with Vietnam. Both events produced briefly the general public support of government still customary in international crises and summit diplomacy, providing a last, fleeting interval for the Johnson administration before the mortal blows of the coming winter. Outwardly, it all seemed the way foreign policy was supposed to work. The White House, suitably firm about American interests, was seen gravely watching the Israelis and Arabs, and, of course, the Russians, until the war lapsed again into the endless diplomatic bickering synonymous with the Middle East. Inside the government, the crisis was managed with all the customary trappings, including due attention to the public imagery. The "Wise Men" were represented by McGeorge Bundy, called back for the occasion by Johnson from the presidency of the Ford Foundation to become a temporary "Special Consultant on the Middle East" and thereby principal administration spokesman on the war. Bundy was to take public charge of a policy in which Presidential Assistant Walt W. Rostow and his brother Eugene, an Under Secretary of State, were thought too conspicuous, the President being worried, as he said to several aides at the time, "how it'd look to have two Jewish boys from New Haven running my even-handed Middle East policy."

There was even a putative confrontation with the Russians on June 10, when Johnson sent the Sixth Fleet steaming toward the Syrian coast after a belligerent hot-line message from Kosygin about the Israeli refusal to observe a cease-fire with Syria. The cease-fire agreement was concluded in hours, however, and the crisis dissipated. Within weeks, the President of the United States, now smiling, now somber, was in earnest conversation at Glassboro, New Jersey, with the chairman of the Soviet Council of Ministers, Aleksei Kosygin. Johnson helicoptered back to the White House after the secret talks to reassure the reporters and cameras positioned to await him on the South Lawn that the meeting with the Russians had indeed "made the world a little smaller and also a little less dangerous." Just how "little" would not be manifest until years afterward.

The Middle East conflict of 1967 was one of those decisive turnings that unmistakably alter the contours of world politics. Between June 5 and 10, Israeli forces smashed the Arab armies on three fronts and stood unchallenged on the banks of the Suez Canal and the Jordan River. It was the model preventive war of Israel's strategists, and, of its kind, the last. Out of the shattering defeat came a massive Soviet rearmament and modernization of Arab forces, the outline of which would be visible to U.S. intelligence almost from the day the war ended. Politically, Israel's occupation of Arab territories in the Sinai, the West Bank of the Jordan, and the Golan Heights embedded new and still more volatile conditions of hostility. The aftermath of the Six-Day War thus presented a rare and urgent opportunity for creative diplomacy before the situation hardened. At the least, it was an occasion for a searching reappraisal of policy. Yet the moment passed with the U.S. government unable to act on the portent.

The surface alacrity and toughness of Washington's public pose in June 1967 hid an inner malaise in the Johnson administration that worked to prevent even official recognition of the new conditions left by the war, much less the creation of a fresh policy. Only once in the fleeting months after the war, in mid-June following the cease-fire, was there an effort to review U.S. interests in the region. The method and the result were telling, typical of the Middle East and others in the making of foreign policy. Filtered through the bureaucracy, the policy papers ordered by the White House emerged as the customary bland consensus of departmental interests. The Pentagon reiterated its long-standing enthusiasm for arms aid to Israel, which should definitely be continued; the Central Intelligence Agency presented as usual an alarming portrait of rising Soviet influence among the Arabs, which would bear watching; the State Department offered an optimistic forecast for negotiations in the United Nations, which should be pursued.

"Same old shit, isn't it?" Johnson once asked an aide, as he ruffled the pages of the thick, top-secret looseleaf notebook filled by the Mideast "review." About all this, as in the deliberations on Vietnam and other problems, there was a fatalistic, almost surreal quality. Below, the vast bureaucracy consciously blurred its language and formulations, resisting changes of policy as a potential threat to institutional and personal interests, surrendering judgment to the momentum of moving the appointed papers through the interdepartmental gamut. Above, the political leadership knowingly scorned and discounted the bureaucracy in its self-protection, its barren papers. Yet lacking the intellectual resources to dispense with it, or the political will to reform it, the President and his senior officials eventually deferred as well to the system. The Lyndon Johnson who moved swiftly to mend the public appearances of "two Jewish boys from New Haven" could not, would not, remedy the real problem posed by the Middle East in the summer of 1967: the absence of an American policy to deal with perhaps the most dangerous issue in world politics. Meanwhile, its bitter results left to work on Arab pride, June 1967 became the parent of October 1973. Ahead lay a far more serious U.S.-Soviet confrontation. And from the next Mideast war emerged the Arab oil embargo, with its still incalculable costs for Israel, the United States, western Europe, Japan, and, most tragically, for millions in the poor nations of the world. There is no assurance that a different reaction by the U.S. government in 1967 and afterward might have avoided the calamity of the October sequel. The success of later American mediation efforts showed clearly, however, that the Arab-Israeli hostility was not immutable. But in 1967, bureaucratic inertia and an indifferent leadership deprived American diplomacy of its greatest asset: its possibilities as mediator and negotiator.

Within a few weeks of the Six-Day War, the Glassboro summit provided the façade for a very different though equally typical phenomenon in foreign policy. For months before the summit, the Johnson administration had been mired in a confused quarrel over the deployment of an anti-ballistic missile (ABM) system. The main protagonists were Secretary of Defense Robert McNamara, initially skeptical of the ABM both as a practical weapon and for its negative effect on possible arms control negotiations, and the joint chiefs, who advocated an American ABM to match what seemed then a fledgling Soviet ABM deployment, though military and CIA intelligence varied widely on the nature and possible effectiveness of the Soviet system. Allied with the chiefs were influential conservatives in the Congress, led by Senator Richard Russell, then chairman of the Senate Armed Services Committee. Between the two factions sat the President, vague on the issue, generally sympathetic to arms control, but more worried that a refusal to deploy the ABM might be used against him by Republican opposition (perhaps spurred by the disaffected joint chiefs) in the 1968 election.

Johnson had nearly decided to go ahead with a major anti-Soviet ABM defense of American cities when he met with McNamara and the chiefs at his Texas ranch in early December 1966. McNamara, always reluctant to lose a policy battle with his Pentagon rivals, averted defeat by a last-minute and largely makeshift bureaucratic compromise. The United States would postpone a final decision on ABM deployment while the State Department hastily proposed to the Russians the first round of negotiations on limiting strategic arms, including in the first instance ABMs. If the Soviets did not "come across," as the President put it, they could build the ABM "with a clear conscience." The administration decided almost inadvertently to enter on one of the most complex and fateful negotiations in the history of diplomacy, not with a careful preparation or a precise understanding of the issues, least of all with a sense of the necessary patience and perseverance, but rather seeing the negotiations as an expedient, a device to paper over bureaucratic indecision and presidential politics.

Through the winter of 1967 followed a series of diplomatic approaches to Moscow, the usually lethargic State Department spurred by McNamara personally. Not surprisingly, the talks were still inconclusive and Pentagon pressures to build the ABM were still mounting when Kosygin and Johnson met in June at Glassboro. "Name the place," Johnson pressed Kosygin nonetheless on the arms control talks; "Secretary McNamara is ready." In reality, Washington was no more "ready" than Moscow for the bureaucratic discipline and rigorous analysis needed for strategic arms limitation negotiations. Ahead for the next administration were months of intricate and tortured bargaining within the U.S. government before agreement could be concluded with the Russians. The purpose of Glassboro was not authentic negotiations; the summit and the first tentative talks before were something to be "tried" for bureaucratic reasons. And the failure to get an immediate agreement with Kosygin now became a pretext for a policy that had little to do with genuine security needs or diplomatic prospects. Less than three months after Glassboro, the Russians not having "come across," Johnson ordered McNamara to announce the decision to deploy an ABM system. It would be a "lighter" deployment than the joint chiefs had advocated, aimed ostensibly against a Chinese nuclear threat. But that only emphasized the underlying fraud of the policy. No intelligence analysis took seriously the prospect of a Chinese missile attack. On the contrary, as Pentagon congressional testimony revealed in 1968, both Russian ABM construction and Chinese missile development were laggard in 1967 and presented no compelling new danger. The ABM deployment decision had been made instead to cater to congressional pressures, White House political fears, appeasement of the joint chiefs who wanted whatever the Soviets might or might not have—and, not least, because of the token demonstration of diplomatic failure hidden at Glassboro.

Joined to the MIRV—a system of multiple warheads for strategic missiles—the American ABM would complicate enormously the coming arms negotiations between Moscow and Washington. The ultimate price is impossible to reckon. In the precious time lost later negotiating the ABM issue, Moscow and Washington missed an opportunity to move on to the more vital issues of controlling offensive weapons before technology created in the mid-1970s an ominous new generation of weapons, including the almost undetectable cruise missile. A decade afterward, a deadly impasse in the SALT talks would be due in some measure to the bureaucratic shadow play at Glassboro, New Jersey.

The men and methods varied from region to region, but almost everywhere there was the mark of another, unacknowledged reality in American foreign policy. In Latin America, for example, relations supposedly centered on the "Alliance for Progress," the multi-billion-dollar economic aid program that defined the U.S. interest in the hemisphere as "the prosperity and independence" of its peoples. By 1968, the less inspiring product of the Alliance was an overgrown State Department bureaucracy clinging to its established projects primarily because they were there, bureaucratically familiar and safe in Washington as well as acceptable among the predominantly conservative Latin governments, regardless of the all too eager effect of

U.S. aid on the real needs of the mass of people on the continent. Yet the sterility of these projects was only a small part of the real U.S. presence in Latin America. From the Dominican Republic to Chile, critical segments of the Latin economies were dominated by giant U.S. corporations. Firms like United Brands, Kennecott, or ITT had vast stakes in the political and social-economic status quo in the hemisphere, its cheap labor and compliant, corrupt governments, and applied their influence and money to preserve those interests.

Still less visible than this corporate power, however, was the dominance of U.S. policy by the Central Intelligence Agency. Unleashed by Washington's anti-Castro hysteria of the early 1960s, the CIA had been empowered throughout Latin America with the ultimate authority in foreign relations short perhaps only of open war: the practical determination of the very governments that ruled there. In Brazil and Ecuador in the mid-sixties when leftist politicians contemplated recognition of Cuba, in Chile when the 1964 elections threatened to vote a Marxist into power, in Bolivia, Uruguay, and other countries whose oligarchic régimes were threatened by revolutionaries, the CIA moved decisively and spent lavishly. Legislatures and newspapers were bribed, unrest and instability "arranged," unruly governments toppled. For friendly régimes there was police training and military aid to carry on counterrevolution. As in all CIA spending, the cost of this covert intervention in Latin America in the 1960s remained secret. But former officials believed later that in some Latin countries the United States had spent more for subversion and political interference than for public economic assistance.

The policy of secret intervention in Latin America bred its own internal momentum. There were the large and powerful CIA "stations," owning so many "locals" and hatching new conspiracies. Numerous military attachés were ever intent to perform their mission, shading their intelligence reports to the Pentagon to that end. And always there were appreciative Latin clients, anxious for more discreet help. In Washington these decisive relations with Latin America were no more than marginally shaped by the State Department or Congress, though that was the accepted public hypocrisy of annual presidential speeches or messages on the "Alliance." The real forum that made policy toward the hemisphere was not even known to exist. Predecessor to the more infamous "40 Committee" of Nixon's administration, the top-secret "303 Committee" was a similar small group of officials from the Pentagon, State Department, White House, National Security Agency, the FBI, and the CIA, who met regularly to approve the covert intelligence operations of the U.S. government. The world of that committee, with its own bureaucratic rivalries and personality clashes, was rarely seen even by other secret realms of government; when it was, the glimpse could be startling and revealing even to high government officials. In 1968, after a hunt heavily financed and "advised" by the CIA, the Bolivian army finally captured and killed Che Guevara, the Cuban revolutionary who had unsuccessfully attempted a peasant uprising in Bolivia. Years later, several officials present would remember the scene as Walt W. Rostow, a member of the 303 Committee, presided over a meeting of his National Security Council staff the morning after the news of Che's killing reached Washington. The President's Special Assistant for National Security entered the room smiling broadly and excitedly rubbing pencils together in his hands. After an expectant silence, broken only by the click, click of the pencils, he turned to his assistant for Latin affairs. "Well," he said to the official, who nervously smiled back, "We got him, we got him!" There was no more comment on the subject. The staff meeting resumed, concentrating on its usual concern with public relations and the current maneuvering of bureaucratic politics through State or the Pentagon, its own brush with the harsh, inner reality of Latin American policy swiftly over, but indelible.

If the CIA and its anti-Communist mission were dominant in Latin America, there was yet another priority and impulse shaping relations with Africa. Africa had enjoyed its brief moment of cold war chic when most of its countries gained independence early in the 1960s. The Congo (now Zaire) had been John Kennedy's first international crisis, and the scene of a sizable CIA covert intervention at the time which installed a pro-Western dictatorship. But as the intractable politics and poverty of the continent became evident and Soviet and Chinese Communist interest in Africa diminished, Africa quickly fell back to an area of lowest priority in U.S. policy. It would be "the last issue considered, the first aid budget cut," as one official lamented in Washington at the middle of the decade. About the same time, Johnson himself had made the point with characteristic color, force, and some brutality in a remark that traveled quickly through the government. Enraged at a State Department press spokesman for an unmanipulated leak on Vietnam, the President of the United States could think of no worse punishment for the offender than to threaten that "From now on, his ass is going to be briefing someplace in Africa."

Left behind in this swing of political mood in the White House and the press, however, were scores of foreign service bureaucrats who, unlike the threatened spokesman, were already in some thirty new U.S. embassies in Africa or the African Bureau in the State Department. Their careers were invested in the importance of the steamy posts of the continent, whatever the fugitive attention of higher levels in Washington. And their inevitable rationalization against the new disregard of Africa (and the U.S. officials there) often drove them into their own isolated and private view of foreign policy. One of the most common and tragic expressions of the problem was the tendency of American diplomats to equate their own responsibility and importance, and ultimately the national interest, with the interests and survival of the governments they dealt with. Most often the results of this cliency in Africa were trivial and obscure, the little bureaucratic deceptions to conceal the client's failures lest the country, and the U.S. Embassy, lose what meager call they had on Washington's programs and attention. But at its extreme cliency could be more serious and costly, its toll taken in human suffering and death as well as in the integrity of American policy.

During the same summer of 1967 that saw the Six-Day War and Glassboro, a sequence of political intrigues and tribal massacres triggered civil war between Nigeria and its secessionist Eastern Region, which became Biafra. When Biafra collapsed more than two years later, hundreds of thousands were dead, many of them children. The vast majority died from starvation caused when Nigeria blockaded rebel-held territory. The war was essentially a battle for power between post-colonial élites. Neither side would subordinate its political or military goals to relieve the enormous human cost. United States policy toward the conflict—the public, presidential policy—was a combination of political neutrality, including an arms embargo, and a major commitment, rising to over $100 million, to the international relief efforts operating on both sides. Behind the relief policy was an extraordinary outpouring of public concern and bipartisan congressional support across the political spectrum from Edward Kennedy to Strom Thurmond. All the major American religious relief agencies were involved in aiding Biafra, along with the International Committee of the Red Cross and several private European relief groups. There were disputes in Washington over whether the United States should play an intermediary role in trying to end the conflict, but no apparent doubt that the country should make a major humanitarian response to the starving children of the Nigerian civil war. Or so it seemed. In the U.S. Embassy in Lagos, ardently committed to its Nigerian clients, it was another of those different worlds.

Only weeks after the outbreak of the war, the wife of an American Embassy official in Lagos startled her Nigerian dinner guests with a toast to "the destruction of Biafra." When numberless Biafran children, dying of protein deficiency, their hair turned rust color, became symbols to the world of the war's wanton suffering, U.S. Embassy officers in Lagos soberly explained to visitors that the clever rebels had found an obscure red-haired tribe, starved its infants, and put them on display.

The mission's zeal had not always been so overt. Diplomats who served in the Lagos Embassy during the early months of the war recall the pervasive suspicion in the form of official restrictions on the contacts of junior officers lest they acquire rebel sympathies. Officials also told of recurrent attempts to alter or altogether suppress reports to Washington unfavorable to Nigeria, including eyewitness accounts of Nigerian atrocities. Dissent, according to many accounts, was severely punished by unfavorable performance ratings.

There was visible irritation with the embassy in Lagos back in Washington, even among the African Bureau's career officers who had served in the country earlier. Letters, then official visitors, were sent to urge more complete reporting. The CIA even sent an investigator to Lagos to discover why the embassy's intelligence was so different from all accounts of the war given in the media and by other governments. But those efforts soon gave way to a weary resignation and State's own growing reluctance to offend victorious Nigeria as Biafra's collapse became imminent.

At the higher levels of the Department, comparatively free of cliency but also generally indifferent to African problems, the same kind of weariness and abdication prevailed that had greeted the Mideast policy review in 1967. When a career officer explained to Under Secretary of State Nicholas Katzenbach in 1968 that the United States could not provide more food to Biafra for fear the

Soviets would gain influence with Nigeria, Katzenbach shot back, "Hell, I'd give the whole country to the Russians if they'd feed these people." It was a remarkable throwaway line in an administration then spending so much in lives and fortune supposedly to stem communism from Saigon to Rio. Nevertheless, the Biafran policy continued, with its outer public compassion veiling its inner bureaucratic callousness. To the end, the Lagos mission resisted the awful reality of Biafra's starvation, refusing to support the presentation by Nigerian relief authorities of vital scientific data on the famine developed by U.S. public health experts. Convinced that the public, Congress, the White House, and the State Department were either duped by Biafran propaganda or else conspiring to dismember an important client, the Lagos Embassy largely followed its own foreign policy for the duration of the war.

Neither the Biafran episode nor most other policies could be understood as the consequence alone of any underlying doctrine or ideology in American foreign relations. There was the equally heavy mark of personalities and organizational politics, influences that cut across ideological bounds whether in Washington, Peking, or Moscow. Official Washington's hostility toward Communist China in 1968 was frozen in place not only by cold war mythology, but also by a timorous bureaucracy and White House whose political fear and inertia on the subject were deeply rooted in the position the presidency occupied in the larger organization of American foreign policy. So, too, the Johnson administration went on from the Six-Day War and Glassboro to evade and temporarily bury the international dollar crisis in 1968. The crisis would reappear ferociously a few years later, forcing stringent measures that might have been avoided by earlier action. This costly postponement owed more to the bureaucratic anarchy in Washington's policy, the lack of a coherent position among squabbling economists in Treasury, State, and the White House, than to any ideology. Then there was the sheer distraction of the Vietnam war. By its relentless attrition of the time and energy of senior officials, and especially the President, the war pushed aside initiatives in East-West relations, for example, from which Lyndon Johnson might well have constructed the détente that was to be a major achievement of his successor. In the summer of 1966, when Charles de Gaulle threatened the survival of NATO, European allies pressed Washington for fresh policies. Dean Acheson, then briefly recalled to government by Johnson to be a special consultant on the NATO crisis, went to the White House with a list of specific proposals to open a new relationship with both western and eastern Europe and the USSR. Johnson listened impatiently, glanced at the memorandum, then drew some small white cards from his pockets. "Yeah, yeah," he waved off Acheson, "but have you seen these polls? Ho Chi Minh's killin' me even in the Gallup." The East-West initiatives eventually returned to State Department files, only to be resurrected by another President a few years later, who saw their value very much in terms of those consuming polls.

The governing character of U.S. foreign policy in 1968 did not lie in the issue that was later seen to destroy Lyndon Johnson's presidency, the impulse toward intervention so terribly represented by Vietnam. Intervention was common enough, although frequently— in Europe, in Biafra, in the Middle East—the decisive force in American policy was inaction. Nor was there always a single institutional villain, as so many would discover later when some of the CIA's numerous abuses were exposed. For example, the Agency's estimates of Soviet missile strength in the late sixties turned out to be lonely models of accuracy and objectivity amid the self-serving military intelligence that encrusted the ABM decision. Moreover, if the CIA conducted its covert machinations in Indochina or Latin America or in the main New York City Post Office with obvious relish and ruthlessness, it was also acting in every case under some authority of a presidential decision. Its intervention abroad invariably operated with the quiet tolerance and often the enthusiastic support of several senior officials in the State Department, Pentagon, and White House.

On the public surface policy was made by impressive, competent men who were in charge. But beneath that surface appearance, the reality was starkly different. The Johnson régime calculated much less the tangled manner and substance of its decisions than the cosmetics of how it all looked. Back in their White House, Pentagon, or State Department offices, after the ritual photographs and press conferences, the impressive men were suddenly shrunken by the weight of reality. Besieged by the organizations they were supposed to rule, they seldom made the thoughtful analysis and unequivocal decisions suggested by the pictures that showed them leaning forward so seriously at the cabinet table or in animated conversation with a foreign leader. More often, their decisions represented the ambiguous, con-

tradictory residue of hidden internal politics constantly waged between personalities and departments. Those politics were arbitrary
and capricious. They could compel grave national choices such as
the deployment of the ABM, or paralyze diplomacy at critical moments, as in the Middle East after the Six-Day War.

What most of the Johnson administration policies did have in
common was the shallowness of senior officials and their repeated
surrender to bureaucratic momentum or sloth. There was a ready
tendency to advocate or sabotage policies purely for institutional or
career reasons often unrelated to the issues at stake. The President
himself was largely unable to understand or to control the forces at
work in foreign policy within his own government, let alone abroad.
And a compulsion prevailed throughout the system to decide and
execute the real policies (as distinguished from the public posturings)
as much as possible in secrecy beyond public debate or accountability. Finally, the necessary condition—congressional and public ignorance and acquiescence in the whole process—was scarcely less common. Least of all did this internal world of foreign policy have a single
center of responsibility, a central command and control. The senior
officials, the bureaucracy, the President, all with their peculiar
strengths and weaknesses, were left in an uneasy stalemate—which
they were unable, or afraid, to change.

The "Wise Men" summoned to the Johnson White House that
March in 1968 represented the nominal leadership of what its members called the foreign policy "community." They had been the cabinet officers, the executives of the great departments, the presidential
advisers, or the ambassadors in the important missions. With few
exceptions they were not career civil servants, though most had
spent a decade or more in government. Their outsider's status with
its seeming independence of the bureaucrats was an important qualification. Presidents traditionally reached for distinguished private
men, preferably from their own party, to take the highest appointments in State or the Pentagon. These men were supposed to hold
the critical administrative and policy power, harnessing to the White
House the huge, halting bureaucracy. It was not only a matter of
political loyalty and efficiency; there were also the important ties to
the financial world, the press, and even to other politicians that came
with the well-connected lawyers, businessmen, or foundation execu-

tives. When the senior foreign policy jobs were being filled, presidents could treat foreign affairs as a species of ordinary politics. Men with careful and cultivated reputations were approved by other serious men who had held the jobs before them, and won ready acceptance in a Washington intent on appearances. Electoral politics rarely satisfied those conditions. Blurred as political campaigns might be, there were unavoidable votes and statements that were still sharper than the opaque expressions, if any, made by the discreet men in line for the foreign affairs posts. In 1961, for example, President Kennedy had considered naming Democratic Senator William Fulbright of Arkansas as Secretary of State, but quickly dismissed him on the basis of Fulbright's all too public and controversial position on desegregation. The office went, of course, to Dean Rusk, whose views on almost any issue, foreign or domestic, were wholly obscure.

For almost a quarter-century, under both Republicans and Democrats, the principal foreign policy positions have been virtually the exclusive preserve of a small, ingrown élite of men clustered in New York and Washington. They awaited the call from the White House to determine America's role in the world, or to judge the fitness of one of their colleagues who would. The call usually came. Selection of the Secretary of State since World War II has been something akin to establishment primogeniture. The élite provided the patrician lawyers like Dean Acheson and John Foster Dulles for Truman and Eisenhower, and for Kennedy and Johnson Dean Rusk, a Rockefeller Foundation president and erstwhile Assistant Secretary of State under Acheson in the Truman administration. No postwar President seemed to worry, as Sam Rayburn once warned Lyndon Johnson, that people like Rusk had never run for sheriff. Of the "Wise Men" who advised Johnson in 1968, only one, Henry Cabot Lodge, had held elective office.

Up to the moment of their swearing in, the process of placing such men did not appear all that different from filling the senior positions in domestic affairs. Each set of high-level jobs had special conventions and constituencies to be consulted. Yet once in office, something extraordinary happened to the foreign policy managers. Unlike their colleagues at the Departments of Agriculture or Labor or Interior, they entered a sanctum of government where the most prosaic business was shrouded in secrecy. A Congress and press which could confidently probe and debate the complexities of domestic issues stood largely mute and a little awed before the subject of national security. A breed apart from other high officials, these careful men of the foreign policy élite were somehow presumed to know more of their grave responsibilities, and to know it more profoundly, than the rest of the country could or indeed should. Much of the tragedy in foreign policy, too long concealed, was that for the most part they simply did not.

Afterward, when the *Pentagon Papers* and subsequent revelations exposed so vividly how much these distinguished men had blundered in Vietnam, there was about their failure a sense of puzzlement as well as disillusionment. Many observers would see the war as a consequence of deliberate, malevolent design. To others, the underlying flaw was the product of a native American ebullience, the overweening self-confidence of successful men come to power in a mighty nation. "They were American," David Halberstam wrote of them in his account of the Kennedy-Johnson decisions on Vietnam, *The Best and the Brightest,* "and they had been ready for what the world offered, the challenges posed." Yet if malevolence and arrogant zeal played a role in Vietnam and elsewhere, there were also those other policies presided over by many of the same men in similar ways—policies in arms control, Europe, the Middle East, Latin America, and Africa—which often lacked initiative and any evidence of high-level command, malign or otherwise. Across the differences of priority and circumstance that separated various policies, what was more consistent was the surprising intellectual mediocrity of the foreign policy leadership, and its inability or unwillingness to master the bureaucratic system below.

Missing in the first instance was a precise understanding of the issues at stake and of the onrushing changes in the world. To mistake utterly the force of the Vietnamese revolution and its relevance to American national interests, to pass over the ominous portent of the Six-Day War, to yield to the vague, haphazard bureaucratic scheming that launched the first strategic arms control approaches to the Soviets and thus the ABM decision: at root so much was traceable to a failure of intellect. The most important international political event of the 1960s, the embittered schism between Russia and China, happened largely beyond the grasp of this foreign policy elite. For most of the decade the split was a cliché among many observers. The Nixon administration would rest historic diplomacy on it, and secretly draw up contingency plans for a Sino-Soviet war. Yet when George Ball, reputed a relative "dove" on Vietnam and one of the most thoughtful and informed of Johnson's "Wise Men," an establishment lawyer who had watched the international scene for more than six years as an Under Secretary of State, in 1968 published his views of foreign policy ponderously entitled *The Discipline of Power: Essentials of a Modern World Structure,* the enmity between Moscow and Peking received scarcely more than passing paragraphs buried deep in the book. Rivalry between these two powerful Communist states was not, apparently, an "essential." Ball's indifference to the problem was not unique. The Sino-Soviet split intruded hardly more into either the public speeches or the secret memoranda of most of his colleagues in the Johnson administration.

It was one of the whispered little secrets of younger aides who worked closely for many of these men that the boss, whatever his respected name, reputation and apparent success, was not really all that bright or informed. Too often he was at the mercy of the memos and intelligence reports siphoned up from the bureaucracy, most of which were shaded by the personal and organizational interests of the authors and much in need of sharp questions and independent judgment (which the aides, who were usually career officers with their own interests to protect after the boss was gone, were loath to provide). Nor, it turned out, did his stature and experience give the typical senior official, even when he had his own view, a grip on the organizational politics that swept along careers and policies. Men like Rusk, Ball, and Katzenbach at the State Department or McNamara and Vance at the Pentagon might devoutly wish for arms control. But somehow they could not "get a handle," as the official cliché went, on issues dominated by the obscure, conflicting reasoning of the joint chiefs or the instincts of allied Southern senators who inherited without challenge both the key committees and Lyndon Johnson's deference. Similarly, there seemed no ready way to restrain the sometimes embarrassing impulses of the CIA, or to check the lethargy and defiance of the State Department's own bureaus and embassies, which could, as in Biafra, quietly carry on their own policies in mockery of presidential declarations. "He's the only Assistant Secretary who can declare war before anyone notices," Rusk once said of the chief of State's African Bureau, revealing a sure sense of the job's paradoxical insignificance to higher officials and its resulting awesome bureaucratic power. He promptly named to the position a stalwart and conventional foreign service officer, and left African policy to its bureaucratic fate. The same fecklessness guided State Department representatives at the critical 303 Committee meetings that approved the CIA's covert interventions. "They always took good notes, lots of notes," one high official remembered of State's officers at those sessions, "but I don't think they ever opposed a major operation."

The intellectual stagnation and bureaucratic impotence were not, however, confined to the random weaknesses of a few personalities. The flaws lay deep in the background from which most of the foreign policy élite had come to the highest levels of government. Whether the preparation was with a prestigious old law firm, a major bank, a large corporation, a foundation, or, as for most at some earlier stage, the middle ranks of government itself, it was not likely to be an experience that nurtured intellect or zeal for institutional reform. One tended to rise in those special precincts for quite opposite reasons. In such institutions it was usually vital to have the patronage of older men, with their own long-acquired vested interests in the policies and practices at hand. In most cases, there was little choice but to adapt, and to accept what could be changed only at the cost of open controversy, and perhaps one's career. Patrons seldom asked first for original ideas or change. Hounded by rivals within and competition without, they asked instead of their younger protégé, was he loyal, was he careful, was he, in that all-purpose cliché of the establishment, "sound"? Where murmured opinions settled careers, the survivors of those questions rarely learned the habits of independent thought or nonconformity. All of them—Acheson and Rusk in their discreet earlier service in State; McNamara as he waited to rise to the top at Ford Motor Company; Ball and Vance and Dillon serving as efficient deputies in government or private firms; Bundy as the arbiter of interests at the White House or Harvard dean; Lodge dutifully taking orders at the UN or in Saigon; and, of course, the generals schooled in the politics of the army—all understood the rites of passage in their universe.

Not that such men lacked convictions, or did not articulate contempt for the "system." Indeed, it was fashionable to curse the "system" quietly, acidly, to show one was apart from it. But, for most, no conviction would ever be more important than the risk it posed for advancement. Changing the system in the law firm, the company, the State Department, or Pentagon would have to wait for the power that eventually came with playing the game carefully. The problem for too many, though, was that at the top convictions were somehow more expendable than ever, compromise more necessary. And there was never quite enough power or time to change the way it all worked. Besides, some of them, Rusk for instance, felt comfortable and proper with the conventional institutional mode. By middle age, bureaucratic politics was after all one of the most familiar and predictable elements in the lives of such men.

The crippling force of the organizational ethic was familiar enough in other areas of American life, but few critics saw its pervasive, frequently decisive influence on the nation's foreign policy. Men who had mainly earned selection by an experience that discouraged intellectual rigor were called to deal with problems of immense complexity and rapid change. To manage and master a bureaucracy of legendary recalcitrance presidents called principally on an élite of bureaucrats whose distinction derived in large measure from their tractability.

This sort of background fortified among the élite the stubborn cold war mythology and sense of American omnipotence so evident in Vietnam. It was an ideology of imperial benevolence, which propounded the development of non-Communist economies and the salvation of régimes with Western democratic forms. An ideology held by men who believed that the United States exercised power unique in world history, both in its intent and its reach. As he would in many ways, Walt Rostow symbolized the combativeness and presumption of the era when he entitled the final chapter of a book written in 1964 as a State Department official "The Way to Victory." Not even the relatively more moderate and urbane Ball, Rostow's too gentle adversary in Vietnam policy debates, was immune from the regional parochialism feeding the myth. "We Americans and Europeans . . . must all continually search for an answer to the question posed by Faust's servitor," Ball began his later book, *The Discipline of Power.* " 'How shall our counsel serve to lead mankind?' " These were not men who readily questioned whether the United States should, or indeed could, "lead mankind."

At the core of the doctrine were three major propositions. The premise was that the United States faced implacable, basically undifferentiated Communist foes in Moscow and Peking, both ready and able to extend their dominance at the expense of vital American interests throughout the world. To this was added the belief that revolution and national experience, whether in Southeast Asia or Latin America, was but a local replica of that universal struggle. Finally, in taking up the conflict at will, by stealth or by open war, the presumption was that government was not only pursuing its historic mission but also conveniently doing what its public expected, even demanded of it. By 1968, each of these generalizations was badly discredited as a basis for policy. Splintered Communist politics in Europe and Asia had shown for nearly a decade that the threat of a competing Communist imperialism was far less certain or formidable than had been supposed at the height of the cold war fifties. National Communist parties tended to succeed, in China, Yugoslavia, or Indochina, for example, where their alliance and identification with authentic nationalism inevitably put them at odds with other already established Communist powers. Events also argued that national circumstances country-to-country were indeed unique. In any case, the singular history, culture, and leaders of each country ultimately shaped its politics and fate. The world was, in short, vastly complicated, and no more accurately described by an American cold war demonology than by Moscow and Peking's warring versions of antique Marxism.

The men who led American foreign policy in the 1960s were largely numb to those nuances. In part, they simply lacked a thoughtful and critical perspective on world politics. Nor did they possess the detailed knowledge or sophistication about any single foreign society that might have led them to question their larger misjudgment. But an element of dogmatism was there too in the conventions of the élite. The cold war and its facile strictures were above all an inherited policy, the unquestioned wisdom of the foreign policy establishment in its postwar rise to power. It was not a wisdom that the serious, eligible successors to that élite debated, any more than they attacked the senior partner in the firm or on the board of trustees. Their social and political isolation further insulated the growing ignorance of these men, and they clung to the prescribed mentality. In or out of government, hurtled snugly in their chauffeured cars past the ongoing life of New York or Boston or Washington on the way to their quiet conference rooms, they were men largely oblivious of their own communities, let alone the rest of the country. It would be one of the many bitter ironies of their failure: presumed to manage the world because they were so worldly, these men tended to be deeply provincial. Their constituency was, in the end, only themselves. They largely inhabited the same insular, establishment confines. There were the corporate clients and overseers, the bland board meetings, the "responsible" discussions at foundation or government-financed conferences, the discreet seminars at their pretentious and ever orthodox New York fraternity, the Council on Foreign Relations. They promoted, demoted, certified, ostracized, shielded, branded, and, most of all, decided what they thought almost exclusively from within. Politics at its most plebeian was the dainty jockeying in "advising" the Congress and the potential presidents. The more common game was the endless incestuous maneuver and cutting gossip among the tiny group of one's peers and would-be protégés. Of the men at the upper levels of foreign affairs in the Johnson administration, of the "Wise Men" meeting in March 1968, none came from much broader experience or associations than this in American life. The sole exception was perhaps Arthur Goldberg, active in the labor movement before joining the Kennedy administration, who was for a short time Johnson's ambassador to the UN. But then Goldberg was clearly not an "expert" on foreign policy. He quietly questioned the Vietnam escalations, was scorned by both élite and career service as well as Johnson, and would be duly excluded from policy decisions in any case because his position at the UN was bureaucratically powerless.

Underneath the discreet, dignified exterior of it all coursed a basic contempt for the public, and by extension for most politicians. That contempt fed on itself as the country turned against the Vietnam war. Ordinary people and most of the Congress had never fathomed foreign policy, the establishment told itself. It was simply a matter of "bringing them along" or, if necessary, acting without them. Like the cold war, this basic irresponsibility in foreign affairs had been fastened on the establishment by the past. If the international analogies for Vietnam or the missile race were Munich or the Berlin Blockade, the historical model for domestic anti-war sentiment of the 1960s was the isolationism of the era before World War II. The theme was monotonous in their public statements. "We shall not unlearn the lesson of the thirties," Johnson intoned in an October 1966

speech before an establishment audience in New York, "when isolation and withdrawal were our share in the common disaster." The
lesson, to be sure, had never been lost on the Achesons or the
younger army officers, on the lawyers and academics who deplored
unpreparedness and favored lend-lease for Britain. Almost thirty
years after the experience, Dean Rusk would tell a gathering of
newly recruited foreign service officers that Hitler and Hanoi presented the same problem. "We fought this battle before in the 1930s
against the people who didn't understand totalitarianism," he lec-
tured the young diplomats. "We were right then, and we're right
now." Rusk spoke for a generation of officials whose superiority to
confused and divided public moods had been vindicated once and for
all by Pearl Harbor.

    This contempt for the public was exhibited in several ways in the
1960s. Most notably, the secrecy and deception surrounding the war
policy were not aimed at the Viet Cong or Hanoi, but rather at an
American Congress and public who in the opinion of the policy
makers did not need to know, and, in their potential for ignorant
opposition, deserved to be misled. The contempt issued forth too in
a defensiveness, a belligerent refusal to face up to the scandal of their
governance, their ignorance and provincialism. Many of them knew
all too well the sometimes shocking incompetence masquerading
behind the façade maintained by respected colleagues and orderly
government. Yet the covenant of discretion was stronger. "There is
no reason," wrote Ball after more than 20,000 Americans lay dead
in Vietnam, "to put ourselves on the analyst's couch."

    A public accounting of sorts did come eventually for several of the
senior foreign policy officials involved in Vietnam, if only in the deft
portraits of some of them in Halberstam's widely read book. Even
that kind of reckoning, however, was prey to furtive malice within
the foreign affairs élite itself. Many of the scathing anecdotes and
selectively leaked documents would come from the younger men of
the establishment struggling to blot out their own complicity in the
disaster. These were non-career officials in their thirties and forties
during the Kennedy and Johnson administrations. They crowded the
middle positions in State or the Pentagon from backgrounds in business, law, academia, or Democratic staffs. Pulled along by various
patrons at or near the top, they became the special aides, the assistant
secretaries, and the ambassadors to the smaller posts, "in-and-outers"

taking their place on the establishment ladder to climb by the rules much as the older men before them. Without Vietnam, they would probably have passed silently from their government experience back to a period of private life before the next appointment. But the extraordinary public revulsion at the war policy changed that. If survival and self-protection prevented senior officials from placing the foreign policy apparatus "on the couch," similar ambition drove some of these junior "Wise Men-in-waiting" to provide the therapy involuntarily. The responsibility for Vietnam was thus saddled on a few well-known names, the policy in Southeast Asia depicted as an unfortunate aberration. Leaking was, as always, done discreetly, not for attribution. And in that obscurity it resembled the anti-war dissent so many of these younger men privately claimed later to have pursued inside the government. The best and the brightest had been there all right—one former State Department Assistant Secretary would tell writers come to interview him—but they were the younger men (like himself) who deplored the war, and were free of all that unsophisticated cold war nonsense believed by the decent but superannuated people upstairs.

In a less important setting, this political cannibalism of the patrons by the protégés might have been dismissed as the petty aftermath of a débâcle, following the precedent of those numberless adjutants through history who as military memoirists saw too clearly after the battle their own suitability to command and the general's fatal weaknesses. But in this setting it only obscured how much what happened in Vietnam ran beyond particular figures to deeper and more enduring weaknesses in the organization of American foreign policy. The middle-level officials, who later raced to position themselves clear of the war's wreckage, were an equally integral part of the system that allowed the ABM decision, the abortive 1967 Middle East "review," the Latin American interventions, and all the rest, as well as Vietnam. Their dissent against the war was so quiet at the time that it left almost no trace. In many cases, their memoranda, cables, and intelligence reports directly fed the rationale and misinformation of the war policy. At the least they looked on quietly while the war not only demanded its own terrible cost, but also devoured the time, energy, and initiative badly needed in other areas. The continuous deception of the public, the shallow decisions, the choices made for bureaucratic reasons—none of these could have happened as they did without the participation and acquiescence, if not support, of such men.

For the most part like their conspicuous (and thus less fortunate) superiors, these men were absorbed in the élite's ethic of propriety and expectancy. Reading their speeches and articles, it was equally difficult to distinguish conviction from ignorance or conformity. The cold war orthodoxy certainly found its echo at these middle levels. But, again, few of these men were educated or experienced as specialists in international politics or foreign societies. Commonly, like the older men above them, they were and continued to be experts in administrative survival. To call them the best and brightest was no less ironic. They were simply the most available, attached in some way to Democratic politicians or older officials. And as they showed in the subsequent scramble to distance themselves from the folly they shared amply, they too lacked a sense of the mediocrity and self-compromise in it all. Of the dozens of such men at the key middle-level positions in the 1960s, there was not a single resignation in public protest against the war policy. Open dissent, after all, damaged one's soundness and threatened reentry. When the attacks slashed at the senior men, they would be untraceable, beyond public view where such things were done. The revelations were made not in spite of careers but to resurrect them. So they banked on the hope that the war and the other less apparent policy blunders would be buried with time and blamed on the Rusks, the Taylors, the Rostows, the Bundys. Meanwhile, they would await in their law firm or foundation or Wall Street exiles another presidential call to govern. The next time it would be their turn.

At the bottom, below the presidentially appointed offices filled largely by the establishment, American foreign policy in 1968 was also the reflection of another group of "people who are expert at it," the career civil service. Here as much as anywhere in government the power of the bureaucrats was awesome. For the few issues besides Vietnam that received consistent high-level attention, the bureaucracy commanded the flow of information to senior officials, variously pressured and lobbied the nominal decisionmakers to protect bureaucratic interests, and then controlled the daily execution of policy. Most policies it simply ruled by default, by just being there, in the vacuum left by executive, congressional, and public inattention. As disillusionment with foreign policy grew in the 1970s amid gathering revelations of official deceptions and abuses, there would be an increasing sense of the sinister and conspiratorial about the conduct of foreign relations. For its major share in the problem, however, the role of the bureaucracy was more banal than mysterious. To U.S. foreign policy, as to Joseph Heller's memorable character in a 1974 novel, "something happened." In both cases it was the absurdity and tragedy of people enveloped in the relentless politics of the large organization.

Over the three decades since World War II, the growth of the foreign affairs bureaucracy had been enormous. In 1939, it numbered a few hundred foreign service officers (FSOs) and clerks in some fifty sparely staffed missions abroad. In Washington they occupied with the War Department and Navy the few high-ceilinged Victorian-Baroque suites of what is now the Executive Office Building adjacent to the White House. By the 1960s, more than 50,000 people (including a classified 16,000 at the CIA) sprawled over Washington and 100 international posts. To the foreign service officer corps, itself expanded several-fold, was added in Washington and abroad a horde of other bureaucrats, including the Agency for International Development, the U.S. Information Agency, attachés of the Pentagon, Treasury, Commerce, Agriculture, and, from the CIA's 16,000, the ubiquitous "case officers" and analysts of what its minions called "The Company."

This burgeoning diplomatic officialdom was not the stronghold of a single class. The prewar foreign service once had its Eastern Ivy League club, the CIA a similar old-boy network when it emerged as the consolidation of various wartime intelligence operations. After the war, however, the ranks of all the organizations expanded with men (and as officers, an occasional token woman) from a broad cross section of social and geographic backgrounds. Much more important than family or geographic origins was what the new bureaucrats became in Washington and the foreign posts—a class of organizational aspirants and dependents whose lives and worth were in some ways more rigidly bound by the canons of career than by any previous status.

At the core of the system, in spirit if not in relative bureaucratic power, was the Department of State. The foreign service became a top-heavy careerist guild, rewarding compliance and routine, punishing dissent, shunning a sense of policy responsibility to the public. The bloat of the organization, in which bureaucrats vastly outnumbered meaningful or necessary jobs, reduced the FSO to a tortuously slow apprenticeship. The careful levitation from slot to slot, promotion to promotion, put a premium on conformity and on the patronage of superiors writing efficiency reports, who were in turn awaiting their own similar advancement through the ranks. It all ended with a dirty little secret of the service, discovered by many too late, after the children were in college, the mortgage too high, the life invested beyond return: that neither the makework on the way up nor the positions at the top, even the crown of the corps, the coveted ambassadorships, really mattered all that much. Abroad there were spacious free quarters, servants, and savings. There was the artificial importance of diplomatic status. The career was probably destined to end in a certain style: quiet Washington retirement amid the exotic carpets and brassware, the insiders' gossip, club lunches, and the handsome pension that marked the spent diplomatic life. For most, however, there was no lasting escape from the tedium and obscurity of dealing with other officials in remote places or in the high-rent, servantless suburbs of Washington, where the FSO was one more commuter in the legion of bureaucrats.

In such a world, idealism was too obviously sacrificed and ability too noticeably atrophied. Complacency and smugness often clothed a profound disillusionment and self-deprecation, and, in many cases, a natural rage at the system and oneself. Ambition survived often only in caution, sometimes in obsequiousness. Duty could take the form of an obstinate defiance of what State Department bureaucrats called with nervous sarcasm "the real world" of the Congress and public.

Among the great agencies of government, the State Department was peculiarly isolated from its public constituency. Not only did diplomats spend most of their time out of the country. Even when in Washington they seldom encountered the people they were supposed to represent. Nearly every other bureaucracy faced some segment of the public: farmers at Agriculture, union leaders at Labor, consumers, businessmen, groups that inevitably drew the agencies, however reluctantly, into some contact with the politics and mood of the nation. For most foreign service officers, there were a few lobbyists in Washington or, abroad, the occasional American delegation entertained curtly at the embassy. Otherwise, they governed almost entirely free of the intrusions of the public that plagued their domestic counterparts—and tended to make them more account-able.

The service's searing brush with McCarthyism in the 1950s only deepened that institutional isolation. In the corporate madness of the time, the senior Far East specialists, some of the most able and inde-pendent men in the Department, were accused as security risks, went largely undefended by their timorous superiors, and were eventually purged. The miscarriage haunted the country long after-ward. The absence of such men during the early decisions on the Vietnam policy left unchallenged the cultural and political ignorance of Asia that made possible the American intervention. Just as insidi-ous and costly were the effects of the purge on the vulnerable men-tality of the surviving foreign service. The episode only reinforced the cautious, compliant, play-it-safe habit in the ranks, the secrecy and evasiveness, and, with a vengeance, the corps's abiding abhor-rence of congressional and public meddling in the Department.

Ironically, however, it was the otherwise customary removal of the State Department from politics that slowed the healing of the worst wounds of McCarthy's savagery. Deliberately aloof and out of touch, with good reason distrustful of swings in political opinion, the foreign service was among the last to see how much the country had changed by the 1960s, that the recrimination and hysteria were no longer there. The lingering fear of reprisal was a significant factor in the failure of the career diplomats to oppose the war in Vietnam. When the nation most needed its expertise, political independence, and sophistication, America's diplomatic service was politically cowed, deprived of its ranking experts, and ignorant of the most important developments in its own society.

The organizational malaise and isolation of the State Department drove it still deeper into an insular preoccupation with its bureau-cratic goals, and hastened its eclipse in the making of much of foreign policy. When the issue involved questions of cold war manliness and a powerful rival agency, the Pentagon matching the Russian ABM or the CIA guarding Latin America from communism, the Department largely retreated. In any Washington battle of memoranda it was chronically weakened in any case by the wooden, elliptical writing style imposed by caution and the obligatory compromise among factions within the Department. Tested in English composition at entry, foreign service officers found themselves in a culture in which the simple declarative sentence was regarded as risky. The real power of the State Department lay not in its ability to challenge prevailing policy or the dominance of other agencies, but rather to preserve its own vestiges of authority and importance after the rest of the bureaucracy staked its claims in foreign affairs. There its caution and vagueness became strengths. Set against change, aided by the normal sluggishness of a large government, the average foreign service bureaucrat did what the conventions of his organization allowed him to do best and most safely: to postpone, to blur, to outwait, and to do it in a solitary confusion of bureaucratic interests with the national interest.

The most widespread and malignant application of this power was in the cliency that consumed policy in episodes like the Biafran famine. To some degree, an attachment to client régimes held FSOs fast to the status quo in every mission and on every bureau desk, except those for the Communist countries and South Africa, which were obviously ineligible for client privileges on grounds of ideology and racism. Cliency flourished in the service's search for a mission. Good relations with a particular régime were important simply because that was what one did. From there it was a short step to the added belief that those relations were, or ought to be, urgent national business. Individual careers and the status of whole embassies were linked to the success of aid programs or other enterprises dependent on the clients.

Over several months in 1968 the AID mission in New Delhi debated with Washington the packaging of condoms; it did not report the casual corruption and misdirection of the Indian government's population control program. What the client was doing represented an investment of the mission's time and reputation, a call on Washington's resources, and thus further proof of the mission's importance. Then there was the basic matter of "access," the service's prized ability to hear and be heard with the host government abroad or their embassies in Washington. Information and influence, by which performance was measured, put a premium on agreeable relations with the foreign régime whatever its eccentricities, whether torture of political prisoners or venality with U.S. aid money. Perhaps the strongest single impulse toward cliency was the

distance—geographic and psychological—between the foreign service and the rest of Washington. Among officers who escorted junket-
ing congressmen and watched the steady shrinkage of aid appropriations, who saw "emotional" public outbursts come and go over
starving children in Africa, who viewed the press and Congress as
troublesome amateurs in policy matters, there grew the persuasion
that one of the major duties of the career diplomat was to protect U.S.
relations with other régimes from the excesses of Washington, the
special perils that democracy holds for professional diplomacy.

The extreme example of cliency, as of much else, was Vietnam.
In a sense, it was a medieval application of the practice; a country
could do no more for its client-states than fight their wars for them.
But to the bureaucracies in Washington and their proconsuls in Saigon, the larger issues of the war policy were lost in the daily pursuit
of individual missions. Behind the lines and sometimes on them were
the endless jurisdictional disputes—ambassadors, AID administrators, political officers, not to mention the generals, the ambitious
colonels, and the CIA operatives, each with Vietnamese clients on
whom he was somehow dependent for success, each suspicious that
his colleagues would expand their domain and promote their clients
at his expense. "They could accept more easily a complete reversal
of objectives and grand strategic design than a revision of their own
roles," said a veteran of the bureaucratic theaters of the war in both
the United States and Vietnam. The war was clearly more complex
than this single dimension. Nonetheless, the dishonesty, the zeal, the
secrecy, the ambitions and fears that drove on the Johnson administration reflected this perverse, parochial execution of foreign policy
by the career officialdom.

As a bureaucracy intent on its own mission and worth, the State
Department was never itself a unified whole. In the characterless
seven-story office building in Foggy Bottom sat a loose collection of
competing baronies, the various regional bureaus, the specialized
offices for intelligence or economics or political-military affairs, and
lesser branches with all their assorted interests and clients. It was in
small a replica of the vast feudal kingdom of bureaucratic agencies
and power that lay beyond in Washington. At the Pentagon and CIA,
and, with generally lesser effect, at the numerous other agencies with
international interests, were a majority of bureaucrats who saw their
responsibility as the preservation and extension of their own institu-

tional mission. It was idle to speculate how such men weighed the policy they supported against personal interests. Career and self-esteem almost always carried along conviction. "Those fellows in the CIA don't just report on wars and the like," reflected Harry Truman from retirement; "they go out . . . stirring up trouble so they'll *have* something to report on." If not quite that simple, for the CIA was usually sanctioned in the "stirring" by anxious presidents and suitably tough-minded U.S. diplomats, Truman's point was nonetheless telling. The programs, initiatives, intelligence, and policy advice radiating from the foreign affairs agencies were all shaped by what the people in them *had* to administer and report on.

To a point, of course, competing perspectives and interests might have provided a healthy variety and debate in government; but by 1968, the weight of conformity in the great bureaucracies made their positions sterile and predictable. The worst tyranny of the organizations was that they deprived the government of an authentic range of specialization and advice. Where were the generals who would argue against the ABM and for cuts in the Pentagon budget? Which embassies had the career diplomats who would tell the unflattering truth about clients and suspend their own aid program to save taxpayers money? To what country went the CIA operatives who would soon recommend their own recall on the grounds that intervention was pointless and the foreign service could handle the occasional intelligence reports of interest?

Men immersed in the system saw their predicament with varying clarity. John Franklin Campbell, a young FSO, left the corps to write a biting book whose title was eloquent of its theme, *The Foreign Affairs Fudge Factory* (1970). (He died prematurely two years later.) But so distinguished a career diplomat and scholar as George Kennan would seem to miss the point. There was a "tragic contradiction" between domestic politics and the national interest, Kennan wrote in his memoirs, bemoaning the former's "frequent intrusions into foreign policy." Like most diplomats, he had worked with "a preference for hierarchy and authority over compromise and manipulation; and a distaste amounting almost to horror for the chaotic disorder of the American political process." Much the same "compromise and manipulation" that horrified Kennan and others like him about the Congress was precisely what went on within the State Department and among the various jousting agencies. Too many officials saw their own "chaos" as somehow more orderly—and, of course, consistent with the national interest.

However dimly acknowledged, for those within it, the system was not some abstract, lifeless process; it was decisions, with flesh-and-blood costs paid at home and abroad. It was also people whose lives cut back and forth across historic events with ironic, sometimes poignant consequences. William Trueheart had been a young FSO with a successful and promising career when he was assigned as Deputy Chief of Mission in the Saigon Embassy during the last years of the Diem régime in the early sixties. As Diem's rule crumbled in corruption and internal dissent, however, Trueheart ran afoul of the fervently pro-Diem American ambassador, Frederick Nolting. Nolting's commitment to Diem as client turned from the usual myopia and intolerance of criticism to rancorous charges of disloyalty among his own staff when the Saigon dictator, and with him Nolting's policy, collapsed. Trueheart by all accounts had loyally supported the policy and joined the embassy's roseate view of Diem; though he also allowed, on one occasion in Nolting's absence, some reporting of Diem's weakening hold. His reward was a devastating efficiency report from Nolting and his career did not advance as might have been expected for nearly a decade. When Trueheart was at last appointed an ambassador to Nigeria in 1969, it was seen by some in the press and government as a belated act of justice for one of the few genuine career martyrs of the Vietnam folly. Trueheart would be among the rare heroes in Halberstam's indictment of the Kennedy and Johnson years.

Yet having suffered so acutely the effects of cliency, having seen so vividly in Saigon the distortions of national policy in embassy politics, Trueheart did not overcome similar forces entrenched in the Lagos mission. He would be the ambassador whose staff refused to pass on scientific data on the suffering in defeated Biafra lest it offend the Nigerian régime in its inept relief effort, much as Nolting had refused to report the scandal in Saigon. In the end, as so often, the clients were ungrateful. Nigerian-U.S. relations generally soured after the war in resentment over relief to Biafra, and Trueheart soon returned from Lagos to an assignment as a political adviser at the Atlantic fleet headquarters in Norfolk. Truehart's experience is a sad testament to the way his government conducts fateful business with the world.

These were the people, the *chinovniki* of American foreign affairs, the poignant, powerful bureaucrats in the ranks who shared the conduct of policy with the non-career establishment élite. For their own haunted reasons they shared, too, a contempt for the public and a weary resignation to the ways of government. In their less prestigious conference rooms, they spoke with similar attention to appearance, careful to appear manly and casual, going always with the flow. They buried their disgraces, the Trueheart affair or a score of others like it, in cynical bureaucratic folklore. They dutifully buried the policy blunders as well. As an example, in 1967, at White House request, officers from the State Department's Latin American Bureau prepared a detailed history based on the official record of the U.S. intervention in the Dominican Republic two years before. Intended to be published as a justification of the policy, the study showed instead that the actions had been based on dubious information and were accompanied by major deceptions of the public. The study was quietly filed, where it remains in Department archives. They were not men who dissented openly. As there were no resignations of high-level protest against Vietnam, there were none below. These men, too, watched; they leaked occasionally, but discreetly. The failures, the policies, belonged to someone else. The important task was to survive, to do the job at hand as they, and they alone, were given to see it. And they did.

Over them all, the establishment and the bureaucracy, stood the President. Of these three major forces shaping foreign policy in the executive, the presidency was supposed to be critically different from the other two. The distinction was constitutional, and basic to democratic government in foreign affairs no less than domestic. Alone among the executive branch, the President and Vice President were elected. The thousands of notables and nonentities under them might administer policy without ever running for office, but ultimately the responsibility lay with the politician in the White House who did indeed run. His background could hardly be sheltered by an élite existence in New York and Washington or by some bureaucratic exile. The presidency was part of what Kennan viewed distastefully as "the chaotic disorder of the American political process." Its occupant ostensibly opened foreign policy to public accountability, if only because he was as dependent for his success and survival on the electorate as the élite was on its elders or the bureaucracy on its efficiency reports. Moreover, the President theoretically had the authority to match his responsibility. The senior foreign policy officials from the assistant secretaries through the cabinet to the ambassadors in the field served at his pleasure. If he understood, if he cared, if he were able, he possessed the legal means to command. Amid all the isolation and narrow self-interest of those who conducted foreign policy, the one figure constitutionally linked to a national constituency and thus to the public interest was potentially the most powerful.

In that power lay a tragic illusion. The authority ran only as far as the President's own sense of confidence and independence in foreign affairs; yet these very strengths were usually missing in presidents precisely because they came to office as part of the larger system, in which foreign policy was the preserve of those "people who are expert at it." Like all politicians, Johnson was largely a creature of his domestic political rise. Just as his presidency reflected the cunning and roughshod style of Texas and Senate politics, it was also a casualty of the prevailing secrecy and exclusion of Congress and the public from foreign policy, an exclusion that left such men in line for the White House without knowledge or practical experience in the responsibilities of world affairs. In most of the victims, the snub produced neither resentment nor skepticism, but instead a heightened sense of awe and dependence toward the men who *were* privy, mainly the establishment. Added to that dependence in Johnson's case was the inescapable ghost of John Kennedy, who, though no less taken with and by the establishment, enjoyed a posthumous reputation as an international sophisticate in contrast to LBJ's country origins. Those origins scarred Johnson with a permanent sense of inferiority and bravado toward men he saw as his patrician betters, including some in the foreign policy élite. But the class envy seldom overcame, and often fed, the ambition to employ them. The myth of a dead rival (with live heirs) thrust Johnson still closer to the serious, stylish advisers dredged from the same reservoir.

Finally, there was myth as well in the presumed responsiveness of the Kennedys or Johnsons to the popular mood of the country. The majority leadership of the Senate, the vice presidency, the presidency, all suffered their own mounting isolation from the nation. In the provincialism and hypocrisy of congressional Washington, in the

upper reaches of power where policies meant increasingly manipulation and appearances, it was as easy to lose touch with reality—
whether in Vietnam or the United States—as it was in the seminars
of the Council on Foreign Relations or U.S. Embassy offices in West
Africa. Nor were presidents, so absorbed in their politics, disposed to
begin sweeping reforms of the national security bureaucracy, though
both Kennedy and Johnson periodically railed against the inertia of
the State Department or Pentagon. There were too many other
issues thought more important, too many possible defenders of
bureaucrats in the press and Congress. For the presidents, as for their
establishment advisers, the bureaucracy was a monstrous thing, but
it was too much trouble; it would have to wait. In practice, then, the
power of the presidency in foreign policy floundered in the long-
cultivated weaknesses and insecurity of the politicians who held it.
Flung into command having abdicated prior experience and responsibility in the issues, isolated and unsure of themselves, drawn to the
myths and traditions of their predecessors to avoid controversy, they
turned to an élite whose incompetence they could not recognize,
and tolerated a bureaucracy whose damage they did not really understand.

In an administration that endlessly photographed its leader in
statesmanlike poses, and released millions of words of official statements on foreign affairs, it was the images unseen by the public that
caught the underlying disarray and pathos. There was the President
of the United States slowly picking his way through welcoming remarks and a state dinner toast for a visiting head of state without once
mentioning the guest's country, Niger, for fear of an embarrassing
mispronunciation. Yet a few months later the President, having seen
a television report on famine in Biafra, would peremptorily telephone Under Secretary of State Nicholas Katzenbach, telling him to
send relief and "get those nigger babies off my TV set." But then
Katzenbach could not enforce the order on the foreign service, who
though never so crude as to call them "nigger," certainly agreed that
the babies on TV were a fiendish inconvenience in maintaining
proper diplomacy.

Biafra was by no means the only example of limits on the presidential writ, however crudely put. Solemn State Department officials
were shocked in 1967 when Johnson, determined to extract long-
overdue agricultural reforms in return for needed U.S. food aid to

Mme Indira Gandhi's régime in India, announced to a White House meeting that the Indians had made a concession and "we've got our hand under the dress." But no one was dismayed when the Indians gradually reneged on the reforms and the U.S. Embassy in New Delhi under Chester Bowles stoutly defended its client. "Tell Mme Gandhi how lucky she is," Johnson ruefully called after a startled Indian diplomat as he left a White House meeting a year later. "She's got *two* ambassadors workin' for her—you here and Bowles out there." For his part, the Secretary of State seemed to notice the problem only when it intruded on his own preoccupation with Southeast Asia. Rusk fell into annual rages when Mme Gandhi sent her birthday cables to Ho Chi Minh. "How long can you kick a cow in the udders and still expect it to give milk?" Rusk once reacted with his own Georgian earthiness in an "eyes only" telegram to Bowles. Otherwise, of course, the President's powerlessness, Rusk's quaint view of world politics, Indian corruption, and U.S. aid went on as always, discreetly concealed from the people who would not understand.

By 1968 it was still too easy for politicians to play the fool inside their own government and in the world. So much was still secret, and seemed bound to remain unknown to the public. Much of the guarantee lay in the gentlemanly co-option of the Congress. Except for a lonely Fulbright dragging the Senate Foreign Relations Committee into Vietnam, the Hill could be counted on to keep its distance. The handful of older members who got occasional glimpses of CIA operations or Pentagon discrepancies were satisfied to have the inside information to themselves. The younger senators and congressmen were still humbled by the mystique of national security and hostage to party or personal loyalty; the Congress also had its patrons, protégés, and efficiency reports of a kind, with equally forbidding punishment for those who went "off the reservation." Like the rest of the system, it was self-reinforcing: the responsibility of the Congress spawned ignorant, gullible, unprepared men like Johnson and Hubert Humphrey whose own irresponsibility in turn went undetected for so long and at such cost because the Congress did not care to know. The final assurance that it would all work rested with a journalism that mirrored the deference of Capitol Hill toward foreign affairs. Though a tradition of skeptical reporting developed from South Vietnam, no comparable investigative habit thrived in Washington. In 1968, the Pentagon Papers were still being written in the government. The weakness of great men or the pervasive force of bureaucracy were not apparent in the communiqués and press conferences that formed the staple of diplomatic reporting. Reporters who dug into the Chicago police beat or a possible scandal in the Agriculture Department, like the congressmen who debated such subjects with relish, could not see foreign policy in the same light, as what it was, simply another inglorious province of politics, played out not in speeches or votes but in flesh and blood.

In the end, it was not the press or Congress, nor the Democratic leaders, much less the State Department, Pentagon, or CIA bureaucracies, who told Johnson that his Vietnam policy had come to an end. The task fell to the "Wise Men" that March afternoon after Tet. Of its kind, the meeting was remarkable: Acheson, Bundy, and the other "sound" men who had once backed the Vietnam policy, telling the President that more troops would not really matter, that he should press for negotiations, that the war was lost. Yet they were divided. The generals, Taylor and Bradley, led a smaller group arguing against, as Robert Murphy called it, "a giveaway" if the United States now sought peace negotiations after a damaging Communist offensive. It was extraordinary. When the débâcle of Tet was clear enough to the public, when an unprecedented electoral revolt over foreign policy was driving the incumbent President from the renomination of his own party, many of the "Wise Men" still could not see. Even the dissent was careful and indirect. There was "concern" in the financial community, some of them told Johnson, that another escalation would hurt the economy. The war was costing Washington in terms of public disillusionment with its other commitments in western Europe and Asia, commitments the establishment had founded and valued above all. This was true; it had been true four months earlier when the same men had unanimously endorsed the war. But the mood was clear to Johnson; the men he had relied on, the men whose reputations weighed so heavily, were against him like everyone else.

"The establishment bastards have bailed out," Johnson reportedly sneered as he stormed away from the meeting, accompanied by Humphrey, who by the same account replied a helpful, "Yes, Mr. President." "I knew they had not seen all the reports I had," Johnson remembered his reaction in its expurgated version in his memoirs. Five days after the meeting, he announced new restrictions on the bombing of North Vietnam to encourage peace talks, and, most dramatically, withdrawal from the presidential race. March 26, 1968, rankled long after he left office. Shortly before he died, five years later, he would recall the meeting with the "Wise Men," bitterly telling an aide at the presidential library in Texas that while in the White House he had been "screwed" by a lot of people—the press, the Congress, even his own staff, but "the big-name foreign policy types did the royal job on me."

Picking up their distinguished passengers at the West Basement exit of the White House, slipping one by one into the Pennsylvania Avenue traffic in the darkening March afternoon, the limousines of the departing "Wise Men" formed in a sense a funeral procession for an administration and its foreign policy. It was also a larger ending, though typically the men in the cars could not have known it. Lyndon Johnson's withdrawal opened the White House to Richard Nixon, a politician of a different sort, whose private visions of the establishment, the bureaucracy, and of himself would make for very different government in foreign policy. With him came a relatively obscure Harvard professor who brought his own similar convictions about the nature of statesmanship.

Henry Kissinger had been a sometime consultant to the Kennedy and Johnson administrations, and one of the house academics of the establishment, writing a series of books under the auspices of the Council on Foreign Relations. But the most significant of Kissinger's impressive intellectual accomplishments concerned not so much problems among nations as the making of policy within them. Masked in abstract, often heavy prose, his telling criticism of past American policy came down eventually to its men and methods, the ultimate failure of "people who are expert at it." For that fatal flaw, for the international problems confronting the United States, he would have a single remedy—himself.

II

---◄◆►---

Coup d'État at the Hotel Pierre

Nearly halfway along its fashionable and historic course up the center of Manhattan Island, Fifth Avenue abruptly leaves a concrete ravine of commercial buildings and enters a softer terrain. On the west are the trees and walks of Central Park, on the east the stolid apartment houses and tasteful philanthropies of the wealthy. The Hotel Pierre at 61st Street is close inside the frontier of this elegant region. Less famous than the Waldorf or the nearby Plaza, the Pierre is one of the most prestigious and exclusive of New York's great hotels. Its own lucrative commerce is carefully muted, from the black limousines outside to the small European lobby and posh shops within. Upstairs, the hallways are dim, the rooms often venerably worn, but that too seems part of the distinction, a stylish refusal to risk yielding to the common mode. In the raw late autumn of 1968, the buff-colored canopy over the Pierre's Fifth Avenue entrance was a note of characteristic insouciance against the gathering filth of the city's air. It was here, beyond that canopy in the aging suites, that Richard Nixon established the embryonic government of his first administration during the pre-inaugural transition to power from November 1968 to January 1969. It was here that he hired Henry Kissinger. From within the Pierre they promptly conceived and began what would become a seizure of power unprecedented in modern American foreign policy.

Their *coup d'état* was not an act of grand conspiracy. They neither plotted nor foresaw its far-reaching consequences. Its origins, like many crucial events, were based in elements no one could plan, the expedient collaboration of two very different men with surprisingly similar perceptions about the weaknesses of other men, the need for hasty improvisations to meet opportunities. The meaning of it all was scarcely noted at the time. Nonetheless, it was a coup. At the Pierre, Kissinger recommended and Nixon readily adopted (provided it could be maneuvered past his other senior foreign affairs advisers without confrontation) a formal new system of decisionmaking for the National Security Council (NSC). The system would install Kissinger firmly atop the bureaucratic structure, with decisive control over both the formulation and conduct of policy, and thus *de facto* power greater than the *de jure* constitutional authority of the Secretaries of State and Defense. Exploited and extended to become a vehicle for Kissinger's extraordinary talents, that position of power created a new pattern of government in Washington for foreign relations. It was instrumental in some of the most important and enduring diplomatic achievements of the Nixon administration. From those successes, from his unique position, can be traced much of Kissinger's personal rise to a rare eminence in the nation and the world. At the end of the Nixon administration, with the presidency in political and psychological collapse, Kissinger's authority would make him at critical moments no less than acting chief of state for national security. His grip on government continued under Nixon's successor, Gerald Ford, who would appear to be visibly in awe of his Secretary of State.

The agreement to the new NSC apparatus was significant, too, for the portent it held of the flaws running deep in Richard Nixon's government, and of the ironic role foreign policy would play in its failures as well as its triumphs. The new NSC apparatus compounded the existing exclusion of the Congress and the public from foreign policy. Later, when abuses and deceptions were exposed, that exclusion made all the more angry and sweeping the public disillusion. The system that was to foster bold initiatives within the administration also worked to rob foreign policy of its essential constituency in the Congress and beyond. It deepened, as well, the wider isolation of the White House. As the new NSC machinery in Kissinger's hands tightened a circle of vast power close about the Oval Office, as the diplomatic feats with their domestic applause seemed more and more a mastery of events, the effect was to reinforce in the President and some of his men a belligerent arrogance and a longing for similar control over American domestic politics. Already visible at the Pierre were the presidential furtiveness and manipulation of government, the strange mixture of private resolve and evasiveness toward subordinates, that were to be ingredients of Nixon's self-destruction. A tangled and complex history lay behind the widespread loss of faith in executive conduct of foreign policy in the mid-1970s. There were many other significant influences in the genealogy of the Watergate scandal. But this unobserved coup on Fifth Avenue belongs in a way to an understanding of both those fateful developments.

There is now almost a tintype quality about the Henry Kissinger who stood, elated but nervous, beside the President-elect at the Pierre on December 2, 1968, as Nixon announced to the press his selection as Assistant for National Security Affairs. Across eight years, with all the thousands of photographs and television images, that man seems suddenly much younger, thinner, less imposing. With a simplicity and reserve soon to disappear from the press, *The New York Times* described him then as a "45-year-old specialist in defense policy and European affairs." On its surface, the biography was that of an accomplished, successful academic whose thoughtful views and contacts had brought him to the respectable edges of power and politics. The most unusual part of his background was the beginning: a smalltown Jewish childhood in Germany during the collapse of the Weimar Republic and through the early years of the Nazi régime. After immigration to New York as an adolescent in 1938, he rose rapidly and steadily to a distinction that seemed largely conventional. Impressive service in army intelligence, including work in occupied Germany, propelled Kissinger in 1947 into Harvard, where he completed an undergraduate degree and a Ph.D. in seven years with obvious gifts that kept him on the Harvard faculty. He came to public attention at thirty-four with the prize-winning book *Nuclear Weapons and Foreign Policy* (1957), developed while he was chairman of a Council on Foreign Relations study group. The next year he directed another special report on national issues for the Rockefeller Brothers Fund, which began a long period of profitable patronage from Nelson Rockefeller. In 1958, Kissinger was back at Harvard as an associate director of its Center for International Affairs. At the

Center he ran a prestigious seminar for foreign students, many of whom later became prominent governmental figures in their own countries. Tenure at Harvard and a growing reputation came with the publication of three more books. There was a brief consultancy to the NSC during the Kennedy administration in 1961–62, more routine consultation for the joint chiefs and the Arms Control and Disarmament Agency from 1959 to 1968, work on the Rockefeller presidential campaign in 1964 and again in 1968, and finally the late 1968 summons to the Pierre.

It was the record of an ambitious, sometimes lucky man, working well within established institutions, without apparent defect or special tempering for what lay ahead. Based mainly in teaching and scholarship, despite the political interludes, Kissinger's career seemed to have little in common with the fitful progress of the politician who was now hiring him. Many of those who knew him in his academic years would later register surprise at his public fortunes. "I could not believe it was the same man," a Harvard colleague said typically. The puzzlement probably owed more to a misunderstanding of the qualities that can make for success in government than to any basic change in Kissinger. Behind his scholarly credentials was a preparation in miniature for much he encountered in the reach for Washington power, including a rancorous, unforgotten taste of defeat and some important similarities of experience with Nixon. The respected but obscure academic adviser presented to the world at the Pierre was already in most respects the artful diplomat he would become.

The ascent to 1968 had involved its own politics, rivalries, expedient alliances, and costly lessons. The early years at Harvard had been consumed in the sometimes elaborate maneuvering for the coveted faculty tenure—a process described by one survivor as having "all the elegance and justice of a cockfight." There had been, too, a running feud with Robert Bowie, a former State Department official under both Eisenhower and Johnson who formally directed the Center for International Affairs. Kissinger had conducted the contest, and similar sparring for status among other advisers in the Rockefeller campaigns, with public decorum, unrelenting private venom, and little damage to his career, as he would later deal with more formidable rivals in the White House. Playing past Bowie and other faculty adversaries to a wider constituency in the university and outside

world, he energetically solicited foundation support for the Center
(including funds from some CIA fronts then backing foreign affairs
research in several institutions), and nurtured the success of his international seminar, with meticulous attention to the *entrées* it opened
in official Washington and abroad. He continued with equal cultiva-
tion his relationship with the Council on Foreign Relations and the
New York establishment. His third and fourth books, *The Necessity
for Choice* (1960) and *The Troubled Partnership,* a study of Atlantic
relations (1965), were again drawn in part from Council study groups
that had included Dean Rusk and other notable figures.

Interestingly, students and colleagues from this period saw Kissinger in much the same ways in which his staff and rivals viewed him
later in government. To those below he was gifted, demanding, colored by the allure and distance of his association with the famous. He
was also capable of a kind of intimate poignancy and self-pity, the
hints given of a man ensnared. In 1958, after the widely praised
Nuclear Weapons and Foreign Policy, the beginning of the Rockefeller patronage, and the appointment to the Center for International
Affairs, he could still advise one Harvard student to "get yourself a
profession that will have real meaning to you. Don't become like
me." That remark was to be frequently echoed in later complaints
to his NSC staff about the frustrations and indignities encountered in
the Nixon White House. But from another vantage point, Kissinger
was charming, abrasive, and ultimately more successful than his
peers expected. His brilliance and ambition were usually controlled,
almost "consciously circumspect," as one academic associate put it.
About one characteristic, however, most recollections before and
after agree—the remarkable care and faithfulness with which he
tended the politics of his advance, whatever his inner doubts or
exterior guise. There were the thoughtful private notes on hundreds
of Christmas cards to public figures he had met, the sudden rages if
an embarrassingly small lecture audience or some other mishap
threatened to offend a visiting dignitary and cast aspersion on Kissinger. In Cambridge as in Washington, he was a man intent on
appearances and the maintenance of personal ties, however slight, to
fortify his reputation against the inevitable enemies. "He was always
counting the votes," remembered a friendly Harvard colleague.

The votes were not always there. His part-time consultancy for
the Kennedy NSC was marred by clashes with McGeorge Bundy

over U.S. diplomacy in Europe, which Kissinger indiscreetly criticized in public at the time. The problem went deeper than policy. Whatever the issue, Kissinger was in an unequal struggle, without a bureaucratic power base in the administration or easy access to the President. He resigned as an NSC consultant in 1962, leaving in their government offices many of his Harvard and New York colleagues, men whom he generally regarded as being of lesser caliber than himself, amid scathing gossip about Henry's lack of political sense. It was a bitter, lasting instruction for a man whose life had been so largely ruled by maneuver and preparation. Defeat of a different though equally memorable sort came in the 1964 campaign for the Republican presidential nomination, which climaxed in the savage outburst of the right-wing galleries against Nelson Rockefeller at the San Francisco Convention captured by Barry Goldwater. According to several accounts, that exposure to electoral politics at their most poisonous made a deep impression on Kissinger. Rockefeller would later describe his otherwise phlegmatic foreign affairs adviser as "indignant" at the incident; another staff member recalled him as "genuinely shocked." As the lost skirmish with Bundy no doubt drove home the stark requirements of White House power, the spectacle at the Cow Palace in 1964 may have implanted another preconception Kissinger would bring to Washington five years later—an abiding fear that foreign policy reverses could arouse a volatile recrimination from the right wing in American politics. By the summer of 1968, another Rockefeller run for the nomination had collapsed, again in part destroyed by conservative forces within the party. At the same time, the Harvard international seminar suffered dwindling support and the prospect of eventual abandonment. Earlier that year, Kissinger had gained brief publicity as a would-be intermediary through academic contacts for one of the Johnson administration's somewhat perfunctory and chronically abortive peace feelers to North Vietnam. As the presidential campaign progressed, occasional calls for advice went out to him as to other academics, from the staffs of both Nixon and Humphrey; but there were no special requests for his participation, and no tangible prospect of appointment by the winner.

The sum of his influence and impact at this juncture was meager —measured, as he saw it, against the obvious grasp of his ambition and his comparatively swift, promising advance in the late fifties. For

his decade of hard work and opportunities, there had been an embarrassing failure in Washington, two campaigns with a losing candidate,
a diminishing academic base, accompanied by the usual acid faculty
politics and the personal trauma of a divorce. The record had an
accumulating sense of the also-ran, the marginal, the unrealized. At
forty-five, his ardently burnished career seemed to have dulled, the
one secure prospect a career of more Harvard lectures and faculty
gossip, broken only by continued jockeying for position in the establishment for another chance. As personal history, it was not so different, in its own terms, from that of the forty-nine-year-old Richard
Nixon, who came to New York after the political defeats of 1960 and
1962 a man of large expectations and early promise to whom disappointment had also taught some vivid lessons.

In character and talent, Kissinger stood apart from the foreign
policy élite whom he courted at the Council on Foreign Relations
and elsewhere. There were inescapable differences of status. He was
an intellectual with a heavy German accent and no practical governmental experience, a house academic in a club dominated by the
lawyers and business men who had held high office in Washington for
years. Aspiring Secretaries and Under Secretaries attended seminars
and conferences, uttered their wisdom, and left the writing of seminar minutes and the books, with proper subsidies, of course, to the
technicians like Henry who had time for such elaboration. "He was
an adornment," said one observer who directed similar studies, "but
still more hired hand than member." The hierarchy was subtle but
real. Of Kissinger's four books, the Council on Foreign Relations held
the copyright on two. There was a prospective category in Washington for such people, a way to fit them into a slot, albeit well short of
the top. When Kissinger telephoned McGeorge Bundy to ask his
advice after the first call came from Nixon for a meeting at the Pierre,
and neither knew what office Kissinger might be offered, Bundy
suggested he might suitably try for the chairmanship of Policy Planning in the State Department. It was, as the Ford Foundation president knew, a powerless, irrelevant position, and not one which a
Rusk, a Ball, or a Bundy would accept, but a natural place for someone like Kissinger. It was indicative of the understood force of such
invisible rules that Kissinger later told an aide that, though he had
been put off by Bundy's pigeonholing, Policy Planning was about
what he himself had expected to get. Adding to this caste distinction

was Kissinger's personal temperament. Most of his fellow workers at the Council and on the Rockefeller campaigns would remember him above all as a "loner." Attentive as he was to his reputation within the establishment, he did not easily mix outside the formal sessions. He preferred to do the bulk of the work (and later claim credit) himself rather than in committee—a method that no doubt preserved the quality of the projects he directed, though at the price of some bruised vanities and resentment.

What separated Kissinger most significantly from the foreign affairs élite was the distinction apparently least recognized by the club: his sizable intellectual superiority and the habitual disdain expressed in his books for the institutions and men who had governed American policy since World War II. As arguments on specific policies, Kissinger's writings were noteworthy but seldom audacious. *Nuclear Weapons and Foreign Policy*, which urged a strategy embracing tactical uses of atomic weapons and limited wars in seeming contrast to the prevailing Eisenhower-Dulles doctrine of massive retaliation, was the most controversial of his books when it was published. But the central point was consistent with the general criticism of Washington's rigid diplomacy at the time, and Kissinger soon publicly recanted the more chilling implication that he was somehow advocating the use of nuclear weapons in conditions short of national survival. Three years later, *The Necessity for Choice* posed in many respects an unoriginal critique of the "fatuous diplomacy" of the Eisenhower régime. The indictment, in which Kissinger supported the erroneous assertion of a "missile gap," was fashionable enough to form part of current Democratic campaign rhetoric at the time. Similarly, his 1965 prescription for European policy, *The Troubled Partnership*, reduced to a recital of U.S. neglect and continental disarray the already accepted wisdom of the best journalism and academic writing on both sides of the Atlantic. By comparison, his most thoughtful work had been scarcely noticed. *A World Restored*, a Harvard doctoral thesis refurbished for publication in 1957, was a penetrating, sometimes wry study of the diplomats and diplomacy of the decade after the Napoleonic wars, and was obviously a labor of intellectual love. Into it Kissinger poured his most creative and practical insights about the politics of foreign policy.

The nexus of his scholarship was the "inherent tension" between bureaucracy and statesmanship, and, in the American case, the dubious quality of the foreign policy leadership on top of organizational inertia. "It was no accident, even if it was paradoxical," he wrote in *A World Restored,* "that in 1821 Metternich had greater difficulty with the Austrian than with the Russian ministers, and that in every negotiation Castlereagh had to fight a more desperate battle with his Cabinet than with his foreign colleagues." Bureaucracy, "designed to execute, not to conceive," paralyzed by "its quest for safety," was "diametrically opposed" to the spirited development of good policy, which thrived on "perpetual motion" and abhorred routine. His analysis owed a primary intellectual debt to Max Weber and others who had explored the bureaucratic envelopment of the modern state. Kissinger's adaptation of the thesis to diplomatic history, however, was fresh and revealing. In a discipline which often explained international politics either as a machine of a larger historical determinism or as an intricate game among protagonists coldly calculating the next move, he saw the statesman in his more pedestrian reality as a politician for whom success began at home. Traditionally, the diplomat struggled with "the inertia of his material" in the form of the alien force and interests of other states. But for Kissinger, "the acid test of policy is its ability to obtain domestic support." This meant not only public political support, but in the first instance "the problem of legitimizing a policy *within* the governmental apparatus."

The same year he published these observations of restoration diplomacy, he brought them with an added dimension to contemporary Washington. "Our final problem," ended his somber list of perils in *Nuclear Weapons and Foreign Policy,* was "the adequacy of our leadership groups for dealing with the challenges we are likely to confront," which he saw as part of the "more general problem" in the enduring conflict between "the requirements of organization and the need for inspiration." The same specter that bedeviled Metternich now plagued American foreign policy: the opposition to statesmanship by a bureaucracy "whose primary concern is with safety and minimum risk." To make matters worse, while the bureaucrats were very much in evidence, there were no statesmen. There were no Metternichs in the Eisenhower régime, nor were there any waiting in exile at the Council on Foreign Relations. The "leadership groups" of businessmen and lawyers had reached the top by being "essentially manipulative" in institutions, while "the qualities required for leadership are primarily creative." Businessmen saw policy administratively, and lawyers dealt with a world of ad hoc cases. Neither of these "two professions which are most dominant in the higher levels of government" was able to galvanize the torpid organizations into creative action or to think in strategic and political concepts. "Our leaders have not lacked ability," he allowed, "but they have had to learn while doing, and this has imposed too great a handicap." Nor was Kissinger reluctant to tally the cost of the basic internal weakness of personalities. "This explains," he concluded in 1957, "many postwar Soviet successes."

He developed the point most forcefully in the final chapter of *The Necessity for Choice,* entitled "The Policymaker and the Intellectual." The United States had not reached a moment of crisis and policy impasse because of some wrong choice made among alternative courses. "The more serious and pertinent question is how qualified our eminent men are for the task of policymaking . . . very little in the experience that forms these men produces the combination of political acumen, conceptual skill, persuasive power, and substantive knowledge required for the highest positions of government." The typical executive, whom Kissinger knew in their numbers at the Council, was "shaped by a style of life that inhibits reflectiveness." Such men became hostage to their subordinates' views, were, in their "lack of substantive mastery" and compromising style, reluctant to stand alone, and succumbed to government by committee and consensus where there was always a "powerful tendency to think that a compromise among administrative proposals is the same thing as a policy." The impact of it all on the U.S. international position was, as he put it in a word, "pernicious." The NSC had become "less concerned with developing measures in terms of a well understood national purpose than with adjusting the varying approaches of semi-autonomous departments." Nor was there any automatic salvation in the recruitment of intellectuals, who were prone in government to be sucked into the bureaucratic routine. In any case, the administrators, the inwardly feeble "men of action," consigned the intellectual by convention to a marginal "advisory" role while reserving to themselves the policy choice. "The intellectual is rarely found," Kissinger complained (some eight years before his conversation with McGeorge Bundy about the obscure job of Policy Planning in State), "at the level where decisions are made." The only solution was for the intellectual to preserve somehow "his independence," to establish over bureaucracy a substantive, reflective leadership that would "transcend routine" and "take the responsibility for innovation." That way alone lay the escape from routine and narrow departmental interests to the broader conception and purpose on which policy should be founded. Again, in a book dealing with the whole range of foreign policy problems from arms control to Communist subversion in the developing countries, Kissinger concluded that America faced "no more urgent" task than to remedy this organizational malaise. It was implicitly a prescription for an intellectual autocracy in the weakly governed domain of foreign policy. If not in 1960, then certainly later, he had no difficulty seeing himself as the sovereign.

Along with the criticism of organization, the outline of Kissinger's particular version of the larger view, the conceptual approach he urged on Washington, also took shape. His definition of policy and creativity argued against an avowed doctrine. But from the vague, consciously detached observations on power relationships at the conclusion of *A World Restored*, he distilled a coherent view of American place and purpose in the late fifties. At its heart was an undisguised preference for a conservative structure of diplomacy, which would produce at once "a notion of quality . . . with the framework of great conception" and "the key to a stable international organization." He saw the purpose of American statesmanship, much as Metternich's, to accommodate yet check revolutionary changes in a new balance of postwar power. The general conditions of the period after 1945, the rivalry of the United States and the Soviet Union, the third-party roles of Europe, China, and Japan, and the unsettled environment and relative powerlessness of the former colonial nations, for the most part he took for granted as the context of diplomacy. He accepted the primacy of Washington's and Moscow's military and political power over the apparent economic diversification of that world. His view of America's international economic interests was conventional, uncritical, and comparatively unsophisticated. The emphasis of his analysis lay much more upon the methods and mentality essential to a new *Realpolitik*. Washington would have to come to terms with specific issues such as arms control and a more general political settlement with both adversaries and allies, or face "a world in which we had become largely irrelevant." His policy arguments centered on the need for a precise calculation of interests, a rigorous preparation of positions, and a flexible yet self-interested approach to negotiations. It was in several respects Kissinger's vision of another "world restored," with diplomats dispassionately accepting the inevitable clash of national interests, and diplomacy conducted toward its time-honored goals: definition, resolution, compromise, order, stability. Security would lie in the essence of power balance, the absence of dominance by any single nation, the acceptance by all of relative insecurity as a condition of their enemies' stake in the settlement. The Rostows notwithstanding it was not, and never had been, a world where the United States could reasonably expect or seek "victory." Peace and stability was its own triumph, and that condition could be achieved only by a continuing adjustment and balancing of interests.

The novelty of Kissinger's intellectual analysis was striking only for an America still in thrall—or at least imagined so by its political leadership—to the chauvinism and ignorance of the cold war. But it was no less important for that very reason. Kissinger's freedom from dogma, his deep seriousness, seemed authentic genius in a foreign policy dialogue heretofore confined chiefly to irrelevant diagram-drawing academics, the fatuous zeal of establishment professors like Rostow, the aphorisms of the élite's memoirs, or the utter emptiness of official statements. Kissinger's gift, a replica of the nineteenth-century statesmanship he studied, was to understand the enduring sway of great power nationalism through the haze of ideological rivalry and revolutionary changes that reached its climax after World War II. "We have come to the end of the policies and of the men that dominated the immediate post-war period," he wrote in 1960. Almost the same words formed the underlying concept of Nixon's first major foreign policy message to Congress a decade later. Like the impact of the machine gun on the relevance of the calvary charge, it was one of those seemingly self-evident observations in public affairs which appear banal in retrospect, yet at the time penetrate encrusted policies and politics only slowly.

In 1960, and to a large degree even ten years later, Kissinger stood out amid a foreign policy mandarinate blinded to the possibilities of diplomacy by the ideological precepts of its rule. Kissinger as historian appreciated no less than the establishment the antagonism between Moscow and Washington, the anti-American impulse in local revolutionary movements. He saw the struggle, however, against the backdrop of a complex, ambiguous world of nations in which there were mutual as well as competing interests. With the same realism that enabled him to understand the broader limits of American power and the self-defeating character of his country's international messianic urge, he also recognized the divisive national interests and politics of Communist states. He accepted the Russian and Chinese revolutions as irreducible, if unpleasant, facts of world politics. Yet the régimes in Moscow and Peking were distinct. In contrast to the prodigal simplicities of the ideological view dominating American foreign policy, he saw nations as nations, as they indeed were, with unique histories and identities. Any settlement between revolutionary and conservative powers would always be uneasy, contradictory, subject to challenge. There would be conflict, and tests of strength that must be met. But many of the most urgent problems of that postwar period—traditional issues of frontiers and military restraint creating instability and risk—were within the capacity and will of these rival governments to resolve. Diplomacy could knit together the elements of their common stake in the resolution and create a tolerable order. One could ask no more. Kissinger's view was a blend of cynicism and practical idealism that could rationalize with ready consistency simultaneous policies of nuclear détente with the Kremlin, reconciliation with Mao Tse-tung, the bombing and blockade of North Vietnam, and the covert subversion of a Marxist president in Chile.

Of the three concepts which would have a lasting influence on his official career, two—his scorn for the bureaucracy, and his faith in the establishment and promise of a new national diplomacy—came through clearly in Kissinger's writings. The third—his view of the domestic political basis of American foreign relations—was less sharply drawn, perhaps for being the more uncertain and ominous element in his vision. The "acid test" of policy, "its ability to obtain domestic support," went beyond circumvention of the bureaucrats within government to the larger challenge of "legitimizing" policy in the country's politics. Yet the statesman would have "great difficulty" in achieving this necessary goal, he wrote in *A World Restored,* precisely because international stability depended on "self-limitation" of states, "on the reconciliation of different versions of legitimacy." Domestic politics, by contrast, were ruled by a consensus, "a parochial version" of justice and legitimacy that inevitably ran counter to realistic diplomacy. The simple uncomplicated domestic context where will and execution coincided was the natural habitat of bureaucracy. It was the burden of the diplomat to tell his country-men the unpopular truth that, in the world of nations, their aims, opinions, and desires were factors without universal value, and that the foreign affairs of their country were destined to be a messy, unrewarding business, whatever their cherished pretenses. "Not for nothing do so many nations exhibit a powerful if subconscious rebel-lion against foreign policy," he observed, without naming the United States but having it very much in mind. And statesmen, he added, "often share the fate of prophets," ending "without honor in their own country." The only solution was for the diplomat to be an "edu-cator" as well. "He must bridge the gap between a people's experi-ence and his vision." At best his possibilities were limited: "A states-man who too far outruns the experience of his people will fail in achieving a domestic consensus, however wise his policies. . . . A statesman who limits his policy to the experience of his people will doom himself to sterility. . . ." In any event, the indispensable condi-tion was that the creative diplomat not be destroyed by domestic dissent while he struggled to attain his historic balance abroad and at home. Societies required "sufficient cohesion so that policy could be conducted with the certainty conferred by the conviction that domestic disputes were essentially technical and confined to achiev-ing an agreed goal."

His portrayal of the dilemmas of nineteenth-century negotiators was again obviously relevant to Washington in the fifties and sixties. A diplomat so bold as to deal with the Soviets or the Chinese Commu-nists as great powers with separate interests, or to discipline the joint chiefs on an arms control bargaining position, would be inviting the wrath of "parochial versions" of U.S. interests, and would soon need the higher sanction of history. On one level, Kissinger's warnings about the problems of domestic politics interfering with foreign pol-icy seem directed at a predictably nativist, perhaps xenophobic reac-tion to the grand postwar settlement he imagined. His foreboding about the people's impatience and lack of subtlety in the face of contradictory international realities was an astute anticipation of some of the problems he would later encounter in sustaining the policy of détente with the USSR. But the more significant character-istic of his concept in terms of the future was its élitist spirit. Deplor-

ing the narrow, exclusionary quality of national politics, he proceeded to endow the statesman with the inherently exclusive powers
of a prophet—eventually perhaps even a martyr. It was given to the
diplomat, neither a bureaucrat nor an administrator, to see the country's proper course in the world. The diplomat possessed a skill in
which his benighted countrymen were naturally deficient; they were
much in need of his "education" to save peace and stability in spite
of themselves. Between the lines in Kissinger's writing, one detects
an almost mythic quality bestowed upon the figure of the diplomat.
Alone he threads his way through a treacherous world, eluding the
grasping hands from the bureaucratic bog. And after all that he must
still deal with the "parochial" public, whose relative ignorance must
be appeased and carefully attenuated lest they ruin it all by failing
to support him.

Kissinger's later obsession with the perils of dissent and division
in American society, the fear of national recrimination that lurked
behind so much of the Vietnam policy, was part of a generally conservative view of democracy, no doubt deepened by the experience
of Weimar Germany, which he saw in vivid terms intellectually if not
in fact as a personal childhood trauma. But his later contempt for
congressional and public opposition can also be traced to this fundamental conception of diplomacy. The body politic owed its own
cohesion to the statesman who assured its survival. It was not a
system in which the public could properly be allowed to challenge
the wisdom of the policymaker. And whatever the virtues of his
conception, it was not a description of a lively democracy, at least in
the conduct of foreign policy. If the establishment's constituency was
itself, Kissinger's statesman answered in the end only to history. He
might fail ("outrun" the popular experience), but that was a technical
flaw; the disaster was that domestic politics could not keep pace.
Keenly aware of the need for domestic support—indeed, having
made it the "acid test" of policy—he nonetheless endowed statesmanship with an aura of superiority that in part enabled him later,
when theory became reality, to flout the very domestic backing he
believed so essential. There was in it, too, a sense of the personal
tragedy of the popularly rejected diplomat, however vindicated by
history. Castlereagh, whose diplomatic brilliance in bringing En-
gland into the post-Napoleonic settlement was admiringly described
in *A World Restored,* eventually was isolated and repudiated by a

nation which, luxuriating in the security he had created, lost understanding of his vision. Broken by his success, the king's gifted minister—Henry Kissinger's hero—committed suicide at fifty-three.

Few public figures so embodied the insular politics Kissinger deplored, the domestic nemesis of diplomacy, as the one who called
him to power at the Pierre. Nixon seemed an unlikely patron of
statesmanship by Kissinger's lights, and even less likely its practitioner. Nixon's early career had been a model of the politician as
opportunist, usually at the expense of national reason in matters of
world affairs. A crude, demagogic anticommunism had fueled his
rise. Throbbing with allusions to treason and conspiracy, his invec-
tive against the Democrats' foreign policy before his 1952 election
as Vice President was characterized by the fury that the author of
A World Restored regarded as destructive of the very political order
as well as ruinous for the conduct of international relations. "To the
extent that 'McCarthyism' means the exposure of individuals who
needed to be exposed for the security of the country," Nixon said in
one of his more moderate statements of 1952, "I think the majority
of the American people favor it." Less elliptically, he had earlier
called a senatorial opponent "the Pink Lady," smeared Dean Acheson as the "Red Dean," and accused Truman of a "defense of Communism in high places." The President and his Secretary of State
were "traitors to the high principle" of their party, licensing his
listeners to wander over the edge of hate and hysteria to which such
language led them. (Twenty years later, Henry Kissinger himself
would speak darkly of America's internal and international "collapse" under the din of much less florid and inflammatory critics.)
Though these excesses stopped just short of McCarthy's dementia
and his rhetoric of betrayal slackened and finally disappeared from
the public utterances as Vice President and presidential candidate in
1960, for many Americans Nixon remained a symbol of those rancid
politics.

The President who proudly saw himself as peacemaker in the
Kremlin and on the Great Wall of China was not so much transformed as naturally evolved from this earlier Nixon. The paradox
went to the marrow of the human being and his administrations,
where a Kissinger governed beside the most mediocre men, and
qualities of greatness co-existed with the basest political instincts.

Lacking any visible ethic save his own promotion, Nixon's original politics reflected and exploited the insecurity and confusion already present in American disillusionment with the immediate postwar world. A people who had won a war at vast effort, who thought of themselves as predominant in the world in both moral and material force, had been suddenly deprived of clear victory by the emergence of Soviet power, posing the sinister prospect of a continuing warfare, political as well as military. It was virtually a model of the collision Kissinger had conceived between international reality and domestic self-image. The search for conspiratorial scapegoats within was one temporary refuge from that threatening world. Like the country, however, Nixon gradually came to terms with the lost peace, reassured by his own success and growing accustomed to the continuing stalemate of U.S.-Soviet rivalry. By 1968, as Johnson had too briefly discovered a year earlier at Glassboro, there was overwhelming national sentiment for a negotiated lessening of tensions with the Russians. That Nixon the politician felt this change and foresaw its opportunities was in a sense no less expedient than the pandering to angry recrimination two decades before. It was proof, not of conviction, but of his abiding astuteness.

The views that made Nixon Kissinger's collaborator at the Pierre —contempt for the establishment and for the bureaucracy, and an insistence on a single iron leadership in foreign policy—grew out of an unrecanted past. There was, and is, a deep vein of populism in the politics of resentment Nixon exemplified among the Republican party and beyond. It was part of the wrath a frightened Kissinger had seen hurled down on Nelson Rockefeller from the galleries at the 1964 Republican Convention, an animus of the plains and the West for Eastern privilege and wealth, a vague but vexing sense that if America has gone wrong, it has been at the hands of the powerful and the established. The strain was seldom blatantly revealed in Nixon, the poor boy from California, though it was never far beneath the surface. In the 1952 campaign he had called Adlai Stevenson "haughty" and "snobbish" in what seemed epithets of equal force with being "tolerant of Communism." His reputation-making trophy of the witch-hunt years was Alger Hiss, patrician State Department official and prominent member of the foreign affairs establishment. He won only meager political support from that same quarter in 1960 and 1968. Its predictable preference (like Kissinger's) for Rockefeller no doubt confirmed Nixon's belief that the establishment—whether in its smaller foreign policy version or in the wider definition of East Coast money and influence—was not to be trusted. This attitude found its practical application in the men who staffed his 1968 campaign and later came to the White House, men largely from the West. It surfaced bitterly in later moments of crisis, after the Cambodian invasion when, like Johnson after Tet, he spoke of the "desertion" of the establishment. And at the end, it was apparent in one of his delusions about the Watergate scandal when he told an aide, "The establishment is dying and they're trying to take us down with them." In any case, consistent with the social and regional tensions which had nourished his career, a mark of how Nixon saw himself and his constituency in 1968 no less than in 1952, he brought to the Hotel Pierre an aversion to the foreign affairs élite quite as potent in its own terms as Kissinger's.

Nixon despised the government bureaucracy on similar grounds of distrust. Here the formative experience was his years as Eisenhower's Vice President. He had watched Ike, he told Kissinger in one of their early conversations at the Pierre, being manipulated and subverted by the bureaucracy with their special interests. He had seen the homogenized "position" papers slowly wind their way to the top, giving the Chief Executive no choices other than what "they" wanted. Besides, even under Dulles it had been mostly "their" State Department, by which he meant the Democrats. This was, of course, a presumption of institutional disloyalty that every President makes. To Eisenhower the foreign policy bureaucracy had been staffed by twenty years of Democratic functionaries. For Kennedy the same department was Dulles's Foggy Bottom, ever too lethargic to perceive or capitalize on progressive trends in the world. To Johnson it was full of "the Kennedy people," out to embarrass him because he was not their dead hero. And to Nixon it was "them," another group with whom he felt himself a vulnerable outsider. Ironically, seen from inside the government, a President's alienation and powerlessness in the face of the bureaucratic mass—particularly in foreign policy, where the contrast between White House initiative and organizational sloth is often most apparent—was a vital exception to the common assumption of ever-growing presidential power. No President attacked the problem so soon and so effectively as Nixon in foreign affairs, however. There should be a reform of the

National Security Council, he told Kissinger, that would "give the people of this country the foreign policy they want," a system that took power from the bureaucrats and placed it where it belonged, in the White House. As he told the story later, Kissinger simply smiled and added, "I agreed."

The quality that may have ultimately assured Nixon's relationship with Kissinger was perhaps the most paradoxical and poignant. For it was in the area of Nixon's divisive irresponsibility as a politician on the make—in foreign policy—that this troubled man found the sole intellectual passion of a quarter-century spent amid public issues. His affinity for foreign affairs may well have begun with his initial Red-baiting. The suddenly fashionable menace of the outside world in the postwar years, plus his swift expertise in unearthing "Communists," would no doubt have drawn him as a senator to some marginal involvement in international affairs. As it happened, in the role of ceremonial traveler abroad, foreign policy was to be the one flirtation with substance he was allowed as Vice President under Eisenhower. There were the necessary briefings from the State Department, the CIA, and in embassies abroad, opportunities for personal encounters with the bureaucrats he subsequently swore to cut out of decisions. In the process Nixon received an education in the politics of diplomacy, albeit someone else's policy. Yet the same sort of vice presidential junkets and briefings made no noticeable dent in the critical insensibility to foreign affairs of Lyndon Johnson or Hubert Humphrey, both of whom emerged from their tours of duty accepting the prevailing orthodoxies of policy, largely hostage to what the system told them. Nixon, on the other hand, was distinguished not only by his visceral distrust of the establishment or his shrewd reading of the bureaucracy, but also by a genuine preference for the content and style of diplomacy over the less ordered, more gregarious politics of domestic affairs. He believed foreign affairs to be a higher calling of the politician.

In some measure, too, Nixon was simply bored and ill at ease with the personalities and brokering of economic or social issues at home. As a result, he clearly saw foreign policy as his major responsibility as well as special competence when he assumed the presidency. He had done "a great deal" of reading in the subject since 1962, he told a still skeptical meeting of the NSC staff early in his administration. Whatever its depth or character, his preparation had an immediate impact. Unlike his predecessor, he was generally familiar with most of the foreign policy issues that flooded before him, at his order, for review at the outset of the administration. It was not uncommon during early meetings of the NSC for Nixon casually to correct mistakes in the opening briefing presented by CIA Director Richard Helms, who, in the prevailing custom of high officials, read with scant personal comprehension a script prepared for the occasion by his underlings. At one meeting Nixon corrected Helms's butchered pronunciation of an obscure nation; at another he pointed out to the director of Central Intelligence that his briefing, complete with maps and charts, had confused the essential fact of just which countries were recognizing and arming which sides in an insurgency, a distant imbroglio in which the CIA was lobbying (fortunately without success) for a covert involvement. Like Kissinger's discovery that the postwar world was changing, Nixon's knowledge was stunning only by comparison to the standard mediocrity and shallowness of the cabinet table talk into which he entered. Again like Kissinger, it would matter very much that he knew more about the subject than the men who were supposed to advise him—except, to be sure, his Assistant for National Security, who would never fail to note the name and allegiance of a country (or the weakness of a bureaucratic rival who did).

When foreign affairs did not provide its presumed excitement and gravity, however, Nixon's reaction could be as crudely personal and unsophisticated as Johnson's. During his first two years in office, for example, he steadfastly refused, much to the chagrin of the State Department, to see a Third World leader who earnestly wanted to visit the White House. There was no apparent conflict between the two men or their countries. The President eventually explained to an aide that he had no intention of seeing "that dope." The last time they met, in 1966, the foreign leader had repeatedly slighted important matters of world politics to question Nixon the private lawyer on such mundane topics as American party organization, agricultural policy, and business regulation in the United States. It was hardly the stuff of diplomacy. What, Nixon asked disingenuously, was the use of talking to this man? Ironically, Nixon treated foreign policy with much the same mystique, the sense of a mission above politics, that the establishment and the bureaucrats generally employed to exclude interlopers like himself. Almost alone among recent presidents, he considered himself an initiate in the mysteries. In the first days of his administration he conveyed the impression of a man who, had he not gained the White House, saw himself as a qualified candidate for Secretary of State in someone's Republican régime.

The interest and enthusiasm Nixon found in foreign affairs may have sprung from the deepest impulses in the President. For the instinctively shy, withdrawn man, still awkward with large groups despite his years as a public figure, for the politician in whom defeat had implanted permanent suspicions of hostility and sabotage on all sides, foreign policy satisfied above all his obsession to control. That urge was most apparent in his mechanical, lifelessly programmed campaign of 1968, but once he attained the office, it readily found lodging in foreign policy. If the bureaucracy could be mastered, diplomacy opened up a vast area of controlled power. Foreign governments, unlike congressmen or governors, or even one's own staff, could generally keep secrets. Dealing with them was more often a clean, neat process: the confidential letters, the personal emissary. It was a world where much could still be done by two or three men, reducing the threat of failure and the need for capricious politics. There were obviously uncertainties and risks, but even the complexities had a certain symmetry, were gauged by the measurable quantities of economic and military power. In any case, diplomacy was not of a kind with the anarchy of vote fraud in Illinois or the shabby practices of logrolling in Congress. In addition, there was always the drama and command befitting a Chief Executive as he announced the secret diplomatic maneuvers, the historic strokes, to an unknowing public—when the time was right. For Nixon as for the Harvard professor he employed, foreign policy had an almost aesthetic appeal that depended on its ultimate removal as a governing function from the democratic process. By temperament and his own characteristic political paranoia, he was drawn to the private, benevolent dictatorship of Kissinger's model statesman.

Nixon's appetite for foreign affairs by no means assured wisdom, nor did it transcend malevolence or prejudice. For Richard Nixon's worst, as well as his best, foreign policy variously provided an outlet, a field of play. Combined with his distrust of the figures and institutions to whom American presidents customarily abdicated so much of foreign relations (with usually disastrous results), the rare assurance that he developed enabled him to move decisively through statesmanlike initiatives his predecessors could not, did not manage. This combination of contempt and self-reliance also fortified him in mistaken or malign policies against which the most thoughtful advice both in and out of his government would argue. Without such independence of action, his greatest achievements in the White House would probably have been impossible; with it, the tragedies of his presidency became more numerous.

Few if any of these portents were visible to the public as Nixon won election and paused in the Pierre to organize his administration. More than most politicians, he obscured the issues, including those of foreign policy. But the American presidential campaign barely requires the candidates to explain their traditionally obscure views on international questions, let alone to explain if they understand how and by whom policy is made, or how precisely they intend to rule in the most perilous and costly region of government. Foreign policy disappears beneath the deliberate clichés and false images manufactured in a campaign—Kennedy's "missile gap" in 1960; Johnson's "Asian boys to fight Asian wars" in 1964; Nixon's "peace with honor" in 1968—emerging only after the election when reality savagely mocks the slogans. But then candidates are not obliged to discuss the seamy inner realities of foreign affairs because their interlocutors generally understand them no better than they. Of all the examples of the pervasive neglect and ignorance of foreign policy among journalists, politicians, and thus the public, none is more telling than the election of a President.

Nixon thus managed easily to run both in 1960 and 1968 without a significant discussion of any aspect of foreign affairs, even if the 1968 election in particular was haunted by the Vietnam war and its destruction of the incumbent President. The two campaigns provided only faint and frequently misleading traces of the methods and positions that would dominate his foreign policy. In a 1960 interview in *The New York Times,* Nixon stated his preference for a Secretary of State who would "work with those in the Foreign Service and inside the State Department and . . . possess initiative, creativeness and a recognition of the necessity to break out of old thought patterns." There was an intriguing incident in the early autumn of 1968 when the Nixon staff telephoned Kissinger, among other academics, to canvass ideas for reorganizing the State Department. Despite his strong convictions on the matter, Kissinger declined to discuss it in a telephone conversation, and when the others consulted were similarly unresponsive nothing more came of the approaches. On at least two occasions during the campaign, Nixon vaguely denounced the "disorder" in Johnson's handling of foreign affairs, charging that decisions were made in "catch-as-catch-can talkfests" among advisers. A Nixon presidency, he promised without further explanation, would "bring back orderly government" to national security deliberations. Otherwise, there was virtually no evidence throughout his election campaign that Nixon had given any thought to the organization of foreign policy or the power relationships of his senior advisers. And yet it was a problem on which he had decided views.

Nixon's cautious, antiseptic 1968 run had given scanty hints of his attitude toward specific policy issues. A year before the election, he had written an article in *Foreign Affairs* seeming to suggest a new initiative toward Communist China. "Taking the long view," it concluded, "we simply cannot afford to leave China forever outside the family of nations. . . ." But the point was monotonously hedged by qualifications, ending with an inauspicious analogy between China and "the more explosive ghetto elements in our own country." In both cases, Nixon saw elements to be "curbed" and "brought within the law," as well as "dialogues . . . to be opened." That article, however, was as close as he would come to foreshadowing Kissinger's historic secret flight over the Himalayas to Peking four years later. And though his speeches were sprinkled with references to "a new era of negotiation" with the Soviets, his prospective policies on arms control or other relations with Moscow were no more precise. On Vietnam, which should have been the central issue of the election, he was, of course, relentlessly evasive. He had a "plan" to end the war, which he repeatedly pledged to do. Just how or when the "plan" would work, he refused to say, on the pretext that politics should not intrude on the Johnson administration's negotiating efforts, and that he could not properly discuss the details of his own future action on such a sensitive problem. This handling of the war in the campaign became in many respects a first example of the control and freedom from public accountability in foreign policy he expected as President. Largely unchallenged by the press or by a Humphrey compromised under the current policy, Nixon's concealment of his intentions in Indochina was successful, and a precedent. If he were qualified for the presidency in terms of his understanding of the institutions and issues of foreign affairs or because most of his policies would enjoy popular support, that was in no way established for the voters by his runs in 1960 or 1968. Then as later, the single most important standard of competence in a presidential candidate, the positions he takes in the field of national security and his ability to command, would be left mainly to image and intuition in the unbroken superficiality of the campaign.

When the President-elect first met with Kissinger on November 25, 1968, it was in part to satisfy those banal reasons of external appearances and personal whim which so often lead to fateful appointments in Washington. The distinguished professor was an uncommon hybrid, a Republican as well as a respected intellectual. Kissinger afforded the victorious Nixon a useful political symbol that the new administration could command such prestige, just like the Democrats. Also, having been Rockefeller's man, Kissinger might have represented another of the old rival's privileges and perquisites Nixon seemed to want to emulate, as in his Fifth Avenue apartments, New York physicians, and the landscaping of various vacation retreats. There were few other intellectuals recruited, however, and fewer still who were Rockefeller protégés. Nixon turned to Kissinger above all because the two men shared fundamental attitudes about the uses of power in foreign policy, and in Washington. "Believe it or not," Nixon told White House reporters early in the administration, "I'm familiar with Dr. Kissinger's writings." Set against the conventional pose of newly elected presidents toward foreign policy advisers, their first conversations at the Pierre were symbolic of the change. John Kennedy knew a lot about delegates and primaries and winning campaigns, as he would plaintively tell the establishment elders he consulted, but he needed their help getting the right men and policies to govern in the world. Lyndon Johnson approached the subject with similar if uncharacteristic humility, just not understanding, he once told Bundy during a talk about Mideast diplomacy, "the black magic you fellows stir up." But it was different now with Nixon, who beneath his plastic surface was apparently so much less substantial than Kennedy, less forceful than Johnson, the figure so many viewed—as Arthur Schlesinger had caustically put it in 1960, as the archetypal " 'other-directed' man in politics."

Elected to office through a weary public indifference to both the depth of his weaknesses and the potential of his strengths—which, such as they were, lay in international affairs—Nixon, for all his fatal flaws, came to the presidency with a rare if narrow sense of self-confidence and purpose in foreign policy. At their initial meeting, he talked with his future chief foreign policy adviser for hours about a broad range of issues, losing himself in the subject, forgetting to offer his visitor the job, making the formal tender two days later only when campaign manager John Mitchell discovered the omission. For his part, Kissinger asked for a week to think over the offer, and after two days of the usual rationalizing and casual phone calls to friends and colleagues, he eagerly took the post.

So they came together at the Pierre, outwardly contrasted in their roles as scholar and politician, yet remarkably similar. On the verge of acceding to long-coveted power, and despite careers devoted to political acceptance in their respective worlds, they continued to see themselves largely as men apart, as outsiders. For Nixon there were always the hostile press, the politicians and the bureaucracy, the ominous, endless "them" ever unreconciled to his victory. For Kissinger the inevitable mediocrity and careerist competition of the rest of officialdom aroused his scorn and alienation. Both expected strong opposition to their rule within their own ranks as well as outside. Suspicion and distrust ran deep in each, the venomous residue of past defeats and the conviction, so often produced by overarching ambition, that other men were equally ruthless and committed. They saw themselves too as reformers, in part on principle, in part because change in the system was necessary to the roles they proposed to play. In their private visions of public service and statesmanship, Nixon and Kissinger seemed to share a basic intolerance, almost contempt, for democracy. To each man, the public loomed in some way as a potential problem to be handled. Finally, there was the larger similarity that both of them had come to authority by default. Johnson, who in a deliberate putdown of both men persistently referred to the German consultant from Harvard as "Dr. Schlesinger," might normally have won another term in 1968, leaving Kissinger in Cambridge and Nixon in his Manhattan law firm. Instead, one of the most extraordinary and tumultuous periods in American life had shattered the pattern of politics. The fact that the two men acceded to power in 1968, and were given the opportunity to change American foreign policy as they wanted over the next four years, was very much, for all their ambition and readiness to govern, an accident of history.

An already uneasy press greeted the Kissinger appointment, as Nixon no doubt expected, as a reassuring sign of respectability in the new régime. The adviser was, after all, a familiar species, at least according to the journalistic authorities who kept track of such matters. James Reston of *The New York Times* duly endorsed Kissinger's selection. Unconscious of the multiple ironies in the comment, Reston pronounced it "significant that he has the respect of most of the foreign policy experts who have served the last three presidents." It was encouraging too, he wrote, that Kissinger had taken his Ph.D "under McGeorge Bundy." This slight confusion of intellectual pedigree and establishment hierarchies (Bundy did not have a doctorate and could not have advised Kissinger at Harvard despite outranking him among the élite) threw the new appointee only two days after his designation into the first of what would be many private rages at the press. The *Times*'s columnist was more thoughtful in pointing out how "odd" it was that the President-elect had chosen his White House Assistant "before" either the Secretary of State or Defense. "This may lead to some friction," he predicted in a sizable understatement.

At the formal announcement, both Nixon and his adviser seemed clear enough on the latter's responsibilities. "Dr. Kissinger is keenly aware of the necessity not to set himself up as a wall between the President and the Secretary of State," Nixon told the press in apparent candor about the old backstairs problem. "I intend to have a very strong Secretary of State." The Assistant for National Security was to concentrate on planning, not on operations. The President-elect did not want his man down there in the White House Situation Room, like Bundy and Rostow, spending "too much time going through cables." Nor did he choose someone who had "spent too much time in Washington." He wanted a "fresh approach," and here was the man. Kissinger himself said little. His most memorable statement came at the conclusion of the conference, when he was asked how he would advise the President on Vietnam. He believed "very strongly," he replied, that his position was "inconsistent" with making public statements on such issues.

Almost unnoticed when it was over went the sole hint of what was really happening at the Pierre. "Dr. Kissinger," Nixon said in an aside early in the announcement, "is setting up at the present time a very exciting new procedure for seeing to it that the President of the U.S. does not just hear what he wants to hear." That dangerous distortion was always, Nixon observed from his experience, "a temptation for White House staffers."

In 1947, the National Security Council had been established in an attempt to remedy the arbitrary and often uncoordinated foreign policy decisions which had flooded Washington from Franklin Roosevelt's White House. The Council had been designed to advise the President on "the integration of domestic, foreign and military policies," and to enable the armed services and other agencies of government "to cooperate more effectively in matters involving the national security." In addition to the Chief Executive, its statutory members included the Vice President, the Secretaries of State and Defense, the chairman of the joint chiefs, the director of the CIA, and the director of the Office of Emergency Planning (the latter a small, powerless bureaucratic vestige of the postwar era concerned with monitoring the availability of critical resources in event of war). But through the fifties and sixties the Council had never really attained the independence, much less the orderly foreign policy, it was established to insure. It had never freed itself from the arbitrary control and caprice of the dominant personalities in the bureaucracy, or from savage departmental rivalries. Under Truman and Eisenhower, Acheson and Dulles respectively had dominated foreign affairs, the intragovernmental disputes being settled by bureaucratic brokering of compromise positions. Kennedy had dispensed with the elaborate NSC structure of staff and policy papers which had been built up around that brokering by his predecessors. But he had not altered the essential mode of its operation. Written memoranda and oral presentations on foreign policy to the President continued to be amalgams of bureaucratic positions, often the product of prearranged compromise among the agencies. At most, they represented a collection of various agreed views and positions generated from within the individual departments.

The NSC system was, in short, a device in which the policies discussed by presidents and their senior advisers were with few exceptions the policies consonant with already established bureaucratic interests. It was a system Roosevelt had utterly rejected, preferring to make his own foreign policy to begin with. Johnson, along with Kennedy, simply thought the NSC too formal, too large (including too many of the wrong people, such as the Vice President), and altogether too prone to that ultimate scourge of his rule: the leak. Johnson thus reserved the NSC for public relations, as a forum at which to announce a decision already made, and conducted foreign policy mainly by informal meetings with a few preferred advisers, who, of course, were alternately advocates or indifferent proxies of institutional interests. Like a flimsy tower thrown up heedlessly atop a geological fault, the structure Johnson constructed to produce foreign policy decisions absorbed all the stresses and strains of government at precisely the weakest points, eventually to buckle and collapse under the pressure, taking its inhabitants down with it.

The real governing body of the Johnson régime's foreign policy was the "Tuesday lunch." In setting and practice, few moments have so vividly symbolized the psychological and organizational confusion of American foreign policy in the last decade as this weekly ritual at the White House. Surrounded by the soft tinkle of fine china and crystal, the deferential service of the naval stewards over the thick carpets, comforted by the sanctity and authority of the statesmen peering down from gilt-framed portraits, Johnson and his men chattily traversed both the menu and the agenda of issues, snugly insulated from the flesh-and-blood consequences of their talk, whether it was an offensive in the Central Highlands of Vietnam, an arms shipment to the Pakistani dictatorship, or another necessary deception of the Congress. These were the "talkfests" Nixon denounced during the 1968 campaign, though more for the apparent disorder of the decisions than for their detached callousness, which Nixon's own new administration was to repeat in its own style.

To this "Tuesday cabinet," Rusk, McNamara, Richard Helms, General Earle Wheeler, and Rostow brought their lists of issues to raise—lists usually prepared feverishly the night before by their staffs, who in turn had solicited the bureaucrats below for problems that could not be routinely handled by formal memoranda for the President. The senior advisers were familiar with some of these subjects, foremost among them Vietnam. But for other questions they were entirely dependent on the briefing materials supplied them by the bureaucracy. Discussion was thus reduced largely to two categories of policy considerations: those in which the men around the table had already acquired a personal stake and position, and those in which they were neither particularly interested nor independently informed. In both cases, there was nothing to oblige the decisionmakers to look beyond their own views or the formulation of the problem by the bureaucracy. Policies which they simply did not understand, or have time for, or consider worthy, did not often make the agenda, whatever their intrinsic significance. Nor did those they disagreed with, or thought might irritate Johnson and cost them his royal favor in other matters of import, the discussion of which at the pleasant lunch might invite open opposition and public rejection. In the tasteful atmosphere and executive style of the presidential dining room, the premium was on agreement. "You just don't go in there," Wheeler explained to one of his younger aides who urged dissent on a Vietnam bombing pause, "and piss in the President's soup."

Like all such institutions for formulating high-level policy, the Tuesday lunch was a reflection of the President. The gathering of this small group of like-minded men indulged Johnson's concern for a government-wide consensus, particularly on Vietnam, and his penchant for the intimate, man-to-man approach in which he could bring to bear most readily the force of his personality over all the "black magic" in foreign policy. Reduced to a few sentences over lunch, spiced with gossip or petty anecdotes, no problem was too complex. It was the method of a President who had been in Washington for nearly three decades without genuinely understanding the isolation of a leader at the hands of his advisers or the grip on cabinet officials of deeply vested bureaucratic interests. The worst of the Tuesday lunch was not that it shaped any decisive turnings in American foreign policy, but that it assured that the current policies and habits would go on. As opposition to the war mounted, the President's advisers became more and more secretive, a besieged group of men in their sanctuary, forbidden from telling any beyond a handful of their closest aides what policy decisions had been made by the U.S. government. Of supposedly the very highest priority, peace feelers toward North Vietnam were conducted in the White House and on the seventh floor of the State Department with an obsessive secrecy that excluded the few lower-ranking Asian specialists whose advice might have given them real life. This practice of secrecy allowed ample room, however, for the Pentagon to plead ignorance when uncoordinated military operations destroyed the tenuous diplomacy, as when bombing raids were carried out in the midst of a delicate Polish mediation effort in Hanoi in December 1966. So the Tuesday lunch increasingly became a forum for handling the public relations crises of a lost war and its inept diplomacy. Johnson's press secretary would have a place set at the table, the problems of press and public relations sometimes totally eclipsing discussion of the actual events abroad.

There was a brief, abortive effort in the mid-sixties to establish a more systematic means for reviewing policies in the Johnson years. In 1966, the Senior Interdepartmental Group (SIG), chaired by the Under Secretary of State, was set up, including ranking representatives from other agencies. An Interdepartmental Regional Group (IRG), a replica of the SIG at the Assistant Secretary level, was organized for each of five worldwide geographic regions and political-military affairs. All were formal committees set up to pass on a range of policy recommendations to the President. In reality, however, the SIG and various IRGs became merely rubber stamps for the process of passing on consensus memoranda, brokered by inter-agency vetos which were already the bureaucratic rule. "There are always three choices," Kissinger later explained these classic bureaucratic memos, "war, surrender, and present policy," or as he put it on another occasion, "current policy bracketed by two unthinkable alternatives." The object always, of course, was to keep on doing what had been done, what was safe, and what was protective of established institutional roles. Where the bureaucracy agreed, the policy continued. Where change or initiative threatened institutional interests or upset the balance of "trade-offs," as bureaucrats called it, the issue usually languished unresolved or was formally dismissed for lack of agreement. In such instances, present policy continued.

In the summer of 1968, for example, the State Department began a routine review of policy toward southern Africa, the periodic make-work drafting of a "National Policy Paper" by the Policy Planning Council. The author, an otherwise unoccupied senior foreign service officer, traveled the area extensively, held numerous afternoon-long inter-agency meetings with his colleagues, drafted and redrafted, and emerged after nine months with the predictable three options: side with the racist white states; side with the violent black liberation groups; or, the only sensible course, maintain present policy. Yet despite its unarguable general position, the paper produced at substantial taxpayers' expense was doomed, like countless of its kind before and after, to consignment to the Department's locked files. Neither the various agencies with interests in southern Africa nor their lame-duck superiors would resolve late in 1968 a series of operational issues that went along with the policy. These issues included the request on the part of American corporations to buy chrome from Rhodesia in a breach of UN sanctions, the proposed sale of U.S. arms to South Africa, requests for more economic aid and weapons from the black states of the region, and the disposition of a NASA tracking station in South Africa with its "whites only" employment policy. The paper was simply completed, the "policy" considered in force, and the bureaucrat's job done. As for those practical questions of chrome, weapons, and racial practices that actually determined U.S. relations in southern Africa, each was quietly shoved aside for the next administration to deal with.

In other instances, to be sure, there was not even the possibility of postponement for a troublesome issue. Two years earlier (in 1966), a low-level State Department economist had proposed a NATO Military Payments Union, a scheme for the sharing of costs for the common defense of Europe as Vietnam and inflation assaulted the dollar. The concept represented a serious response to a mounting problem for the Johnson administration and its successor. The burgeoning price of the U.S. forces on the continent was to be one of the factors in the later congressional clamor to reduce troops in Europe, affecting Washington's relations with the NATO Alliance and the Soviets. But the Payments Union was never formally broached with the European allies, never given the systematic examination it deserved by the IRG-SIG structure nominally designed to treat such new initiatives on their merits. The proposal died a premature bureaucratic death because of the early, formidable opposition of the State Department's European Bureau and the Secretary of Defense, both worried about the likely offense to European clients. It was not abandoned because it was a bad idea, but for the lack of any strong patron willing to take on its enemies in the battle necessary simply to place it on some high-level agenda for further consideration.

Kennedy's corrective for the sloth of the State Department and the autonomy of other agencies had been to create a strong NSC staff under Bundy in the White House. The task of this small presidential organization was to draw out the unconsidered alternative or point up bureaucratic omissions and misrepresentations. It possessed a formidable weapon in American government: the cover memo, a capsule summary and analysis attached to all departmental policy memoranda and sometimes even intelligence reports going to the President. But the cover memo was only as effective as the intellect and bureaucratic courage of its writer or of the NSC staff head. In Bundy's case, the sometimes exceptional talent of his assistants was offset by his own co-option by the system. He tended to see his role as coordinator of bureaucratic positions rather than as a critical adversary on behalf of the presidential interest in provoking the widest spectrum of discussion.

There was a still more basic weakness. Despite retaining the power of the last word, as it were, the NSC staff necessarily worked largely within the context of what the bureaucracy passed up to it. Like an editor who comments on a book's deficiencies but cannot rewrite it, the NSC staff monitor—usually one man charged to watch over the reports emerging from one or more bureaus in State, an office in Defense, and a regional branch in CIA—generally had neither the power to force proper consideration of an issue below nor the resources and time to provide the missing perspective himself. Under Walt Rostow, the blunting of this presidential tool was nearly total. Rostow gratefully saw himself as one more enthusiast at the Tuesday lunch. His cover memos on most issues were a dry rephrasing and seconding of the bureaucratic recommendation. The ultimate powers in the making of American foreign policy—the control of agenda and the timing of decisions, the ability to frame issues, the power to shape and shade and withhold information, the authority to ordain only those particular questions for the available answers— all that awesome authority abdicated by Johnson remained outside the White House. And it was at seizing those powers that the coup at the Pierre aimed first.

In their initial talks together, Nixon and Kissinger discussed the need for a major reorganization of decisionmaking in foreign policy. As with the other subjects they covered in these sessions at the Pierre, they spoke in broad terms but with an easy mutual agreement and reinforcement that began to form the pattern of their relationship. Nixon made it clear that Kissinger had immediate authority to "revitalize" the NSC. His instructions for reform, as Kissinger relayed them, offered wide latitude. There were only two conditions. The new system was naturally to center in the White House; and it was to yield up to the President a full range of options for every issue.

They must avoid "the Eisenhower problem," as Nixon called it, an NSC process which was orderly but deprived the Chief Executive of a genuine choice among alternative courses. Otherwise, Kissinger was free to devise any system satisfying these requirements. During the next four weeks in December, there followed the usual pattern of organizational planning, compounded of scheming, accident, and the chance conjunction of personalities—the unmystical and unstately stuff of so many important decisions in foreign policy.

The draft plan for the new NSC apparatus came, almost inadvertently, from Morton Halperin, a young Pentagon official whom Kissinger had known in Cambridge. Only thirty, Halperin was a New Yorker, nominally a Republican, with a Yale Ph.D. and some published studies on arms control written while still a Harvard instructor. When faculty tenure seemed unlikely, he had come in 1967 to the then powerful Office of International Security Affairs (ISA), the Defense Department's largely civilian foreign policy arm. There he swiftly acquired a record as a bright, versatile, aggressive, and very ambitious bureaucrat who operated shrewdly through the interdepartmental maze. He was among a handful of officials in ISA who opposed escalation of the Vietnam war, and had played a persuasive role in the gradual conversion of Clark Clifford against the Vietnam policy the winter before. While neither he nor Kissinger could know it, however, Halperin's internal dissent on Vietnam had attracted the ubiquitous suspicions of FBI director J. Edgar Hoover, the squalid antecedent to the later episode of phone tapping that was to be one of the more ironic of the Nixon administration's scandals. The episode eventually spurred the passage of Halperin from aspiring government aide to civil libertarian, and was to haunt Kissinger years later.

But in early December 1968, the setting and personalities were quite different. Kissinger had asked Halperin to come briefly to the Pierre to write an advisory paper on how systems analysis techniques might be applied to presidential handling of foreign affairs, a paper he envisioned as a first step toward the reforms ordered by Nixon. Telling colleagues he expected a position in the new régime, Halperin promptly came to New York. And when in their first talks he told Kissinger that he could best respond to the request by charting a government-wide structure for decisionmaking of the sort eventually planned, Kissinger readily agreed, passing on the President-elect's general strictures on White House authority and provision for a full range of options on each issue. Whether or not Kissinger initially intended Halperin to provide only a fragment of the reform, whether or not he may have intended to construct the system himself, what mattered now was that he was already hard-pressed by other demands of the new job. Halperin, whose abilities he respected, was there, apparently eager to seize the opportunity. The drafting began.

In Halperin, as in others who would be involved in the coup, personal ambition mingled with a larger purpose. His zeal for bureaucratic reform flowed as well from his frustrations with the clogged arteries leading to and from Johnson's Tuesday lunch and through the SIG-IRG committees. After often struggling in vain to make felt from his corner of the Pentagon his disagreement on Vietnam and other issues, he came to the Pierre determined to guarantee that differing policies would have access to the highest levels for consideration.

Halperin's distrust of officialdom was neither so visceral as Nixon's nor so philosophical as Kissinger's. A book he wrote after leaving government, *Games Bureaucrats Play* (in which he neglected to assess his own contribution of December 1968), represented an impersonal, sometimes humorous view of organizational politics, and a certain cynical resignation about it all. The system he drafted for Kissinger in 1968 was not designed to eliminate bureaucratic delay and evasion—which Halperin knew from his battles on Vietnam could be used to thwart bad policy as well as good—but essentially to balance those natural institutional forces by compelling full presidential consideration, pro and con, of all the available options. In that respect it clearly satisfied one of Nixon's initial conditions. The other, ultimately most important condition—White House control over the process—was in a sense a by-product of the scheme. The decisive powers of the new system, the assignment of policy reviews and the chairmanship of the high-level committee set up to screen issues coming before the NSC, might just as easily have been vested among Assistant Secretaries of State and Defense without contradicting Halperin's main purpose of providing a hearing for differing positions. But he was not offering his ideas to the new officials in the Pentagon or at Foggy Bottom, who, had they known or cared, might have used the design for quite other purposes. He was now at the

Pierre, working out the system *before* the senior officials had even been appointed, and working *for* a man with a clear grasp of the significance of bureaucratic control; a man who saw the need for preemption of his rivals, as well as the rewards of satisfying a President with obviously strong opinions on the subject.

So it was that Kissinger came to occupy the controlling positions in the system and consequently changed history. Halperin's role was to be doubly ironic, even aside from the later tapping of his phone and his public confrontation with Kissinger. A decisionmaking structure originally designed to assure dissent later served only to strengthen the control of men who soon would brook no opposition to their policies. A reform born out of the frustration of oppositon to the war was to fortify a régime that willfully continued the slaughter.

Outwardly, the framework of the new organization was relatively simple. At bottom Halperin kept the IRGs, still chaired by State Department Assistant Secretaries. They were renamed Interdepartmental Groups. The new IGs were directly responsible to the Review Group, a body of senior representatives drawn from the various agencies and chaired by Kissinger. National Security Study Memoranda (NSSM), ordering the preparation of specific policy reviews by specific dates, originated with Kissinger, were approved by the President, and assigned to the appropriate IG over Kissinger's signature. With a member of Kissinger's NSC staff sitting at each IG table with *de facto* Assistant Secretary rank, the Groups then produced a policy paper covering, in the words of a typical NSSM, "the full range of policy alternatives," and forwarded it to the Review Group according with the NSSM due date. The Review Group in turn considered whether the paper had dealt with all the options, then either returned it to the IG for redrafting or scheduled it for formal NSC consideration. The President was to make his decision on a given policy only after reading all the options and in the wake of a full discussion of the issues among the statutory members of the NSC at one of its regularly scheduled meetings. Once a decision was taken, its implementation was to be monitored by the Under Secretary's Committee, chaired by the Under Secretary of State with a membership of his peers from the other agencies represented on the NSC, and including Kissinger.

In addition to the unprecedented power and command he vested in Kissinger, Halperin made only one other change in the customary inter-agency representation on the various policymaking bodies, but it was significant. He excluded the CIA from the system, save for providing NSC intelligence briefings, on the altogether logical grounds that the Agency was not by law or mission a policymaking institution. Though initially approved by Kissinger and even Nixon, it was the only substantial element of the new scheme as first drafted that did not survive.

The lines of control in Halperin's design ran from every level of the system to the White House basement office of the new Assistant for National Security Affairs. By means of his authority to originate and sign the NSSM, Kissinger determined the context of policy review, the questions to be asked, and the calendar of discussion. In an intellectual sense, this endowed him with something like the power of his own executive order, an instrument of bureaucratic enforcement that had formerly been exclusively the President's. Kissinger's NSC staff monitored the preparation and approach of the assigned papers in the Interdepartmental Groups, interjecting their (or his) views, prodding for wider consideration or new information, voting if necessary against clearance from the IG. The scrutiny continued as the papers came to the White House, where another Kissinger staff member specially designated to supervise the flow of papers to the Review Group (in the first months this key role would be Halperin's) examined the policy options independent of the regional staff member, scheduled the Review Group meetings and agenda, and made recommendations to Kissinger. As Review Group chairman himself, Kissinger could veto, order redrafting, insert amendments, and generally shape the content and tone of the paper. Finally, of course, though it had not been described as part of the formal system, there would naturally be the cover memo accompanying the NSSM into the Oval Office, analyzing, often attacking the bureaucratic positions, and supplying, for the President's eyes only, Kissinger's personal recommendation.

In later practice, there would be intimate talks between the President and his Assistant before *and* after the NSC meeting. On an abstract diagram of the structure, Kissinger appeared only as the chairman of a committee, the neutral manager of the paperwork for the President and his cabinet officers as they pondered foreign policy, just as the law intended, around the NSC table. But for those who understood the bureaucratic reality, Kissinger's grip on the presentation of issues, combined with his sheer physical and psychological proximity to the Chief Executive as a member of the White House Staff, conferred upon him wide and authentic power. Most important, however, it was power Kissinger intended to use, and his appreciation of its potential colored the deft but cautious politics he practiced in pushing the reform past any real or imagined rivals to final adoption.

After a first reading of Halperin's design, Kissinger immediately gave the draft, without Halperin's knowledge, to another aide for comment and criticism, a practice he was to maintain in the White House and the State Department with mixed results in work quality and staff morale. The aide was Lawrence Eagleburger, a thirty-eight-year-old FSO dispatched by the State Department when Kissinger called Under Secretary Nicholas Katzenbach for temporary staff help in the first days after his appointment. A Republican from Wisconsin, where he had earned a graduate degree in political science at Madison and as a young man worked in Earl Warren's unsuccessful 1948 presidential campaign, Eagleburger came to the Pierre on the crest of a brilliant rise in the career service. After only two of the usual apprentice posts abroad, he had entered that élite and upwardly mobile category of younger men in the Washington bureaucracy, the Special Assistant. There he moved progressively upward as a deputy to Dean Acheson during the latter's 1966 consultancy on NATO, as an aide for European affairs on Rostow's NSC staff; and in 1968 as Katzenbach's principal assistant, the position he left to go to New York.

When Kissinger told Katzenbach he wanted a good officer to help with the schedule, Katzenbach replied he could even do better than that. "I'll send you one who's a Republican too." Like Halperin's, it was another accident made up of personality and circumstance with a far-reaching sequel. Eagleburger worked for a time on the NSC staff until forced by extreme exhaustion to leave later in 1969. He then served at NATO, at the Pentagon, and reappeared as Kissinger's closest aide for the final period in the Nixon White House and the first months at State in 1973–74. He eventually became Deputy Under Secretary of State for Management, the second highest and in some ways most important career position in the service—all the while supplying Kissinger on a range of issues from congressional relations to Cuban policy with the kind of reviews of staff memoranda that he had first given Halperin's draft in early December 1968.

In his review of the Halperin draft, Eagleburger's reaction was brief and to the point. He thought the system would fulfill its purpose, but there was the problem in that the coup was perhaps too obvious. "Whatever happened to the Secretary of State?" he asked Kissinger. "We must do something about that," Kissinger answered solemnly, though both he and Eagleburger left the design unchanged.

The problem of legitimizing the reform, or at least of masking its meaning for its victims long enough to win its adoption, centered on a third personality at the Pierre. General Andrew Jackson Goodpaster, fifty-three, slim and erect under distinguished gray hair, was, as one of his colleagues put it, "the kind of man you can spot for an officer even in civilian clothes." Goodpaster was a West Pointer who commanded a combat engineering battalion during World War II, earning several decorations. He rose steadily through the grades to general rank, and took a Princeton Ph.D. in international relations after the war. But what had suddenly singled him out from many other officers of similarly impressive records was his assignment in 1950 as staff assistant to the commander of the allied armies in Europe, Dwight Eisenhower. Four years later, just thirty-nine, Goodpaster became defense liaison officer and staff secretary to President Eisenhower, and for the remainder of his two administrations played a largely behind-the-scenes role coordinating NSC machinery. Now, after exile as a lowly assistant division commander under the Democrats, he had been asked by Nixon to come to the Pierre as an informal adviser on the national security reorganization begun by Kissinger.

Another Special Assistant made good, Goodpaster occupied a curious and critical place at the Pierre. His record of prominent achievement had been compiled mainly on the basis of a mechanical staff efficiency, and his critics claimed he did not possess an exceptional grasp either of world problems or of the bureaucratic realities in Washington. He had been a chief participant in and supporter of a system of consensus and inertia that the new régime was sharply repudiating. Yet because Nixon had known him in the Eisenhower NSC, he was now somehow the Republicans' general, much as Maxwell Taylor had been the Democrats' general eight years earlier for comparable reasons. To the men involved in the new NSC system, to Nixon and the new Secretaries of State and Defense, to Kissinger who shrewdly saw and feared his potential role, he would become the authority, the endorser of the reform, his Eisenhower past surrounding him with something approaching reverence. Yet when the system had been approved and installed, Goodpaster, whose dispensation was decisive, was promptly sent to Brussels as NATO commander, far removed from the decisionmaking process that was supposedly the area of his singular wisdom.

Kissinger treated Goodpaster with deference and caution, however, acknowledging his status as a would-be Taylor, an independent and influential presidential adviser. In giving him the draft system to review, for example, Kissinger concealed its authorship, fearing Halperin's Vietnam dissent at the Pentagon might be known to Goodpaster, who might then point out to the President-elect that his new foreign policy machinery was being built by a man of questionable views, or at least a figure whom the military services at Defense found dubious. It was the kind of wedge, Kissinger worried aloud in telling Halperin to stay in the background, that could give Goodpaster an argument for constituting himself as a check on such matters in the new régime. So Halperin's authorship of the paper remained secret, and in mid-December, after only a few days' study, Goodpaster presented Kissinger with his unquestioning approval of the new system. Kissinger then sent the draft to the President-elect with a certifying note, "I have shown this to General Goodpaster who approves."

Nixon's response to the new system was equally swift and positive, though marred by the first appearance of what would be a major flaw in his leadership. He did approve the reform, Nixon told Kissinger, but it would have to be passed too by the future Secretary of State, William Rogers, and by Secretary of Defense Melvin Laird. "Now you'll have to get it by Rogers," Nixon told a puzzled Kissinger. Though the President-elect had privately endorsed the reform, he wanted to avoid any more controversy. If there were opposition from Rogers or Laird, he clearly implied, the plan was in jeopardy. He would not directly confront his cabinet on the issue, however important. It was a pattern of evasion to be repeated from this pre-inaugural period at the Pierre to the disgraced end of his presidency. Nixon obviously had encouraged and now approved a plan to deprive his cabinet of power; throughout his term in office he repeatedly decided against their recommendations in favor of his own or Kissinger's positions; he frequently cursed them in private for their political disloyalty, stupidity, and worse. Yet somehow, the prisoner of a profound aversion to such direct human conflict, he could not bring himself to face the men he had appointed to the highest ranks of government with a straightforward statement of his feelings or policies. There was only a hint of that in his talk at the Pierre, yet the experience made a lasting impression on Kissinger who, in the first of many instances, told a friend after Nixon's "approval" of the reform that the new President seemed at times "very strange." At the end of their conversation, Kissinger related, Nixon had seemed oddly certain that the plan would succeed without the dreaded fight. "Don't worry about Rogers," he had called after Kissinger as he left the suite where they talked.

The men to whom the new draft NSC system was now sent for approval, a virtual sentencing to their own bureaucratic impotence, were very different individuals, yet similarly unqualified to judge the implications of the first major issue of their new positions. William Pierce Rogers, at fifty-five a successful New York lawyer, had arrived and moved easily in the upper reaches of American businesses and government organizations, where affability and banality often count for as much as talent and intelligence. After graduating from Cornell Law School, Rogers had been an assistant district attorney in New York and, following his navy service, a Republican counsel to several postwar Senate investigating committees. His contacts on Capitol Hill brought him a place as a deputy attorney general in the Eisenhower administration, and in 1957 he was appointed Attorney General. In Eisenhower's cabinet he became friendly with Vice President Nixon, and it was to Rogers's home that Nixon went for friendly advice during one of the "six crises" when word came of Eisenhower's first heart attack. Handsome, often smiling, given to working in his shirt sleeves, Rogers left the impression on some who knew him in government as Attorney General and Secretary of State of a man who appeared unaware of the seriousness or depth of the business moving about him. "He's a fine man," pronounced one State Department bureaucrat who briefed him on a preferred position on a controversial policy during the transition period in 1968–69, "cool and agreeable to everything." His sole experience in foreign affairs had been as a member of that bipartisan group of public delegates annually appointed by presidents to the U.S. Delegation for UN General Assembly sessions. Rogers attended the more than usually uneventful session of 1965. His participation was notable in one respect, however, since he liked many of the FSOs he happened to meet at the U.S. Mission to the UN and subsequently appointed them, frequently without regard to their qualifications, to key positions in the State Department four years later. He had little visible knowledge of foreign policy, no background which prepared him for the bureaucratic swamp he was entering, and least of all no adequate appreciation of the adversary he faced in Henry Kissinger. Rogers lacked the acquaintance with the people and problems of foreign affairs which members of the foreign policy establishment possessed. He was a man Nixon apparently liked at some personal level, perhaps preferring him as Secretary of State precisely for his inexperience with foreign policy.

Elliot Richardson, Rogers's Under Secretary, was no better prepared to measure the meaning of the new system. To the degree that he did recognize its impact, Richardson seemed ready in December 1968, as so often later, to make his own accommodation with the flow of power. Another former Eisenhower official whom Nixon knew, Richardson had been first an Assistant Secretary, then acting Secretary of Health, Education and Welfare in the late fifties, having risen early and easily from a Boston Brahmin family, gone through Harvard Law, and benefitted by the patronage of Massachusetts Republicans Leverett Saltonstall and Christian Herter. He returned to Boston in 1959, appointed by Eisenhower as U.S. attorney, and since 1964 had won two terms successively as lieutenant governor and attorney general of the state. Now at forty-eight, a gifted sketcher with an agile mind and a chafing, though calculated, ambition, he was an Under Secretary of State whose foreign policy experience was largely confined to his heavily decorated service as an army corpsman in World War II. He would soon present a sharp contrast to his superior. If Rogers often seemed groping, his wiry, aristocratic deputy down the hall was crisp and alert. But Richardson's exterior assurance was only a more effective disguise for his similar lack of experience with issues of foreign policy. Intent above all on his own advance, perhaps sobered too by Kissinger's Harvard credentials, Richardson reviewed the new NSC structure and gave it his enthusiastic support. When Kissinger, armed with Goodpaster's endorsement, came to Rogers's State Department office later in December to discuss the proposal, Richardson urged its immediate adoption, impressing Kissinger as an ally and swaying Rogers, already reassured by General Goodpaster's endorsement of the plan. The meeting took less than an hour. Afterward, his State Department aides argued heatedly against his approval, and begged him at least to ask for more time to study the structure; but Rogers waved off their objections by saying that "Ike's man" had said it was all right. "What do all these committees mean anyway?" he asked an aide. Once, after Kissinger, Goodpaster, and Richardson had gone and his agreement was given did Rogers hint at some doubt. "It doesn't make any difference," Rogers said to one assistant, "I have a relationship with the President."

Designated as Secretary of Defense in the new administration, Melvin Laird, the former Wisconsin congressman, was less a mismatching of man and responsibility than Rogers, though enough to assure the success of the coup. Just forty-six in 1968, Laird possessed a fifteen-year record in the House as a vigorous and much-honored legislator. Beside Kissinger the professor, Rogers the New York attorney, even Nixon the self-conscious introvert, Laird was in many ways the quintessential politician and the most interesting. After six years in the Wisconsin state legislature, he had come to Washington in 1953, serving with increasing influence on the powerful Appropriations Committee, rising in Republican ranks by taking on many of the party organizing tasks most of his colleagues spurned. His voting record was conservative to moderate. Laird's 1962 book on defense problems, *A House Divided: American's Strategy Gap,* was the simplistic and partisan inspiration of his work on the Defense Subcommittee of Appropriations, but unlike Rogers he was generally familiar with some of the programs and ranking officers of the department he was about to take over. His more impressive background by far was in the fields of health, education, and welfare, where his legislation and parliamentary maneuvering won him numerous citations ranging from one by the American Cancer Society to distinguished service awards from United Press International and the American Political Science Association.

His crew-cut, balding head too suggestive of a bullet, his eyes slightly askew, Laird later fell easy prey to cartoonists on grounds of his hawkish policy as well as his physiognomy. But behind the counte-

nance lay an acute, recurrently underestimated intelligence, an educated political sense for the country beyond Washington, and yet
another outsized ambition, which conjured up visions of the presidency. The attribute he lacked in 1968 was what he needed most as
Secretary of Defense, an equally adroit sense of the bureaucratic
politics within the executive branch. As Nixon and Rogers had been
before him, Laird was duly impressed with Goodpaster's imprimatur
on the proposed system. Meeting with Kissinger and Goodpaster in
his temporary offices in the Pentagon, he gave his approval. There
was one extraordinary sequel, though, when Laird, having second
thoughts about one detail, flew to Boston a few days later to see
Kissinger, who had returned briefly to complete the semester's
teaching at Harvard. It was not that the new system robbed the
Pentagon of the power to enforce its will on consensus memoranda
against a feeble State Department, nor that Kissinger's position gave
him almost unlimited scope to meddle in strategic and arms control
questions in which the joint chiefs customarily supplied the appropriate briefings. Instead, Laird told an anxious Kissinger, he was worried
that the CIA was not represented on the various groups. The Agency
was part of the process and should have a voice, even if, as Kissinger
briefly pointed out, it was not technically a policymaking institution.
Kissinger promptly agreed to the change, the amendment a seemingly small price to keep Laird's full-fledged support. Whether Laird
requested the change on his own initiative, or whether he was approached by a CIA aware of and concerned about its absence from
the proposed reorganization, the restoration was not in itself decisive
in the CIA's continuing interventions under the Nixon administration. The new NSC system left untouched the apparatus for covert
operations, the 303 Committee (rechristened the 40 Committee),
which gave the CIA its singular role in American foreign policy. But
Laird's change destroyed what might have been at least a symbolic
precedent—a bureaucratic expression of the heretofore unacknowledged fact that the CIA had no proper policymaking role. To have
formally excluded the Agency from the policy machinery on those
grounds might have been the beginning of a long-needed reassess-
ment. The price of passage of the NSC structure, however, was that
the new administration failed even to go that far toward facing the
problem, which was to break scandalously into the open a few years
later.

One effort was made to stop the reform, but it too foundered on the personalities involved. Days before a scheduled meeting of all the principals at Nixon's Key Biscayne vacation retreat to promulgate the system, Kissinger was visited in New York at the Pierre by U. Alexis Johnson, the senior career officer of the foreign service. Now sixty, Johnson had been Deputy Under Secretary for Political Affairs, the ranking career position, under both Kennedy and Johnson, serving as ambassador in Vietnam and Japan in the years between. At the close of 1968 he was about to assume the same job for the third time, appointed by Rogers as by his predecessors for want of any equally unexceptionable bureaucrat of comparable seniority. In the stagnant pool of State Department officialdom, Johnson was, as Kissinger acidly characterized him, "each administration's gift to the succeeding administration." His endurance at the highest levels was an example of both the best and the worst of the foreign service. As a young FSO, he had served courageously in Japanese-occupied China until interned and finally repatriated after Pearl Harbor. Over the next twenty years he rose swiftly to ambassador, and won praise in the mid-fifties as a patient negotiator with the Communist Chinese for the release of U.S. citizens held in China. But as one of the Department's few Asian specialists to survive McCarthyism, he was also a dutiful, unquestioning onlooker while two presidents sank into Indochina. Dour, cautious, fleshed with the ubiquitous paunch usually accompanying seniority in his profession, Johnson, like many FSOs, was shielded from ultimate responsibility for policy, his job being to execute the cable instructions. As a result he was most of all, as his record showed, acceptable; acceptable to superiors appreciative of loyalty, acceptable to peers and subordinates unthreatened by his authority. Johnson embodied Kissinger's prototype of the bureaucrat who rises to the top as a result of longevity. And it was Johnson who came to the Pierre, primed by the frustrated men around Rogers, to persuade Kissinger to change the system to allow more role for the State Department. Johnson was vague. Perhaps the Secretary of State should review the papers from the IG before they went to the Review Group. As men on both sides of the argument remember, Kissinger was coolly unyielding, reassured by his encounters with both Rogers and Laird. If Johnson or the Secretary of State had problems, he replied, they should go to Nixon, bearing in mind, of course, that Rogers, Laird, and the President-elect had all approved the system. The matter was considered closed. Johnson returned to the State Department and made a last effort to persuade Rogers to oppose the system. Once more the Secretary refused and the brief counter-coup collapsed.

A slightly farcical meeting at Key Biscayne on December 28 sealed the issue. Following a talking points paper written by Kissinger, Nixon went over the outline of the organization with Rogers, Laird, Vice President Agnew, Kissinger, and Goodpaster. It was Nixon's first meeting with all his senior foreign policy advisers, and a foretaste of the NSC sessions to come. Rogers hesitantly suggested there might be some unspecified problems with the arrangements, a comment Nixon seemed not to hear as he went on to solicit the approval of Laird and Agnew. Agnew, as he later confessed to an aide about the description of the structure, did not quite understand "what I'm supposed to do with this." Most of the five-hour meeting was consumed by a Nixon monologue, with occasional interjections by Laird and Kissinger, on the priority of getting a complete policy review on Vietnam. Kissinger, having heard the monologue before at the Pierre, was already preparing the lengthy list of questions that would constitute the later famous NSSM 1 on Vietnam. The meeting in Key Biscayne, observed *The New York Times* the next day, had been about "machinery and procedures for developing alternative courses of action" in foreign policy. The new President "clearly intends to elevate the prestige and enlarge the role of the NSC," the report continued from sources in Key Biscayne. In the next few weeks Kissinger would provide plans for a sweeping reorganization, plans "to which the President-elect," concluded the *Times*, "is expected to give a sympathetic reception."

Around noon on January 20, 1969, a White House messenger carried to the State and Defense Departments and the CIA copies of the top-secret National Security Study Memorandum number 1, the first formal document of the new system and, as it were, its birth certificate. Over Richard Nixon's signature, the policymaking machinery was instituted very much as Halperin had first drafted it at the Pierre nearly two months earlier. Most senior foreign policy bureaucrats returned from lunch on Inauguration Day to find on their desks what many of them recognized, if their novice superiors had not, as a seizure of power that went well beyond the usual impact of the day's ceremonies on the steps of the Capitol. Over the next several months, as Kissinger's control became more and more tangible in changing policies, there were efforts at the State Department to recover some of the lost ground. A "planning and coordination" staff grew up around Richardson to monitor the papers streaming from the Interdepartmental Groups. Assistant Secretaries were ordered to clear the State Department's "option" with Rogers or Richardson before it traveled its usually unsuccessful course through Kissinger to the NSC. "We got better at it," said one State Department official of the policy reviews, "but I don't think the people below ever really understood what was happening." What was happening, however, was not so strange. Kissinger had largely reversed the traditional bureaucratic system in foreign policy, giving the departments their ostensible hearing much as they had once deferred "decision" to the President. Yet now the White House no longer waited to pass on what it was given, but instead reached deep into the process to mold and control policy alternatives from the first draft to Nixon's final choice.

In the end, of course, the system mattered much less for its abstract merits in decisionmaking than as a technique for establishing the government of Henry Kissinger and Richard Nixon over the peculiar feudalism of Washington's foreign policy. It worked where they cared to fix their power, failed or had only limited impact on issues to which they were indifferent. There was a sense in which the whole process was a sham, a fraud played out over weeks and months and endless meetings when the policy—Kissinger's policy, Nixon's policy—might have been sent down with a stroke of the pen. But the system gave President and bureaucracy alike the comforting illusion of legitimacy and participation, however arbitrary the reality. The illusion masked the further shrinkage of American foreign policy decisionmaking from the bargaining of the few departments to the will of two men.

From the original Halperin plan, sanctioned by the pattern and precedent of authority as the months passed, Kissinger's control grew pervasively. Before the first year was out, in addition to the Review Group he chaired the Verification Panel directing arms control strategy, the Washington Special Actions Group for crisis management, the Vietnam Special Studies Group to check intelligence and trends in the war, and the Defense Program Review Committee dealing with the Pentagon budget. The structure displayed his talents at their best. The constant flow of papers put a premium on intellect, preparation, versatility, in all of which he excelled his bureaucratic rivals. But it was the man who ruled, and not the mechanism. As Kissinger's power and fame widened, the system became less and less used. There were seven NSSMs assigned on January 21, 1969, some fifty-five in the first four months of the administration, and only eight in the first four months of 1970. In part, the reviews were fewer because policies were established; but increasingly the most important decisions were to be taken outside the NSC. The Cambodia invasion, the secret Kissinger negotiations with North Vietnam from 1969 to 1973, the interventions in Chile, the China trip —all happened without benefit of NSSM options. Yet for his position with Nixon and his accepted dominance in the bureaucracy, Kissinger owed much to the system designed at the Pierre.

Most important, perhaps, the system nurtured the secrecy and evasiveness that afflicted Nixon's personal style of government. In a system in which there were no Tuesday lunches, in which decisions were reduced to lifeless, unthreatening words set down on paper, Nixon could increasingly wall himself off. "You handle it, Henry," became the main operational mode of the decisionmaking process. Unable, unwilling, and, by the protective pretense of neutrality in the NSC discussion, unmoved to confront subordinates on differences of view, Nixon retreated deeper into the distrust and suspicion he had brought with him to the White House. And in the reduction of government to disembodied dicta, he was eagerly abetted by the men around him who, as he ironically told the press at Kissinger's appointment, suffered a dangerous "temptation" to please presidents.

Several months before his summons to the Pierre, Kissinger had told a seminar audience that a new President who wanted to change and control foreign policy had to accomplish the takeover "within the first four months." "He need not complete it within this time," Kissinger added, "but he must give enough of a shake to the bureaucracy to indicate that he wants a new direction, and he must be brutal enough to demonstrate that he means it." The coup at the Pierre provided that shake and the change, complete with the necessary brutality. When American troops massed for an invasion of Cambodia in the spring of 1970, the President's principal constitutional advisers on war and peace, the Secretaries of State and Defense, would be very nearly among the last to know.

Yet the more far-reaching tragedy was not the dubious methods and questionable effects of the coup on the government of foreign policy, but rather that it failed to be a genuine revolution. Two men with rare understanding of the internal stagnation in American foreign policy might have sustained a true opening of the process, might have broken the hold of convention and bureaucracy in the interest of new public debates and congressional participation in determining the future course of America's role in the world. But Nixon and Kissinger brought about their coup to seize power for themselves, not to share it. The brutal truth was that, at heart, neither man had a steadfast faith in the democratic process, least of all as applied to the conduct of foreign policy. And for all their historic impact over the following years, their reform, whatever its wisdom and flaws, would not survive their departure.

III

---◆---

Power in the West Basement, 1969–1970

"The President appointed me to do creative thinking about foreign policy," Kissinger began the first meeting of his National Security Council staff in January 1969. "I've been in the White House for days, and I haven't had a thought yet."

It was an early rendition of the wry, self-deprecating lines that would amuse and win so many of his audiences over the next eight years. On this occasion the small deceit in the humor was sharper than most. No figure in the recent history of American foreign policy entered high office more reflective about the substance of the issues, more absorbed with the bureaucratic politics of his own power. If not always "creative," the "thinking" was visibly constant. The staff meeting itself illustrated part of his preoccupation. There was no discussion of foreign relations, yet the subject at hand was crucial to Kissinger's position, and ultimately to his preeminence in policy. President Nixon had ordered, he told his new assistants, that they were never "under any circumstances" to talk to the press. "If anyone leaks anything, I will do the leaking," he said with substantial prophecy, adding in a similar understatement that the new Chief Executive had "strong feelings" about secrecy. In a ceaseless consuming maneuver to accommodate to the singular demands and opportunities of the Nixon presidency, to gather power and wield it and defend it, Henry Kissinger would never really be without "a thought" from his first moments in office.

Overshadowed by the headlines that flared later from Peking, Moscow, or Indochina, the first months of the Nixon administration in foreign affairs appeared uneventful. Yet under the seemingly quiet surface, it was a remarkable period. The outpouring of policy studies channeled by Kissinger through the new NSC system produced of its kind the most sweeping official review of American foreign relations and national security since World War II. From policies changed or continued, issues confronted or shunted aside, there were far-reaching consequences and, in some cases, enormous human costs. The tangled origins of the administration's Vietnam strategy lay in these first months, largely unseen or, if visible, misunderstood by the press, Congress, and a public widely opposed to the conflict. The domestic political calculations, Kissinger's tortuous secret diplomacy, the plans for savage new escalations of the bombing, the influences determining that the war would go on for another four years, all took shape between the early autumn of 1969 and the invasion of Cambodia in the spring of 1970.

The period revealed the texture and quality of the people as well as the policies of the Nixon administration. It was a régime often more divided against itself than any foreign adversary, often more distrustful of itself and scheming in its own councils than in any diplomatic encounter. Ignorance, distraction, and undisguised racism ruled alongside intelligence, energy, and, intermittently, a sense of justice. And beneath it all was a still darker recess of government whose phantoms haunted Kissinger from the beginning—flickering yet unavoidable evidence that the President of the United States, the most powerful human being on earth, was at times unfit for his awesome responsibilities. In public or among any but the closest aides, Nixon was stiffened to the role, composed and even decisive. Yet in private he could be suddenly transformed, anxious, wandering, swept by the impulse of the moment. On certain nights during these first months of the new administration he was drinking heavily. Incoherent or unreachable, he was a commander-in-chief swerving between command and uncontrol, slurring obscenities over the telephone to Kissinger as they discussed the order of American troops into the invasion of Cambodia. This was the reality of human weakness in the White House, a hidden but chronic crisis of leadership, years before Watergate or resignation. It was in this setting—in an uneasy, costly bargain with contempt, loyalty, conviction, and ambition—that Kissinger began his extraordinary role in American foreign policy.

The new régime was in many respects at its best in the early foreign policy reviews of 1969, a process in which it began to expose and dismantle some of the hoary myths of national security. Most important was the encouragement of a new official perspective on the Soviet Union and China. "We will regard our Communist adversaries first and foremost as nations," announced a presidential report to the Congress in February 1970, "pursuing their own interests as they perceive these interests, just as we follow our own interests as we see them." In the dainty evolution of diplomatic and bureaucratic language, it was a lengthy jump from the penchant of a Johnson or Rusk to speak of the "international Communist conspiracy," "Red China," or simply "the enemy," the latter an interchangeable strategic concept applicable from Berlin to the Mekong Delta. The sophistication would not have been possible without Nixon's own education in world politics. But the lesson was originally Kissinger's, the preaching of the Harvard scholar since the mid-fifties now come to policy.

The change was neither immediate nor arbitrary. Such new rhetoric and its diplomatic implications had been nurtured in the NSC system, and given a wider legitimacy within the government by being "discovered" as it were by the bureaucracy, albeit under force of a presidential order. As the policy reviews were assigned, subjects long skirted were reopened. NSSM 63, a study of the Sino-Soviet rivalry recommended by Kissinger and so ordered by Nixon in July 1969, was typical of the valuable yield in this early turning over of bureaucratic rocks. Four months later in November 1969, more than a decade after the Sino-Soviet rift began, the U.S. government produced its first concerted analysis of one of the more fateful international developments of the time. Their disputes had prevented the Russians and Chinese from "concerting anti-U.S. policies," said the study. In Peking, the result of the Russian threat was "a less belligerent posture toward the U.S." Moreover, the Soviet "readiness to negotiate on issues such as SALT and European security" was also a "favorable by-product of the rivalry." Waxing on the theme once having found it, the review if anything tended to exaggerate the benefits of the split for Washington. It obscured, for example, that there were other powerful motives in the domestic politics of the two countries spurring the Russians into arms control and the Chinese out of their isolation, motives that would still be strong even if the rift between them were somehow healed. The NSSM neglected as well signs that the rivalry of ideology and power provoked both nations to more aggressive policies which in some areas, as in the arming of India and Pakistan or their competitive zeal in backing North Vietnam, might have damaged American interests more than otherwise. Perhaps most important, the bureaucratic experts nervously skirted around the gravest danger of the split, the prospect of a Sino-Soviet war. It was still a customary premise in policy papers that vagueness and brevity of attention can somehow diminish the most disagreeable contingencies. The NSSM did venture that war between Russia and China would "drastically reduce" their "capabilities" to conduct policies against the United States. It concluded, without depressing elaboration, that a nuclear exchange in such a war might also be "disadvantageous" to American interests.

Worried that such a potential calamity was not being taken seriously, Kissinger a few months later commissioned, in secret from the rest of the government, his own NSC staff study of contingency plans for a Sino-Soviet war, including the use of nuclear weapons. In that sense, too, NSSM 63 was characteristic of many of the early policy reviews. Flushing out the neglected if obvious point, giving the ranks of the bureaucracy a new orthodoxy to embellish and protect, the studies exposed with sometimes harsh clarity the intellectual limits of relying too much on the bureaucracy at large. "They" might be educated, brought along to avoid future sabotage, made to believe the policy was their own. But beyond that, many issues were too important to leave to "them." If the President did not agree instinctively, the inescapable wafflings of the NSSMs, helpfully pointed out by Kissinger's cover memos, only proved again that what mattered most was best done in the White House. Despite its flaws and evasions, however, NSSM 63 was a formidable document in its context. Like similar reviews, it began the task of making the government purge itself of some of its most stubborn and significant stupidities. The policy implications of the analysis had been present for years, of course, jammed into the corners of CIA estimates, State Department memoranda, the daily cable traffic from Moscow, Hong Kong, and a dozen other posts. But those documents had dropped on the Kennedy and Johnson White House as unassembled fragments, separated by that fatal gap between what a government knows and what it wants to know. For the authoring bureaucrats, doing their job, it was someone else's responsibility (and risk) to point out that if the world had altered so radically, perhaps policy should change too. For the senior men like Rusk and Rostow, the reports of the Sino-Soviet schism were merely more "pieces of paper" to be fitted into their sclerotic experience with the world struggle, passed on to the trusting presidents only with the properly skeptical cover memo. Now, however, if the bureaucrats remained ever cautious and detached, there was a critical difference at the top.

The early NSC studies not only changed in general terms the official outlook on issues like the Sino-Soviet rivalry; included within the obligatory options presented in each review were sometimes specific operational decisions that bureaucracies did not usually afford presidents, and that presidents did not take without some immunity from bureaucratic reprisal. The administration's 1969 initiative to curb chemical-biological weapons (CBW) was a revealing example of how Kissinger and the new system breached that institutional and political inertia. Few issues had so embodied the unequal struggle between rational public policy and the fetishistic politics of national security. Since the 1950s, the Pentagon had spent billions in secret funds to develop and refine lethal or incapacitating chemicals and grotesque bacterial strains. Though there were increasing doubts among scientists and military intelligence that such technology was practically manageable as a weapon either for the USSR or the United States, the arsenals grew apace. Typically, the programs continued mainly because they were there, claimants for a defense budget in which to renounce the need for one established force might only invite unwanted questions about others. In the Eisenhower years, as Nixon recalled during the NSC discussion of the issue on 1969, "the whole subject was taboo, one of those things not even a President talked about." To Kennedy and Johnson, who by then might have unearthed evidence that the CBW program was dubious at best, the question presented the distasteful prospect of one more clash with the joint chiefs, already doubting presidential manhood in the endless squabble over how far to escalate in Vietnam. Then, too, the war eventually gave the program its only practical application thus far in the use of chemical defoliants and "riot control agents" to deal with an unappreciative citizenry both at home and abroad. By the late 1960s, a few lonely voices had raised misgivings about the issue on the floor of the House. But for most of the Congress, chemical-biological warfare remained one of those many esoteric and apocalyptic matters of national defense understood only by the generals.

That the Nixon administration reviewed policy on chemical-biological weapons in May 1969 and changed it six months later was the sum of random influences. The issue arose in part because the British planned that summer to introduce at the Geneva disarmament conference a draft convention banning germ warfare. This in turn triggered a routine State Department request for White House guidance in how to react to that proposal. A year earlier the same request would have drawn an automatic Pentagon objection to U.S. support of the convention, and a weary presidential acquiescence in the veto, if indeed the question had survived the brokering of the Secretaries of State and Defense. But for Kissinger the issue presented both a diplomatic and bureaucratic opportunity. Well aware as a Defense consultant of the waning enthusiasm for CBW in the Pentagon's strategy if not its budgets, he saw in a review the prospect of a relatively painless unilateral arms control initiative valuable in setting the stage for later diplomacy with the Soviet Union. Whatever the outcome, a review would satisfy the new President's instruction to probe long-neglected policies and would serve to lengthen Kissinger's reach into the joint chiefs' no-man's-land of strategic posture and military budgets, a region his predecessors had never penetrated. For his part, Nixon readily approved the study, less from any visible doubts about chemical-biological warfare than from his accurate instinct and experience that it was a policy in which the bureaucrats governed essentially without the President. This and other policies would be reviewed not so much for change as for the sake of the review itself, the restless striving of a President to assert his control over what he saw as a recalcitrant government.

More important than White House motives in instigating the study, however, was the process itself in terms of organizational politics. It was the system as it was supposed to work, though circumstances were seldom so neat or vested policy interests so expendable. Under the charge to present all realistic alternatives, the bureaucracy produced a review which included the option to eliminate or reduce reliance on chemical-biological weapons. The Pentagon also had its option to maintain current programs. Yet the agreement of the joint chiefs to the range of options was a reluctant but implicit admission that change was still within the bounds of national security. They could not easily claim afterward with their congressional supporters or the press that their expertise was unheeded. Moreover, the onus for advocating change fell on no department or individual. The presidential choice would not depend on a Secretary of Defense bringing himself to oppose the army or a Secretary of State mustering his courage and credentials to infringe on military affairs.

At that the study took months to write amid constant haggling. When it finally came to the White House in late October 1969, it was wrapped in committee prose so bleached as to be nearly unintelligible. "I can't even read this paper, let alone understand the issues," Kissinger complained to assistants. But he understood well enough that the review had indeed uncovered an opportunity. Passing the NSSM through the Review Group with compliments to the bureaucracy for their thoughtful work on a complex issue, he quietly ordered the options rewritten by his own staff to make plain to the President that he had before him that rarity of American statesmanship—a unilateral step in disarmament without military sacrifice or significant Pentagon opposition. The NSC meeting in early November was perfunctory. The chiefs argued that CBW had "symbolic" value, despite admitting, as their representatives had in drafting the NSSM, that the weapons were largely impossible to use. Laird and Rogers were vaguely in favor of curtailing the programs. In his cover memo and later discussion with the President, Kissinger pressed for a unilateral initiative. On November 25, emphasizing the novelty of the review and the historic nature of the decision, Nixon announced that the United States would renounce first use of both lethal and incapacitating chemicals, and disband biological warfare programs entirely except for "research for defensive purposes." The administration was submitting to the Senate the 1975 Geneva protocol to bar chemical and biological warfare, and fully supported the British draft convention. The new policy did not affect defoliants or forms of tear gas, all then actively used in Vietnam. But a subsequent review led to the additional renunciation of offensive use of toxins. The general effect of the November decision was to end a costly, hazardous, and senseless program.

The reviews of Sino-Soviet rivalry or chemical-biological weapons reformed policies that were most vulnerable, positions so overtaken by events that any systematic study would have pointed to change. But such accomplishments were no less important for being relatively uncontested. Outmoded orthodoxies and irrelevant strategies survived for so long in foreign policy because the critical studies were simply never undertaken. The eighty-five NSSMs assigned by Nixon and Kissinger in 1969 constituted an unprecedented questioning of the status quo in any area of government. If noticeable departures in policy took place in only a handful of those cases, nevertheless the reviews breathed some fresh intellectual life into the departments. Largely invisible benefits accrued simply because of the introduction of alternative options and arguments. For two decades, American diplomacy had sprung from habits of thought that had silenced any authentic debate of issues as distinct from bureaucratic jockeying. The new NSC system began to change those habits, as Kissinger himself would ruefully discover later when his own interests turned from revision to the comfort of consensus. The reviews had another immediate effect on the general tenor of the foreign policy dialogue within the government. Even where specific policies remained unchanged—in issues like the maintenance of U.S. troops in Europe or belligerent relations with Cuba—the studies reflected a fresh sense of the retraction of American power and the passing of the interventionist urges of the 1960s.

In part the new realism was given expression because the bureaucracy anticipated on the basis of Nixon and Kissinger's reputations that it was the note the two men wanted struck. But it appeared also because the NSSMs required the explicit definition of U.S. national interests with the pros and cons for each policy detailed, a process that let out into the open in many issues the government's own deep disillusionment with Vietnam and its adaptation to what it saw as the changing public mood. Just as it had not been safe after the McCarthy era to point out any critical distinctions among nations in assessing the Communist menace, it was now in 1969 no longer always respectable to defend policies or programs by their mere existence. When an Assistant Secretary of State that summer listed as an argument for present policy, "This has been traditional U.S. posture in the region," his colleagues on the Interdepartmental Group gently but firmly declined to approve the statement, on the grounds that it jeopardized the approval of the option. In that sense the NSSMs allowed the bureaucracy to articulate at least the new politics of foreign policy, much as they formally acknowledged international realities like the Sino-Soviet rivalry. Progress in matters of the official mind was glacial and uneven at best, however, and the NSC system was often seen as one more inconvenience to be absorbed while clients and careers went on being tended. In the autumn of 1969, senior State and Defense Department officials opposed clearance of a NSSM on South Korea because an option for partial withdrawal of U.S. troops had somehow acquired in the drafting more "pros" than the current policy.

Yet the limits and failures of the new foreign policy emerging from the NSC system can be traced to the White House and Kissinger in particular, as well as to the bureaucrats. If the reviews of Sino-Soviet affairs and chemical-biological weapons reflected Kissinger's sophistication and far-sighted concern for arms control, the schedule of studies also mirrored his ignorance or calculated indifference toward other important issues. Among more than 140 NSSMs in the first three years of the administration, there would be, for example, only one formal review of international monetary policy. On the agenda of the National Security Council, the subject thus enjoyed equal rank with U.S. policy in Haiti, relations with Malaysia and Singapore, or the status of Namibia (South West Africa), and less than Korea, Peru, or the Indian Ocean. Fateful questions which were to have bearing on the later crisis of the international economic system at the end of 1971 were left in these months to bureaucratic improvisation. Like the opposite tendency to probe and exploit subjects such as CBW, this neglect was due to several factors, some of which originated far afield from the substance of the topic. At root was Kissinger's profound lack of knowledge and interest in economics. The diplomatic historian so at home in the other measures of national power regarded matters such as currency exchanges or trade balances as somehow minor technicalities. The bias became self-reinforcing. Kissinger was reluctant to bring before the NSC issues he believed trivial and, accordingly, issues in which he did not readily enjoy superior or equal expertise as against the bureaucrats. Such priorities tended to subordinate most economic problems, and exclude altogether issues like population control, human rights, or environmental problems. Moreover, this studied inattention had its benefits in protecting his Washington flanks. Heavily engaged in extending his province on political or military issues at the expense of both State and Defense, he was glad to avoid, as one former aide put it, "the additional bureaucratic explosions which would inevitably emit from Treasury, Commerce, Agriculture, etc., if he forayed into economics." The practical result was Kissinger's resistance to his own staff's proddings on economic issues and a quiet acquiescence in the drift of policy much the same as the Johnson White House. Kissinger's inability or unwillingness to face up to economic problems continued at mounting cost even after his ascendancy seemed complete during the last years of the administration, in part because the complexities and constituent politics of international economics were not amenable to his one-man diplomacy so successful elsewhere, in part because he continued to underestimate the importance of the subject and shrank from added bureaucratic or political battles. But the outlines of that weakness were already apparent as economic issues were generally given short shrift in the policy reviews of 1969–70. In a system conferring singular power on one man to ferret out the ingrown prejudices and evasions of the rest of the government, no safeguards against the same flaws in the man himself had been provided for.

Nor was there any check, save Kissinger's own insight and courage, on the potential bungling of the presidential power that burgeoned out of the new White House command of policy. Foreign economic policy languished not only because the bureaucracy clung to the status quo and because Kissinger decided it was not worth the trouble, but also because Nixon was similarly parochial. Bored, uninformed, confident that the departments could handle it—precisely the opposite of his approach to other international issues—he did not question the relative absence of economic policies from an NSC agenda which was examining, he assured the Congress in 1970, "all the most fundamental issues." The wider reckoning for such neglect in the form of the dollar's fall did not come in the first half of the administration. But the fecklessness toward economic problems, combined with the new unilateral White House diplomacy which preserved ignorance as well as secrecy, took an early and ironic toll. The day after his inauguration, Nixon approved Kissinger's recommendation for an urgent review of relations with Japan. Pressure for the return of Okinawa to Japanese sovereignty had been building steadily as the Johnson administration tried to ignore it. Kissinger immediately saw the need to deal with the problem before it brought a rupture with Tokyo. The NSC review and decision that followed was the first and perhaps least appreciated act of statesmanship by the new administration. In the teeth of Pentagon efforts to postpone if not block the decision entirely, Kissinger forcefully steered through the system an options paper which starkly presented the case for reversion and the costs of delay. The President, again on his Assistant's recommendation and over the objection of both Laird and the joint chiefs, chose to take the initiative in returning the island. When Japanese Prime Minister Sato visited Washington in November 1969, the agreement was made. Subject to further lower-level negotiation of details, Okinawa would revert to Japan in 1972 and U.S. bases there would be governed under arrangements similar to those for American bases in the Japanese home islands.

The settlement was announced with self-congratulation in Washington and considerable acclaim for the Sato régime and its pro-U.S. diplomacy among the Japanese. What was never made public, however, was an extraordinary secret coda to the November meeting which would have far greater impact on relations between the two countries. After their formal talks had covered the subjects carefully prepared by both sides, Nixon asked Sato to meet him and Kissinger alone in an anteroom of the Oval Office. There he confronted the prime minister of Japan with what Kissinger's notes called "a necessary private agreement" related "informally" to the Okinawa reversion. His Okinawa initiative, Nixon explained, had been one of his most difficult decisions. He had been opposed by his own military, and some members of Congress would be quick to charge a "giveaway." In return he would like Sato's concession on an issue that affected domestic politics in the United States: the control of Japanese textile exports. Only minutes before in the scheduled meeting the two leaders had discussed the subject inconclusively. Textiles from Japan posed severe, often shattering competition for the American industry in Southern states where Nixon had important votes and congressional supporters. Yet trade issues were typically even more volatile in Japan, where policy was an intricate process of parliamentary and industrial bargaining beyond the control of any government. Now, oblivious to those politics, believing that a complex economic clash could be erased by a last-minute deal arranged privately, far from over-cautious advisers, Nixon sought his quid pro quo almost casually. Sato's reply is lost to history amid the warring interpretations of the two sides. The prime minister later believed he gave only a promise to attempt a solution. Nixon came away convinced, however, that he had a commitment to ease textile competition and thus a first vindication of secret and personal presidential diplomacy. Kissinger's official notes of the conversation reportedly supported the President's assumption, but may have reflected, typically, as much what the Americans wanted to hear in their brief huddle as what Sato actually said. When over the following months discreet White House assurances were given to Southern senators and the Japanese made no concessions, Nixon's glee turned to impatience and then rage at what he called "the Jap betrayal." The textile negotiations proceeded intermittently at lower levels; but the anteroom "agreement" remained a secret from both governments, as well as the public, an unseen wound steadily poisoning the relationship. It was this venom that lay behind Nixon's deliberate refusal to inform Tokyo in advance of the U.S. opening to Peking in 1971, a diplomatic shock in Japan and throughout Asia that seemed at the time an inexplicable oversight. In a cryptic public apology in 1975, Secretary of State Kissinger would admit only that "Our own tactics contributed" to the "painful . . . misunderstandings with Japan."

The contrast between the Okinawa decision and the Sato débâcle —prudent, considered policy accompanied by furtive, willful blunder—marked the basic compromise Kissinger made with power and policy under Nixon. To the issues he regarded as critical in these first months, Kissinger brought conviction and a willingness to advocate the potentially controversial choice, as he did with CBW or Okinawa. Yet such issues were carefully chosen and comparatively few, confined mainly to policies in which he sensed that the drift of Nixon's mind was already amenable or at least uninformed and vulnerable to skillful briefing. Out of his own short-sightedness or unconcern or sheer expediency, however, he frequently indulged Nixon's impulsiveness and misjudgment. He was an unquestioning accomplice in the original fiasco with the Japanese because he understood the trade issue no better than Nixon. He played to the ensuing belligerence—though he came to learn that it was senseless and the product of "our tactics"—because it was one of those issues never quite important enough to risk educating this volatile President.

Japan was hardly the only hidden example of such irresponsibility. Two reviews of Latin American policy lurching through the bureaucracy during 1969 led to an autumn NSC meeting which might have come to grips with the range of festering problems in the hemisphere, from self-generating CIA penetration in a half-dozen countries to scandals in American aid and corporate exploitation. But the meeting was a pathetic, dangerous farce of the kind so common in the previous administration. "I know the Latins," began a President who a decade before had been stoned in Peru and spat upon in Venezuela, "they don't care what you do as long as you pay attention to them." The statement set the tone of the discussion, which was largely concerned with another fact-finding trip to the continent by Nelson Rockefeller and a forthcoming speech by the President, thereby "paying attention." The National Security Council somberly agreed that policy should not be based on slogans such as Kennedy's "Alliance for Progress," and promptly adopted as its major decision of the day the President's suggestion that the theme for his speech and future diplomacy should be "Action for Progress in the Americas."

Another presidential review of Cuban policy in particular was more pointed but no less shallow. "There'll be no change toward that bastard while I'm President," Nixon said of Castro in a conversation with an aide before the meeting, adding as he often did with inadvertent irony that he had "too many good friends" among the Cuban exile community in Florida. The policy decision, including Kissinger's recommendation, went unerringly to the maintenance of Cuba's isolation. Kissinger watched these performances with a sour equanimity, joking with aides about the "idiocy" of such NSC meetings, but readily accepting it all as the price of his presence in the West Basement. Had the same insensitivity and banality been dominant in the China policy or SALT, there would have been no trip to Peking, no strategic arms agreement. As these reviews revealed two Nixons in foreign policy, one enlightened, one benighted, there were by his side two Kissingers. The intellectual and would-be statesman alternated with a caricature of the very qualities Kissinger had ever deplored in officialdom—neglect of issues beyond one's specialty, suspension of judgment and suppression of facts to suit the preconceptions of a less competent superior, and not least, a growing inability to see the pernicious cost of self-compromise. By midway into 1969, Henry Kissinger had become, in some measure, one more bureaucrat.

Foresight and folly were entwined at every level of the administration's foreign policy. No single episode caught the mixture more vividly than the review of southern Africa. On paper it seemed to be an orderly examination of U.S. relations with the white minority régimes of South Africa, Rhodesia, and the Portuguese colonies of Mozambique and Angola. NSSM 39, later to gain misplaced notoriety when the bureaucratic response to it was leaked, ordered in April 1969 "a comprehensive review" of tensions in the area, "alternative views" of American national interests in southern Africa, and "the full range of basic strategies and policy options open to the United States." In the event, it was more nearly a study in the tensions inside Washington and the sometimes self-defeating strategies of officials toward one another. When it was over, the NSSM order notwithstanding, one policy was decided, and another conducted in its name, with too little attention to the national interest however defined.

Southern Africa presented one of the classic dilemmas of diplomacy. On the side of the 30 million repressed blacks in the area were the Soviets, the Chinese, and most of the rest of the world, as well as justice and, eventually, history. The first wave of African independence in the early 1960s had broken against the "white redoubt" of 4 million Europeans in the southern sixth of the continent. Yet by 1969 a fitful guerrilla war in the colonies had killed or wounded 100,000 Portuguese troops and taken a heavy toll from Lisbon's economy; Rhodesia was an international pariah branded by UN economic sanctions; and the growing political consciousness of the silent black populations, even under the most tyrannical of the white régimes, South Africa's *apartheid,* was an unmistakable omen of change.

The question bedeviling American policy from Kennedy to Nixon was when and in what form that change would come. In 1969, Portugal's Fascist government seemed determined to pay the cost to hold on to the colonies for their considerable economic wealth, and the divided guerrillas lacked the strength to force the Portuguese out. (Five years later a coup in Lisbon, not the victory of the guerrillas, ended Portuguese rule.) Defiant and well armed, Rhodesia's vastly outnumbered white settlers had survived increasingly unenforced sanctions and a flagging guerrilla threat. In South Africa, the Afrikaner and English populations traced a centuries-old history in much of the land that predated the first black migrations south, fortifying it with a stern racist theology and a modern military machine with the capacity for nuclear weapons. Confronted with this resistance, black African resolve itself had shrunk. Populations within the white-ruled states were quiescent. Neighboring countries like Zaire, Zambia, and Tanzania publicly deplored the minority régimes yet clandestinely traded with them, including sanctioned Rhodesia. Behind the strident talk of liberation, African financial support for guerrilla groups had dried up by 1969. Zambia quietly but nervously denied sanctuary to Rhodesian rebels in a secret agreement with the outlaw government in Salisbury. On deeper examination, the seemingly clear moral and political issues finding voice in the UN and elsewhere were well larded with hypocrisy, deception, and betrayal.

Then, too, other U.S. interests in the region joined to oppose taking a position against the moral and political anathema of the white states. Portugal was a NATO ally whose Azores base was a staging point for U.S. military operations in the Middle East, principally the rearming of Israel in a crisis. In 1969, South Africa housed more than $1 billion in U.S. investments (greater than U.S. capital in all the rest of Africa put together), produced 75 percent of the non-Communist world's gold, and had what the Pentagon regarded as potentially important naval facilities in the South Atlantic and Indian Oceans.

And over the whole tragedy of American African policy lay its obvious connection to U.S. domestic politics. The savage discrimination practiced in the white African states was a special affront to every black American and the professed ideals of the nation. At the same time, the cause of the white minorities and the specter of their inundation touched in surrogate form deep strains of racial fear and resentment among some American whites.

The instinctive response to southern Africa in the U.S. government had been to avoid as much as possible thinking about the harsh questions it posed. Policy in the 1960s had amounted to the shifting sum of contradictory bureaucratic interests pursued on an ad hoc basis. Thus the State Department soothed pressures in the UN and among its black African clients by celebrating the imposition of Rhodesian sanctions and by rhetorical ostracism of the white régimes. The CIA maintained chummy professional liaison with the suitably anti-Communist security services of all the white governments, while simultaneously giving covert money to the rebels in the Portuguese territories. The Commerce Department encouraged lucrative trade with the whites. In South Africa, NASA ran a vital moon-shot tracking station to which no blacks need apply. The navy planned refueling stops at Capetown for its fleet, where the non-white crew members were to enjoy "separate but equal" shore leave on the way to the war in Southeast Asia. Meanwhile, at periodic intervals presidents and their Secretaries of State declared Washington's abhorrence of the minority régimes.

Events occasionally exposed the fakery. In the summer of 1967, for example, American black civil rights leaders got wind of plans for segregated shore leave at Capetown for the crew of the carrier *FDR*. The instant political storm around the White House moved Johnson to cancel further refueling stops, leaving an indignant navy and the larger policy question to his successor. The diplomatic pretense wore most thin against the friction of evolving debate at the UN. In 1963, the United States had led international opposition to the white régimes of Africa by introducing an arms embargo. Yet only five years later, the Third World applause too brief, the American representative pursuing the same policy guidelines was nervously voting with the French and British to prevent an Afro-Asian majority from imposing economic sanctions and even UN military action against South Africa. The new Nixon administration inherited in southern Africa an aimless, overtaken policy, the sole but sustaining virtue of which was that it satisfied for the moment the needs of the interested departments in Washington.

Like many of the first policy reviews, the study of southern Africa was spurred in some part by the impetus and bias of Kissinger's NSC staff aide assigned to oversee the region, in this case the author. My own motives in recommending NSSM 39 to Kissinger were mixed. Bureaucratically, American policy was obviously a shambles and a natural subject for NSC review. And in the reforming zeal of the new White House in 1969, to initiate a review of a bureaucratic horror like southern Africa was to demonstrate the staff assistant's loyalty and abilities to Kissinger, much as the same process was a showcase for his talents with Nixon. The NSSM fell on the bureaucracy as an assault on its jurisdiction and dogma. But for the NSC staff it was a call on Kissinger's mounting power and shrinking time. Not least, with the staff man sitting on the Interdepartmental Groups, his colleagues knowing that his approval and influence were critical all the way to the top, each study conferred a cachet of personal authority to the NSC staff member, reflected from the higher White House control of the system. For some, this in itself was enough. Though he privately agreed with most of the prevailing policy in his area of responsibility and fought its change as fervently as any vested department, one senior Kissinger aide showered the West Basement with recommended NSSMs, his strategy toward his employer and peers, as he often said, being "just to let them know I'm here." Organizational grasping played its distorting role at these upper reaches of the NSC structure no less than in the linoleumed partitions of State and Defense.

Beyond any bureaucratic incentives, however, the southern African review also sprang from my conviction that there should be some alternative to the current drift and hypocrisy of U.S. diplomacy. Unfortunately, two factors limited the realistic options. First, no President, least of all a conservative, relatively uninterested Richard Nixon, could be expected in 1969 to abandon the substantial U.S. material interests in the white-ruled states. Weeks before NSSM 39 was assigned, Nixon had told the Portuguese ambassador in a conversation kept secret from the State Department that the new administration would stop "lecturing" Lisbon on its African difficulties, adding that the United States valued highly Portugal's cooperation in providing the Azores base. Second, if the genuine (as well as public) purpose of policy were to be peaceful change toward majority rule in the white states, the clear historical lesson in southern Africa, from nineteenth-century British colonialism to the Rhodesian sanctions, was that outside coercion only hardened the unity and repressiveness of the beleaguered white minorities.

An acceptable policy would have to rest on those twin premises, accepting the expedient American stakes in the tyrannies, but using that presence wherever possible to encourage racial progress in the region. Rather than loudly spurning the whites while quietly dealing with them, such a policy would openly foster contacts with the isolated minorities, lifting their siege mentality and encouraging internal moderates, promoting the economic growth that would undermine barriers of prejudice, and showing by the assignment of black personnel to the area and in nondiscriminatory practices by U.S. corporations an example of multi-racial justice at work. There would be no question of officially condoning racism; the new strategy would be to expose it to its own inevitable contradictions.

Christened "tar baby" by a State Department critic who foresaw early in the drafting that its only real result would be to mire the United States deeper on the side of the oppressors, this was ostensibly the option finally chosen by Nixon from the policy review. In retrospect, it was a disaster, naïve in concept, practically impossible for the government to execute, and thus a ready cover for pursuing the most reactionary and short-sighted U.S. interests in the region. That outcome, though, traced not so much to the intellectual flaws in the policy itself as to the way it was decided and carried out.

Originally scheduled for completion in two weeks, by April 25, 1969, the response to NSSM 39 was not forwarded to the Review Group until late November. There would have been some delay in the schedule because of the logjam of studies already building by spring on Kissinger's desk. But the hiatus was mainly the result of the classic bureaucratic battle ignited by the study. The initial reaction to NSSM 39 in the State Department was to redraft with only slight variations the policy paper on southern Africa prepared at the close of the Johnson administration, replete with its two straw options framing present policy. Through nearly a score of meetings and a half-dozen drafts over the summer, the arguments raged in elliptical bureaucratic language. Only by early autumn was agreement reached that there even existed two or three legitimate policy choices for the President lying between the two extremes of aligning with the white states or supporting their military destruction. The technique then was for the FSOs writing the successive papers to portray such options—whether "tar baby" or a relative disengagement from the white states threatening various bureaucratic interests—in deliberately objectionable terms. An early draft thus described the objective of present policy as "to promote constructive change in the area," while other approaches were either "to draw closer to the minority régimes" or "to force change in the white states"—the latter in particular calculated to send cautious policymakers hurrying back to the middle option where they (and the authors) presumably belonged. "Remember," the Assistant Secretary of State for African Affairs said to the Interdepartmental Group that summer in a revealing justification for government inertia, "This policy has to have good reasons or we wouldn't be doing it."

Battled out over verbs and commas, vague intelligence estimates, and nuances of diplomacy that would never be practiced, the conduct of the review was alternately childish, venomous, dull, colossally wasteful of official time, and very much the daily stuff of government in foreign affairs. Yet, unlike the charade of the policy planning paper months before, it provoked the most thorough and sharply debated examination of U.S. southern African diplomacy in the decade since the region had become an international problem. It proceeded not as a harried reaction to crisis but in a setting rare for the making of policy: an opportunity to set goals and anticipate events before circumstances forced a decision. But the inherent strengths of the new NSC system could not surmount the weaknesses of the institutions and people involved. The review unearthed in the bureaucracy an often appalling ignorance of the history and politics of southern Africa. For example, in many Rhodesian schoolrooms hangs a vivid painting of the Shangani Patrol, a nineteenth-century Custer-like last stand by a small white military force against overwhelming African warriors. The massacre was a symbol of settler folklore and the racial belligerence of the Rhodesian whites, not to mention one of the few triumphant moments of black history in a hundred years of subjugation. In the summer of 1969, however, not even the "Country Director" for Rhodesia, the ranking State Department desk officer for the country, much less his superiors, had ever heard of the event. It was as if diplomats dealing with Franco-German relations before World War I knew nothing of Sedan, or a European observer predicting continued Mexican rule over Texas in 1836 had not bothered to learn of the Alamo. More aptly, it was reminiscent of the obliviousness to history and tradition that foredoomed policy as the United States plunged into Vietnam. But then Washington generally saw the present and future of southern Africa no clearer than its past. Intelligence projections in NSSM 39, for example, did not analyze the likely prospect that a revolt in Portugal could, as it did five years later, free the African territories and accelerate drastically the black-white military confrontation.

The failure of information in the bureaucracy belonged in large part to the ever-present blight of "cliency." The State Department (and CIA) officers presumably most knowledgeable about metropolitan Portugal, those in the European Bureau in Washington or in Lisbon, were naturally most loath to discover any weakening of Portuguese resolve or stability, their inclination being to resist the downgrading of their clients that might follow such confessions. The deeper futility of the review was that such bureaucratic politics so absorbed the energy and attention that should have been given to substance. The summer-long struggle just to present a genuine range of options for consideration in the NSSM increasingly obscured the contradictions of "tar baby," and made its very inclusion the central issue. In the same way, the grating ignorance and parochialism of State Department officials blotted out midjudgments, embedding the conviction in my thinking that policy had to be changed as much because it was so ineptly sponsored as because "tar baby" was preferable. As with the guilty defendant mistried by a suborned jury, the facts of the case were lost in the corruption of the procedure. And the psychology of it all, totally hidden from the public, enveloped the foreign policy of the United States in a thicket of personal rivalries and self-justification from which there was no escape, and for which I bore ample responsibility along with the other participants.

The episode was played out at the upper levels in the same petty tangles. By November, the response to NSSM 39 was finally brought to the White House with essentially four options: a *normalization* of relations with the white states, based on a paper given Nixon that spring by his old political target, Dean Acheson, who had long argued that condemnation of the racist régimes was an example of excessive moralism in diplomacy; *tar baby*, defined as "limited association" with the white states and economic aid extended to black states, plus a conscious effort made to encourage moderation; the *present policy*, described as "balancing" interests on the two sides; and a *disengagement* from the white régimes, eliminating any but the minimum diplomatic official relations and discouraging economic ties.

At an NSC staff briefing prior to the Review Group meeting, Kissinger was plainly skeptical about the concept of "tar baby," doubting that any outside influence could change the whites. "This is a genuine tragedy," he said then. "Both sides are acting from what they believe to be basic principles." The following day, however, his apparent readiness to accept the current policy vanished in contempt. Worried as always that "tar baby" would shed the conventional hypocrisy and raise a storm among black African clients, yet anxiously believing even before the first consideration that past policy would be rejected by Kissinger and Nixon, the new Assistant Secretary for African Affairs, a career officer named David D. Newsom, suddenly introduced at the Review Group a "new" option. The last-minute policy was essentially "tar baby," but with the added condition that the United States consult with black African states to seek their approval *before* adopting the posture. Having squabbled for eight months to deny such a policy even a place among the possible choices open to the President, the State Department now in effect advocated the position, provided various African governments gave their permission. Whether the policy actually served U.S. national interests in southern Africa itself was not—and seldom had been—the decisive question. On Kissinger the personal effect of this unusually naked cliency and bureaucratic expedience, the qualities he saw as most destructive in American policy, was infuriating, and in a sense historic. Smilingly accepting the change, now joking, now somberly uncommitted in the company of the Review Group, he returned to his office after the meeting to rage at the "intellectual squalor" of the State Department.

On December 17, 1969, the National Security Council met to consider southern Africa. The result was a fitting sequel to the lower-level review over the summer and fall, and a typical cameo of foreign policy a year after the administration took office. As usual, Nixon opened the meeting by reciting the talking points prepared for him by Kissinger. The day's subject was not only a complex foreign policy problem, the President began, but also a matter of extraordinary moral and political dimensions. He would like to have a frank discussion and not try to reach any final decisions (the final choice, as everyone knew, was reserved for a later time when he would act on Kissinger's recommendation). In the fat blue briefing book before Nixon were NSSM 39, which he very probably ignored, and Kissinger's cover memorandum and agenda summarizing the review in a few pages, which he invariably did read. The Kissinger briefing also included in this case a special separate paper on "Domestic and Moral Factors" in southern Africa, which argued in philosophical terms that racial tyranny was the most odious for being inescapable at birth, and that U.S. policy toward white states could well become a volatile domestic issue in American politics. The case for disengagement "on the basis of foreign policy alone is not persuasive," said the memorandum, and "partial relaxation (option 2) is a justifiable act of consulting our interests." But that policy "should be pondered against the domestic and moral dimensions." Of the U.S. interests in the area, the special paper concluded that "none is sufficiently important to run even the potential risks of southern Africa becoming a serious and divisive domestic issue," and it recommended disengagement.

Written by an NSC aide, Winston Lord, the special memorandum was another example of the relative virtues of the NSC system and Kissinger's control over it. Under this system a fresh and thoughtful view, very differently argued in contrast to the bureaucratic NSSM, could be put before the President without dilution or institutional bargaining. Whether Kissinger or Nixon wanted to hear such arguments, the pretense of open choice and sharply argued alternatives which underlay the system clearly sanctioned papers of this kind. Perhaps the greatest failure of the NSC staff under Kissinger was that they did not provide more of such dissent, challenging their own staff positions and Kissinger, as this paper challenged "tar baby," as well as the departmental positions. But if Kissinger put forward the unconventional argument on southern Africa and Nixon took note, it did not prevent what followed in an all too conventional meeting of the National Security Council.

To Nixon's solemn opening lines on the complexity of the subject, Secretary of State Rogers interjected that the issues could not be all that hard since so many of them around the table—John Mitchell, Vice President Agnew, Richardson, Rogers himself, and the President—were "lawyers who must have had clients in South Africa . . . I know I did." The reference was to the more than twenty huge U.S. corporations operating in South Africa, among whom Rogers's former firm did indeed have clients, but the remark was irrelevant. The real clients at hand appeared next in the standard CIA intelligence brief on the area, read with occasional mispronunciations and fractured syntax by Director Helms. So transparently pro-white was the CIA presentation, so disdainful of black African opposition, so reflective of the views of the white security services on whose reports CIA analysis was based, that at one point even the customarily cynical Kissinger passed a puzzled note to an aide, "Why is he doing this?" At the one-word reply, "Clients," he gave a knowing scowl. Southern Africa was one in a train of NSC briefings, intelligence estimates, and field reports during 1969 that convinced Kissinger of the Agency's preoccupation with its established role and sources, and of Helms's basic inability or unwillingness to control the resulting bias. Like Rogers, Helms would survive the first administration, but

Kissinger's disregard grew from incidents like this one and made Helms one more bureaucratic opponent. Following the CIA brief, Kissinger in marked contrast summarized the policy options with scrupulous dispassion and balance, his sole jibe reserved for Newsom's eleventh-hour concoction of "tar baby" with its African veto. This option, Kissinger said acidly, was somewhat "complicated," involving a strategy we would decide to pursue only "if other countries did not object."

The discussion then rambled over much of the ground already covered, albeit tendentiously, in the initial CIA briefing. Nixon acted here as he frequently did in NSC meetings, in the role of interested impartial questioner, almost as a judge questioning witnesses from the bench independent of the contesting attorneys, often to get answers he already knew but to steer the meeting. What was the extent of U.S. trade with the white states? And with the rest of Africa? How did the other African states react to South Africa? What was the situation at the UN? In reply came the halting, sometimes contradictory answers from senior officials striving to stay respectably close to the questions yet insert their own special points. Around the cabinet table with the NSC no less than at the Pierre, the explanation of Nixon's command and Henry Kissinger's preeminence often lay less in the two men themselves than in the mediocre quality of the rest of the government. Officials who argued doggedly for their bureaucratic interests and convictions at lower-level meetings or in impersonal memoranda to the White House swiftly wilted in the presidential presence. "We can live with the Portuguese problem," UN Ambassador Charles Yost assured Nixon when asked if the United States could "roll with the punch" in the General Assembly, though Yost's cables before and after the NSC meeting consistently claimed just the reverse, and the UN mission would complain long afterward that the White House had no appreciation of the peculiar pressures on the East River. "Are we doing the right thing?" Nixon put to the group. Newsom, not to be outdone by Yost in the hardheaded, can-do approach, observed that the UN was no reliable gauge of the rightness of U.S. policy because the black African ambassadors there tended to be "self-generating, uninstructed extremists," whereas their home governments were somewhat more rational. The whole problem was "containable," said Newsom, as long as you could talk to the docile Africans who stayed in Africa. Afterward, in private,

Newsom would reportedly tell colleagues, congressmen, and both sets of Africans that the State Department had fought to the last for a hard line against the whites.

Between this kind of conversation at the NSC and the realities outside, whether bureaucratic or diplomatic, the senior officials erected their own wall of ingratiation and hyperbole which only shut them off further from the final decision. Rogers argued, for example, that the American Consulate in Salisbury, Rhodesia, should be closed because "every African foreign minister" the Secretary had met at the UN the preceding autumn had urged closure. In fact, the record of the Rogers conversations showed that of the some twenty African ministers he met, only three brought up the consulate; Rogers himself prompted the issue with four others; and the rest were indifferent to the subject, at least proving Newsom's thesis of African foreign ministry mentality. In the same vein, Rogers, who was scheduled for a trip to Africa the following month, argued that "my life will be miserable" if the consulate were not closed. For an important act of policy in southern Africa which involved considerations of international law, protection of American nationals, and perhaps future diplomacy in a troubled area, the Secretary of State and his highest aides could give only reasons of client pressure (in this case arguable) and political convenience. At this juncture Helms asked if he might make a comment, though of course the Agency took no "policy role." It seemed "counterproductive" to close a consulate like Salisbury, he said. "We get blind and buy very little in black Africa"; adding about the Africans, "They need us. They'll always be mad at us, even three years from now." Like Rogers's opposite approach to keep the State Department and its black counterparts variously content by closing the post, Helms's chief concern was the CIA station in Salisbury, to which the efficient white fellow officers in the Rhodesian Security Service helpfully funneled intelligence about Soviet and Chinese subversion in Africa.

At another point, having otherwise been a quiet listener to all this, Vice President Agnew read from prepared notes a fervent statement pointing out that "South African independence" in 1965 (sic) was similar to the United States in 1776, when black inhabitants did not have the vote. He expanded on the original provisions of the U.S. Constitution counting only a fraction of slaves for purposes of apportionment. After Agnew ended there was an embarrassed silence, and

Nixon leaned forward to admonish, "You mean Rhodesia, don't you, Ted?" And following another palpable pause in which Agnew remained mute and red-faced, Nixon concluded, "Times do change." The NSC thus completed its discussion of the Rhodesian Consulate without reference to Rhodesia, except perhaps for the Vice President's difficult excursion into historical parallels of repression.

Throughout these deliberations Kissinger remained silent in his putative role of neutrality, turning occasionally to show a small sardonic smile to aides sitting behind him. Like the Johnson men before them, the fleshy figures at the table spoke in self-consciously poised and manly tones, but what they uttered in that studied control gave the meetings a tragicomic shade. Nor was there any single moment that seemed to make the participants face the obvious banality of it all. Helms's gaffes from his scripts were commonplace; Agnew's ham-handed efforts to stop the show with a conservative insight were too easily squashed by Nixon. The only visible emotion at these gatherings of the highest foreign policy officials of the U.S. government was the undercurrent of personal contempt among themselves. With southern Africa it flashed into the open only once when, on the issue of implying recognition of the minority régime by closing the Rhodesian Consulate, Laird curtly reminded Rogers that recognition should not carry moral approval in any case, which drew murmured agreement around the table and prolonged throat-clearing from the Secretary of State. By December 1969 Laird, like Kissinger, could be brusque and offhand in challenging his cabinet colleague at the State Department, sometimes almost too openly to uphold protocol.

The meeting also broke with the usual public stereotypes of foreign policy decisions, both liberal and conservative. After Helms's ritual briefing, at no moment in some two hours of talk did the terms "communism" or "national interest" interrupt the advocacy of organizational goals or personal biases. According to men who have attended both, the Nixon administration NSC sessions in style and content were little different from the board meetings of large corporations, foundations, or other institutions. Yet in the Cabinet Room, of course, the price of misrepresentation and clashing egos or departments was far higher. "Foreign policy is not Palmolive Soap, but it's managed the same way," said one witness of several NSC conversations who left the government only a few months after this meeting. As for how the southern African discussion compared to other NSC considerations of subjects of higher priority, after the meeting an aide remarked to Kissinger's deputy, Alexander Haig, that it had been "unbelievable." "Not only is it believable," answered Haig, who recorded the notes of most NSC sessions. "It sounds like one of the best they've had."

Two weeks later, Kissinger sent Nixon the standard decision memorandum, the most important document of the eight-month process which saw hundreds of pages drafted and redrafted. The memo recommended "tar baby," including a "lower profile" at the UN, a "less doctrinaire approach" to mutual problems with South Africa, reduced pressure on the Portuguese, and increased aid of some $5 million to the black states of the region. On the specific operational issues left dangling from the Johnson administration, Nixon approved a relaxation of the arms embargo on South Africa and Portugal and an extension of trade promotion for American firms exporting to South Africa. Naval calls in South Africa were still prohibited. A decision on Rhodesian chrome was deferred for lack of evidence on the legality of allowing imports under sanctions. The Salisbury Consulate was retained (with Kissinger discreetly supplying Nixon the documentary evidence of Rogers's error at the NSC). As it happened, in a few weeks the British formally asked for U.S. withdrawal since they were ending the fiction of their own commonwealth tie to Rhodesia. The consulate was then pulled because it was important to London. The CIA station simply adjourned to the U.S. Embassy in South Africa while some of its agents discreetly became private Americans in Rhodesia. Very little genuinely changed with the implementation of the long-fought change in policy, and nothing of importance in the basic dilemma of American relations in the area. The administration soon allowed some "hardship" imports of Rhodesian chrome technically purchased before sanctions. With the help of White House indifference, industry pressures a few years later forced through Congress an amendment lifting the chrome embargo altogether, though this did draw some fire from Africa and the UN until it was rescinded in 1977.

At first indignant and sullen at their defeat, the State Department eventually embraced "tar baby" with the fervor of those for whom the sheer existence of orthodoxy matters more than its content. Newsom became the public advocate of a new "communication" with the white states, though in reality there would be over the next four years no official effort to encourage moderate domestic measures by either the white governments or U.S. corporations. Cloaked in new rhetoric and rationale, the Pentagon, Commerce, NASA, CIA, and myriad private interests continued business as usual in southern Africa while the racial confrontation quietly festered. In the end, Kissinger accepted "tar baby" because his encounter with State Department officialdom convinced him, rightly, that present policy was no better. Still, it was folly to believe that the same men, in their ignorance and self-interest, could effectively carry out an even more sophisticated and difficult approach which would be attacked in Africa and the Congress. For his part, Nixon approved the new course because it was new, because the opposition to it was so weak, and because Kissinger recommended it. Neither the President nor his Assistant for National Security had strong, settled views about Africa, and in their indifference, once more, the internal politics of foreign policy became decisive. For the continuing farce of American diplomacy in a troubled region the White House (including the author) was ultimately to blame. But the real "tar baby" was not to be encountered in a flawed strategy attempting to deal with the racial agonies of southern Africa; it was found in the mind and habits of a government that could not escape its own self-serving and incompetence.

In southern Africa the worst effect of such foreign policy was to deprive the United States of a chance to stop or at least slow its own heedless descent, along with other Western powers and the Africans, into the coming disaster of a race war. But that reckoning was still years ahead and the cost difficult to measure. Only a month after the NSC met on southern Africa, the collapse of starving Biafra brought to a climax a similar episode of official vacillation, hypocrisy, and deception. This time the physical and moral toll was all too immediate, measured in thousands of lives that might have been saved in Africa had there been different men and politics in Washington.

The Biafran famine exercised a strange hold on Nixon, and by natural extension on Kissinger. It had been an issue in the 1968 campaign when, to the horror of the State Department and their Federal Nigerian clients, the Republican candidate pressed for more vigorous relief efforts and Mrs. Nixon even appeared on the steps of St. Patrick's Cathedral in New York to encourage donations. Kissinger saw the concern soon after his appointment, and at the Pierre he commissioned a staff paper on options for expanded relief. The formal policy review of the Nigerian civil war ordered by Nixon on January 24, 1969, was one of the first NSSMs. The review encountered the predictable resistance—including a marathon nine-hour session of the Interdepartmental Group over the inclusion, among six options, of the possibility that the United States might support Biafra and that Biafran independence "might" not lead to the disintegration of almost every other state in Africa. At an otherwise desultory NSC meeting on February 9, Nixon and Kissinger alone seemed knowledgeable or interested in the subject. Nixon adopted none of the six specific options in the NSSM ranging from support of Nigeria through mediation to recognition of Biafra. Instead, a brief decision memorandum, drafted by Haig from notes on the meeting, called for continued political and military neutrality and a "high profile" on relief, though the memo included a throwaway line for the State Department that the NSC "considers" the victory of a unified Nigeria "in the long-term interests of the United States." From that aptly vague beginning there followed a year of tragicomic disunity in American policy toward the famine and starvation—the State Department set against the White House, the White House secretly pursuing its own policy at odds with the NSC decision, and the President wavering within himself. At one moment Nixon impatiently strained to act. At another he could be utterly indifferent to the most moving events abroad and the most blatant insubordination in his own government. It was Kissinger who indulged, yet ultimately deflected, these careening moods on Biafran policy, and in the process remained carefully atop the yawning divisions of both the presidential mind and the government.

The only tangible outcome of the NSC meeting on Biafra was the appointment later in February of C. Clyde Ferguson, a forty-four-year-old law professor at Rutgers, as a State Department special coordinator for relief. The new appointee had lacked foreign affairs experience. For the African Bureau officials who were anxious to blunt the mounting congressional pressures for aid to Biafra, led by Senator Edward Kennedy, Ferguson's chief qualification was his race. When asked why Ferguson headed the State Department list of recommended coordinators, a senior diplomat replied, "What could be better than giving Teddy a black man to lean on?" Whether or not Ferguson's appointment provided a public cover of color over U.S. policy, it did little to relieve the onrush of disaster inside Biafra. Ferguson conducted relief negotiations over the next ten months with the double burden of his Washington superiors and his African clients and with apparent reluctance to offend either. Cross River, Nettle, Black Bishop: exotic place and code names marked a series of often desultory and always futile efforts by Ferguson to arrange some added corridor past the blockade in order to supplement the perilous and meager nighttime airlift into Biafra by the Red Cross and various Church agencies. Obstacles to adequate relief towered on all sides. Both combatants feared military risks in a corridor. Both took callous advantage of the famine, Biafra for the international sympathy it evoked, Federal Nigeria because hunger killed the rebellion along with the people. To make matters worse for humanitarian efforts, the nightly relief flights were interspersed with a sporadic but vital traffic of gunrunning planes into the enclave from neighboring Gabon, where the French under De Gaulle had cynically supplied just enough covert arms to maintain the rebels as an irritant to the British. London in turn armed Nigeria and supported the starvation blockade with equal cynicism to protect its own post-colonial economic and political interests in West Africa. The Wilson government was beset by the widespread British public concern with the disaster, to which Whitehall's policy was, as one senior Foreign Office official put it to his American counterpart, "To show conspicuous zeal in relief while in fact letting the little buggers starve out." On one occasion late in the war, Wilson would tell Ferguson that casualties of the famine were no object. He would accept a half million dead Biafrans, said Wilson earnestly, if that was what it took to secure the old Nigeria.

The United States stood uneasily between the belligerents and their sponsors, embargoing arms to either side, financing the relief flights to quiet the public clamor, sending Ferguson ostensibly to try to enlarge the flow of food and medicine. Yet the State Department remained committed as always to the eventual triumph of the Nigerians, and was thus loath to push too hard for a relief agreement or to denounce the obstruction of it on all sides. And while governments practiced their various forms of *Realpolitik,* the human toll in Africa relentlessly rose. In a June dusk in 1969 the Nigerians by sheer chance finally shot down a Red Cross food transport. From that moment, the relief flights shrank to a trickle, sealing the fate of tens of thousands among the more than 3 million people trapped inside the blockade.

As Biafra starved, a similarly Byzantine and sometimes bizarre sequence unfolded in Washington. Having decided in February to stay neutral in the politics of the Nigerian civil war, leaving the State Department to weather the public storm with gestures such as the appointment of Ferguson until the blockade worked the collapse of Biafra, by spring Nixon chafed to become involved in the conflict, in part as an ally of the Biafrans. "He wants to recognize them," Kissinger told his astonished staff aides in May, and related a lecture from Nixon that morning on the virtues of supporting Biafra, largely to teach the State Department a lesson in authority. Presidential musings on recognition continued through June, apparently sparked by intelligence reports or press summaries on the subject. To each statement, Kissinger by his own account gave an unquestioning and sympathetic hearing. He then returned to his office and proceeded as if the conversation had never taken place, ordering his staff to do the same with a knowing smile and a reference to the increasingly common West Basement explanation of periodic behavior upstairs in the Oval Office: "He's a little crazy, you know." What distinguished these tendencies to intervene in Biafra from similar excursions in other areas of foreign policy was that they seem to have passed as quickly from Nixon's memory as from Kissinger's consideration. Elsewhere, as Cambodia would soon demonstrate, the compulsion of the moment could endure to become national policy. But after only six months in office, Kissinger possessed a remarkable grasp for measuring the difference between what he could disdainfully ignore and the more serious exertions of presidential will. Being the former, Biafran policy went on unchanged, the State Department blissfully unaware of the threat to its African client casually contained in the White House.

In July, Nixon formally ordered Kissinger to attempt a mediation of the Nigerian civil war. Reacting to a newspaper advertisement appealing to him to help stop the African fighting as he had promised to halt the war in Vietnam, the President dictated a terse memo to Kissinger recounting the ad and saying, "I agree. Give me a plan." With Kissinger taking this request seriously, the NSC staff prepared detailed terms of reference for a peace negotiation, received a subsequent Nixon approval of the terms, and even began meetings with representatives of the two sides for exploratory talks in August and September—all in deliberate secrecy from the State Department. The episode produced on one occasion the contrast of myself and another NSC aide negotiating with the Biafran foreign minister in publisher Norman Cousins's apartment high over Park Avenue, while a few blocks away State Department officials at the UN met other Biafran envoys for the usual denial that the U.S. government would have anything to do with a mediation effort. The NSC talks with the Biafrans dragged on through the autumn without progress. The Federal side sensed its coming victory, while the Biafrans remained insistent on their dwindling independence. But even had the rebels survived and even had the two sides responded to the U.S. mediation, it seems doubtful whether the negotiations would have succeeded. Sooner or later the truncated White House diplomacy would have become known in the State Department. There it would have encountered powerful forces of cliency for whom the objective of U.S. policy was not to put an end to the war, nor least of all Biafran self-determination, but the maintenance of the traditional Anglo-American patronage in Nigeria at almost any price. And against that inertia, as events were soon to show, the presidential authority that launched the secret mediation would be suddenly powerless.

As the White House concealed its mediation efforts from the rest of the U.S. government, the State Department prepared with comparable furtiveness for the onrushing fall of Biafra. Late in the summer of 1969, after repeated bureaucratic delays, a team of American public health doctors from the Center for Disease Control (CDC) in Atlanta flew into Biafra under the auspices of the Ferguson mission to measure with precise data the depth of the famine. Experienced in West Africa in previous smallpox eradication programs and working against the backdrop of a CDC historical study of famines as well as the most advanced methods of nutritional measurements, the doctors produced the only comprehensive scientific survey ever made of Biafra's catastrophe. The resulting Western Report, named for the head of the team, was sent to the State Department in November 1969. Its findings confirmed the worst. "Slow, creeping starvation of almost the entire population is the key impression today in Biafra," began the summary of the report. It went on to document severe edema, the swelling of tissue that accompanies starvation, in nearly a third of the more than 3 million people in the enclave. Children under four and adults over forty-five suffered most, and over 2 million people needed daily or weekly rations to survive. The population had starved to this point, the report made clear, under the existing night airlift of some 2,000 tons of relief food per week. In cold statistical logic the doctors concluded that by the fall of 1969 at least 1.5 million people in Biafra were literally starving to death despite the emergency airlift.

The same month Dr. Western's findings were sent to him, Ferguson held a conference of private relief agencies working in Biafra. The conclusion of that meeting was that any interruption of the outside airlift by the war—given the notorious inefficiency of the Nigerian relief operation on its own in previously captured areas—was bound to be, as the official notes of the conference put it, "catastrophic." In military and political terms, the meaning of the Western Report was unmistakable. The thirty-month blockade was at last strangling the rebellion, and Nigeria's victory, often unsure, was now only a matter of weeks. For the State Department long backing its Federal clients, this expectation only hardened further the resistance to any action that might offend the Lagos government, even including a suggestion that current Nigerian relief operations or planning might not be adequate to deal with a postwar food crisis inside fallen Biafra. As 1969 drew to a close, the Western Report went ignored by the U.S. Embassy in Lagos, was not given to the Nigerian authorities, and was mentioned to the White House with no analysis of its meaning beyond a routine accompanying memorandum that was overlooked, buried in the flood of bureaucratic paper. As for the starvation, American relief planning continued after the Western survey as before, on the basis of 2,000 tons a week, with no special provision for the predicted "catastrophic" interruption of the airlift.

In the early morning hours of Saturday, January 10, a FLASH cable arrived in the White House Situation Room. From Paris, the telegram relayed the last message of a clandestine French military group inside Biafra. The southern front of the enclave had suddenly collapsed, many of the Biafran soldiers too weakened by hunger even to leave their positions under Nigerian attack. The Federal forces were racing to close the lone Uli airfield, symbol of both the relief and the arms that had kept Biafra alive. As discreetly as they had come, the French advisers had fled on the last plane from Uli, the message added. Left behind were Biafra's millions, now completely cut off from outside food supplies. Over the fateful weeks that followed, the Nixon administration again conducted in effect two foreign policies toward the Biafran crisis. In public appeared a presidential diplomacy of alacrity and compassion. But inside the government, another, more decisive policy of bureaucratic delay and evasion prevailed, at once held in contempt yet fecklessly tolerated by the White House.

Within two days of the collapse, Nixon had ordered the alert of C-130s and helicopters, and had sent to the Nigerian head of state, General Gowon, a personal message offering the aircraft, an added $10 million in relief aid, and all U.S. information on the famine so that the occupying forces would be "totally aware" of the situation inside Biafra. As this message was sent, however, a State Department press officer assured reporters that relief conditions in Biafra were in "pretty good shape," adding that, "We don't even know that a need will develop for an airlift." On January 13, Under Secretary Richardson briefed the press that "normalcy is returning rapidly" to the overrun enclave, and that the Federals were conducting relief "competently," statements for which the evidence was arguable at best. That evening, alarmed that their superiors were ignoring its implications, junior aides to Ferguson quietly slipped to the NSC staff the Western Report, including a postwar estimate by Western that the population of conquered Biafra now required 10,000 tons of relief per week to avert further catastrophe. Because of the earlier failure in bureaucratic communication, it was in effect the first time the report and its ominous implications, filed three months earlier, had been grasped in the government beyond the State Department and the CDC doctors themselves. Kissinger was briefed on Western's study the same night and telephoned Richardson. Richardson recalled the report only vaguely, but suggested that the findings be given immediately to the Nigerians. It would take nearly two weeks for the State Department and the American Embassy in Lagos to bring themselves to deliver Dr. Western's study to the Nigerians. As the days passed, the Western figures of relief tonnage and deaths, mere abstractions of the bureaucratic battle in Washington, became human reality.

On January 14, at Kissinger's instruction, I sent a memorandum directly to Richardson on the serious implications of the Western

Report, urging an immediate high-level approach to Gowon to explain the findings, increased shipments and production of emergency food rations, a renewed offer of trucks, helicopters, and cargo aircraft, and several other steps. That day in Lagos, having been on a routine tour of West Africa before Biafra's fall, Assistant Secretary Newsom told a press conference that all available evidence "does not suggest large-scale starvation" in Biafra. At another Washington press conference the following morning, now fully informed of the Western Report, Richardson turned aside questions by saying the United States was only trying to "assure itself" of the facts and the "adequacy" of relief operations. A meeting of State and AID officials that afternoon under Richardson's chairmanship formally rejected the NSC staff recommendations and confirmed earlier planning for 2,000 tons a week. On Friday, January 16, relief workers who had just escaped from the enclave, including the chief of the large-scale Catholic Relief Operation, came to the White House and gave eyewitness accounts supporting Western's projections of need. But when the party attempted to see Richardson a few hours later, they were shunted off to lower-level officials of the African Bureau. Over the weekend, I called Dr. Western in Atlanta to ask if there was any doubt about the validity of the report. Answering that he and his colleagues would "stake our professional reputations" on the study, Western then called back later to say that by chance he and his associates would be in Washington the following week for consultations on other matters at the National Institute of Health. On Monday, January 19, Western and his team briefed Newsom, just back from Lagos, and Ferguson, the man who had hired them to begin with. As with the relief workers, Richardson did not see the public health doctors. But the effect of the briefing of Newsom and Ferguson, replete with predictions of 1 to 1.5 million casualties, was enough to spur some action. Finally, on January 20, ten days after Biafra's collapse and three months after the submission of the Western Report, the State Department blithely cabled Lagos to ask about the "variance" between the Western data and current U.S.-Nigerian planning, requesting that the embassy give the report to the Nigerian Federal authorities. Yet even as that cable went out, the bureaucracy clung to its preferred vision of the tragedy. In the only meeting between Nixon and his senior officials during the crisis, Rogers, Newsom, and Ferguson briefed the President on the afternoon of the twentieth, assuring him that the situation in Biafra was in hand. They did not mention the Western Report.

Within twenty-four hours, the first accounts from American journalists traveling inside the enclave depicted widespread death, suffering, and a breakdown of Nigerian relief operations. With characteristic panic at the public relations damage and a transparent readiness to shift the blame to the field, State now telegrammed the Lagos Embassy requesting "new evidence" to put "in better perspective" what the drafter called the "lurid" reports of disaster. That cable had scarcely gone when the first official observations arrived. From one of Ferguson's aides, the report confirmed the most terrible of Western's prediction. "Disaster of major proportions appears to be developing here," began the cable, and went on to give a recital of starvation as well as looting and rape by the conquering troops. "At least one million people are in acute need now and situation grows worse daily." Under pressure in the press and from Senator Kennedy (to whom the cable reporting the calamity was promptly leaked by an African Bureau already moving to repair its bridges), the State Department the next day adopted the emergency measures recommended by the NSC staff and rejected a week before. Still, the Lagos Embassy, without senators or "lurid" newspaper stories to move it so directly, remained immovable. Not until January 23 did the mission deign to hand over the Western Report to the Nigerians, and then only to lower-level Nigerian officials, with a curt telegram to Washington that the embassy "could not support" findings so at odds with previous positions. After a de facto disciplinary mission from Richardson had been sent to Lagos and a member of Western's team had briefed senior embassy officials, the Western Report was given to the head of the Nigerian relief effort on January 27. It had been two weeks since the White House first learned of the report and suggested its immediate dispatch to the Nigerians, two weeks since the President of the United States publicly promised the Nigerians all available information on the humanitarian crisis inside the overrun rebel territory. Less than 200 tons of food had reached the enclave during these weeks, a period in which the need, according to Western, was some 20,000 tons. On the day that the U.S. Embassy at last delivered the report to proper authorities, intercepted Nigerian Red Cross messages spoke of "incredible disaster" and "great numbers dying by the roads."

Throughout this sequence of events, Kissinger and Nixon were suddenly transformed: the responsible, powerful men who had so forcefully seized control of other policies for good or ill now became distracted, cynically detached onlookers. Kissinger remained typically intent on the appearance of it all. Telephoning Kennedy late one night early in the crisis, he assured the senator against a background of barking dogs and crying children that he, at least, was doing all he could to help the Biafrans. "You remember, Ted, that I worked for your brother," Kissinger added as proof of his reliability. On another occasion, when Harvard nutritionist and White House consultant Jean Mayer met Richardson at Kissinger's house and promptly demolished the Under Secretary's canned report on relief measures, Kissinger called Mayer aside afterward and whispered, "You see what I'm up against. The State Department is incompetent." These touches left both Kennedy and Mayer with much the desired impression, that Kissinger was a lonely force for compassion against the lethargy and client-myopia of the rest of government. The reality was less heroic. Though he repeatedly informed Nixon on the implications of the Western Report and the bureaucratic refusal to heed it, though he was visibly moved by a personal briefing by Western and his colleagues, Kissinger shrank from any direct confrontation of the deceit and evasion. In large measure, he held back because Biafran policy belonged so much to Richardson, his only ally at the upper reaches of the State Department. A clash could only scar that relationship, and Biafran relief became a casualty to his calculations of the need for Richardson on a host of other issues.

But the most decisive influence in Kissinger's abstention on Biafra was Nixon's. The President who toyed with recognition of Biafra in order to defy the State Department, who had begun a clandestine mediation to end the war, was, at Biafra's collapse, secluded in his Executive Office Building hideaway writing his first State of the Union address. There was no longer time for starving Africans or even insubordinate American officials. When Rogers and his assistants presented their chimeric briefing on January 20, Nixon, who understood Western's data and authority, knew he was being misled. "They're going to let them starve, aren't they Henry?" he asked Kissinger in a brief telephone conversation after the Secretary of State had gone. "Yes," came the almost perfunctory answer, and the two men went on to discuss foreign policy passages in the coming speech. At some level touched by the tragedy and still contemptuous of those indifferent to it, yet unwilling and in part unable to confront his own government, Nixon would treat Biafran policy over these fateful weeks as he later dealt with much of the Watergate scandal, as if somehow it had nothing to do with him.

In the end, as Western had also predicted, there would be no final count of those Biafrans who did not survive the weeks before the need was finally faced and adequate relief organized. Still highly secret State Department estimates put the losses at 20,000, a figure most relief workers on the scene regard as only a fraction of the actual catastrophe. In postwar Nigeria the census in the former rebel territory is a volatile political issue. No one—not the Federal or Biafran élite who made war for their own purposes, not the United States or Britain who covet Nigeria's oil, not the French or others who fed the carnage—quite wants to know the number of those missing. But there is one sign. The schools of Iboland, jammed before the war, are no longer crowded.

In the Nixon administration as in those before and after, American foreign policy ultimately reflected the people who practiced it. Far more than any coherent doctrine or design, it was the collective force of habits, fears, and human relationships that molded much of the use, and misuse, of national power. Those influences were seldom simple, and sometimes bitterly ironic. The Pentagon officers who clung to chemical-biological weapons no longer relevant to the national defense; the foreign service blindly scheming to preserve a sham policy in southern Africa largely because it was familiar; the bureaucrats in Washington and Lagos who watched Biafra starve while squirming to deny information that might have lessened the disaster—nowhere were there easy villains. Intelligent, compassionate men produced stupid, callous policies not on some evil impulse, but most often because in 1969–70, despite the advent of Henry Kissinger and Richard Nixon, those men were still variously trapped in the closed, shadow world of the foreign affairs bureaucracies. No reform of NSC procedures had touched the deep impulse by which stagnant civil services identified the national interest with their own parochial mission. No White House grasp for power at its upper reaches could alter the institutional obsession in the lower ranks with continuity, safety, the survival of career. Kissinger and Nixon in many cases simply abdicated to those abiding forces, finding principle or human costs inexpedient. Behind the façade of their successes, the blunders like Biafra would seem nearly indistinguishable from those of the régimes they succeeded and whose weaknesses they so deplored.

Least of all did the new government escape the squalor of prejudice and personal rivalry among its highest officials. Hovering over the fitful, yeasty attention to African affairs—and over the most basic public issues foreign and domestic—was a pall of racism in the West Basement, and even in the Oval Office. The mentality, of course, was rarely overt and never public, revealed only in isolated gestures or unguarded candor. But the signs were thinly coded. To the amusement of Kissinger and his colleagues, Colonel Haig would quietly pretend to beat drums on the table as African affairs were brought up at NSC staff meetings, or other assistants would joke contemptuously about so-and-so who bought a house in a racially mixed neighborhood of Washington "to be near his dusky friends." Yet it was Kissinger himself, the Jewish immigrant from Germany, the accomplished scholar, who was even more ingenuous on the subject. At the fall of Biafra, he was briefed on the prospects of ethnic slaughter of the captured Ibos by northern Nigerian troops with a long history of hatred and atrocities against the dominant tribe in Biafra. How would the Ibos be recognizable, Kissinger asked. When I explained that the northern tribes tended to be more Semitic in appearance and the eastern, coastal Ibos more Negroid, he was visibly surprised and confused. "But you have always told me the Ibos were more gifted and accomplished than the others. What do you mean 'more Negroid'?" These Kissinger descents into his own private sociology were mild, however, compared to the periodic utterances of the President of the United States. "Make sure there's something in it for the jigs, Henry," Nixon telephoned Kissinger from ship to shore at Key Biscayne in February 1970, while the latter was putting the finishing touches on the first presidential message to the Congress on foreign policy. "*Is* there something in it for the jigs?" the President pressed his Assistant, who assured him in the usual respectful "Yes" that there was. That in Richard Nixon's mind "the jigs" could co-exist with authentic if unsustained sympathy for Biafra's famished children was another emblem of the larger cleft between the disgraceful and the admirable in this paradoxical man and his presidency. There is no documentary evidence—save perhaps the inaccessible White House tapes on national security subjects—that this racism was the decisive influence in Kissinger-Nixon policies in Africa, Vietnam, or elsewhere, policies for which there were other arguments and reasons, however questionable. But it is impossible to pretend that the cast of mind that harbors such casual bigotry did not have some effect on American foreign policy toward the overwhelming majority of the world which is nonwhite.

Kissinger's power grew out of his constant readiness to play on—and compromise with—such seamy undercurrents in an administration that often turned much of its ignorance and bias against itself. As at the Pierre, he had a decisive advantage in the personal weaknesses of his bureaucratic rivals. In the State Department, Rogers appointed his senior aides chiefly from among the few officials he had chanced to meet while on the UN Delegation. Since in the peculiar Darwinism of Foggy Bottom the UN Mission and its home bureau of International Organization Affairs was customarily one of the most ingrown and least demanding provinces, Rogers thus populated the vital jobs in the Department with a narrow group of officers and their protégés. Key positions not filled in this manner were otherwise left to the natural selection of the foreign service hierarchy. The new appointments all but ensured the submersion of a secretary of state whose only hope of approaching Kissinger's assets was to assemble a fresh, creative, and aggressive staff.

Still, the systemic power of the State Department to delay and distort remained formidable. There were also the sometime benefits to State of the capricious, hypocritical relationship between Nixon and Rogers. Again as he had at the Pierre, the President was willing to ridicule and undercut his Secretary of State on policies minor and major, so long as he could also avert any direct controversy or confrontation on the issue. "He'll never say no to Rogers," was another frequent growl from Kissinger, whose remedy was to appease Rogers with the ritual hearing of NSC meetings and then to guard the isolation of the presidential decision afterward. But that effort depended in the last account, like the coup at the Pierre, on Rogers's inexperience and thus his inability to pursue his own policy interests. Kissinger became *de facto* Secretary of State early in the régime in large part because the incumbent endured the humiliation of denied access to the President. To measure this decisive role of personality, one has only to compare Rogers's tenure with a later Secretary of the Treasury, John Connally, whose refusal to submit to the game made for a very different relationship with Kissinger and Nixon, and thus allowed him a far greater impact on policy. Held (and holding himself) at a distance which insulated Nixon's weaknesses, Rogers was prey to other bureaucratic blows delivered from the West Basement. Kissinger readily joined, for example, in the backstairs derision which grew with the Secretary's record of policy defeats, which soon sank to the level of locker-room braggadocio. With favored journalists like Joseph Alsop (who thereby gratified a coveted intimacy with power), with a staff disdainful of their State Department rivals and prepared like all underlings to laugh at the boss's joke, with other White House assistants always anxious to certify their own status and power, their own machismo. This snickering amounted to more than the usual office gossip. It fed into the larger White House atmosphere of swagger, arrogance, and contemptuousness which was to have vast consequences in all areas. Not least, it was an atmosphere which made almost automatic the discrediting of any State Department alternative to presidential foreign policy whatever its merits, and guaranteed the impossibility of genuinely understanding and reforming the ineffectual performance of America's career diplomacy.

Another telling weapon against the State Department was Kissinger's gradual but none too subtle co-option of some of the higher-ranking officers around Rogers. Deliberately shunning the Secretary of State, Kissinger was at the same time careful to cultivate a few men at the second echelon whose quiet alliance would be useful to the NSC process as well as in operational questions. For older career FSOs, whose vanities had suffered in the relative eclipse of the Department under Johnson and who soon saw the even worse omens emanating from the Pierre, the intimate phone calls and brief chats with "Henry" after inter-agency meetings proved irresistible avenues back into the action. In return they gave him important intramural intelligence on positions surfacing in Foggy Bottom to be directed toward the White House. At times, too, they lent him discreet support in opposition to their own superiors from meetings of the NSC down through the web of lower committees and task forces. Such ties also offset Nixon's penchant for appeasing his obviously disenfranchised Secretary of State by "giving" him those areas and policies which the White House thought of secondary priority to issues like Vietnam or arms control. "For the moment," Kissinger told a staff meeting early in 1970, for example, "we're leaving Rogers the Middle East." The result was nearly four years of the usual inept U.S. diplomacy and bureaucratic politics there. But Kissinger's ties to the Assistant Secretary for Near East and South Asian affairs, Joseph Sisco, gave the White House a backstairs purview and control over the negotiations. When Kissinger became Secretary himself and at last turned his attention from Vietnam and détente to the Mideast, Sisco would be at his side, promoted to Under Secretary for Political Affairs.

The most potent of the bureaucratic marriages of convenience was with Rogers's deputy, Elliot Richardson. At weekly luncheons in Kissinger's West Basement office, these two men of matching arrogance and opportunism exchanged their views on issues and conjoined in a weary, acerbic commentary on the comparative incompetence of the rest of the government. To Richardson, the relationship made possible a relative autonomy and independence in policy matters, such as in Biafra, which other senior officials did not enjoy. More important in the long run, it positioned him sufficiently clearly from the undertow of the growing White House contempt for the Rogers State Department. "Except for Elliot," became a well-worn preface to the regular curses pronounced on the administration's foreign ministry. The arrangement survived because Richardson did seem visibly superior to his colleagues as well as eager to collaborate with Kissinger in the very shadow of Rogers, who saw the outflanking and yet did next to nothing to discipline his deputy. The latter moved on later in 1970 to become Secretary of Health, Education and Welfare, an advance in rank sped by the "Elliot-Henry" entente. Yet these innermost politics of foreign policy were never simple. If he could flatter, praise, use, and exempt Richardson from responsibility when it suited him, Kissinger did not let the friendship tarnish other necessary relations. Hence during the Biafran crisis the sneering aside to Jean Mayer about Elliot and the State Department. Mayer, after all, for the moment represented another constituency to whom Kissinger must seem to be standing alone against all the primitives around him.

The power of the West Basement in 1969–70 grew most directly at the expense of the Pentagon, which had enjoyed a discreet but almost unbroken preeminence in important foreign policy issues under the previous Democratic régimes. The decline of Defense now traced in part to Kissinger's personal and institutional assets, and to an emptying of much of the Department's civilian talent assembled under McNamara. By the summer of 1969, the International Security Affairs office was a shell of its once awesome self. The "little State Department" that had run or vetoed so much of American diplomacy from Vietnam to NATO became a refuge for some of the less capable foreign policy academics of the Republican right and soon lost most of its authority within the Pentagon and beyond. But the power of the Department remained in the shape of Laird, the shrewd politician, and of the joint chiefs, with their considerable constituency in the Congress and the general public. The Defense Department thus constituted the single greatest bureaucratic challenge to White House command. And again, as with State, the politics of personality were critical to Kissinger's success and to the shaping of policy. From the outset, Laird was at a disadvantage because of the role he chose to play as Defense Secretary. On most issues, with the notable exception of Vietnam, he was to see himself mainly as an arbiter and spokesman for the competing views within the military rather than as an independent force. It was a method which frequently consumed most of the energies he might have spent combating Kissinger's encroachments. To cut off his rival in that stance, Kissinger unerringly reached past Laird to conduct an ardent courtship of the uniformed services. The Defense Secretary was therefore often confronted in his own Department with a policy position or review already partly distilled by Kissinger. The joint chiefs and their staff were among the first Washington power centers to be paid obeisance by the newly appointed Presidential Assistant even before the inauguration. After assuming office, the contacts continued, by phone, in person, through the mediation of Haig, whose elevation as Kissinger's chief deputy in early autumn 1969 owed much to his military credentials and in turn to the certification they lent Kissinger. A former JCS consultant, himself a scholar of military options, Kissinger was to all appearances a "safe" Pentagon intellectual come to the White House. Only slowly did this image disappear and the irony become clear that the same man would oppose and defeat the generals and admirals on their most cherished issues. In fact, the chiefs reached such a point of bureaucratic desperation and craven-ness in the face of Kissinger's tactics that they would eventually assign an enlisted man seconded to the NSC to spy on Henry Kissinger almost as if he were an enemy commander. But in the first two years of the administration, Kissinger employed warm, trusting relations with the military to neutralize Laird as well as to lull the joint chiefs for the battles ahead.

Unlike Rogers, however, Laird still possessed, in addition to a talent for inside bureaucratic maneuvering, a native political gift for using the weapons of leaks and "inspired" lobbying via both the press and Congress, which provoked his bitterest clashes with Kissinger (who, after all, was using the same methods). Here the antidote was to turn Laird's own success against him in order to discredit him in the White House. Just as Rogers was portrayed as weak, Laird was described by similar innuendo as too strong, his forays into Congress seen as part of a design for promoting his own political future. By late 1969, for example, the Secretary of Defense's office would be labeled the "Laird for President Committee" by some of Kissinger's closest aides—a charge that touched a raw nerve in Nixon's inner circle and achieved much of its intended impact. Nothing more poisoned Laird's White House influence, however, or fortified Kissinger's, than the attribution to the Defense Secretary of foreign policy leaks which enraged Nixon and of course drove the administration to the use of phone taps. "Tell Laird this time he has gone too far," Kissinger said to an assistant when the *Pentagon Papers* appeared in *The New York Times,* a reaction that gives the flavor of the White House attitude toward the Secretary of Defense by 1971.

What made these politics all the more serpentine was that Kissinger conducted them surrounded by assistants who were almost entirely career bureaucrats from State or Defense, and among whom he maneuvered with some of the same distrust and scorn, the same alternating tactics of manipulation and expedient indifference.

Kissinger himself was in a sense the sole infusion of truly fresh talent into the new NSC staff of the Nixon administration. The background and selection of the men around him were largely conventional to the inner workings of government. Three career bureaucrats in their early forties, Helmut Sonnenfeldt, Viron Vaky, and Richard Sneider, handled Europe, Latin America, and East Asia respectively. Vaky was recommended by the foreign service establishment; Sneider by Halperin and Eagleburger, who knew him at State as the Country Director for Japan under Rusk and had urged him on Kissinger at the Pierre. Sonnenfeldt had been a personal friend of Kissinger's since World War II, from which he had proceeded to a long ladder-climbing career as an intelligence analyst in State. The other two regional areas went to the only holdovers from the Rostow staff. The Middle East was given to Harold Saunders, a former CIA analyst in his late thirties who had worked his way up as an NSC aide under both Kennedy and Johnson and had been recommended to Kissinger by McGeorge Bundy; the author, then thirty-one, dealt with Africa and the UN, after working briefly in the foreign service and under both Bundy and Rostow. Staff responsibility for international economic affairs belonged to C. Fred Bergsten, thirty, who came with credentials in a still esoteric field from State Department service and a fellowship at the Council on Foreign Relations. To direct a new NSC systems analysis staff, a group which would play an important role in major policy decisions from SALT to Vietnam escalations, Kissinger chose Lawrence Lynn, a young and gifted analyst from the Pentagon who came on the strength of praise from McNamara and others. Richard Moose, a former aide to Rusk, became in function if not in title the Staff Secretary of the NSC, overseeing the flood of paper in and out of the operation. Halperin dealt with the NSC agenda; Eagleburger and Haig were Kissinger's personal assistants—all bureaucrats catapulted upward from their service in the Johnson administration. Behind these officials, their assistants in turn were chiefly careerists from State, Defense, or CIA. Alone among the senior staff, the director of Policy Planning, Robert Osborn, was from outside government. An academic contemporary of Kissinger's, Osborn had taught and written on foreign policy at Johns Hopkins University. Also new to power were Richard Allen, head of foreign affairs research for the Nixon campaign, and his aide John Lehman. But both were excluded from all but marginal substance, casualties of a West Basement reaction to their unconcealed conservative zeal.

It was a staff with unprecedented power reflected from Kissinger's wholly unique position, and with widely varying degrees of talent and independence. A few, like Lynn, Bergsten, and Eagleburger, challenged the presumptions of both the bureaucracy and Kissinger. Beneath an unassertive, almost shy manner, Saunders wrote meticulously detailed staff work that had the effect of exposing policy foibles if not confronting them openly. Yet in the majority they were like their peers across Washington, remaining after all the men that they had been, simply trying to sense the current mood and do what seemed expected—in this case to abide by and abet Kissinger's sometimes savage methods just as they had adjusted to Rusk's demonology or McNamara's bogus efficiency. Most were operators and survivors, not given to excessive thought or articulation of the long-run policy issues or to probing the deeper questions of political ethics behind the endless maneuvering. When Kissinger in the fall of 1969 assigned each of his senior men a chapter of the forthcoming presidential foreign policy report to Congress, a description of problems and goals of policy in their own areas, he discovered to his consternation that they, like the rest of the bureaucracy, were largely unable to set down in clear concepts or readable English what was supposedly the essence of their work. At that, however, there was also a certain secure acceptance in Kissinger's reaction to this weakness. "It doesn't matter," he said to an aide complaining about Sonnenfeldt's inept rendition of European policy. "My policy's the only one we have to explain."

As he treated other colleagues, Kissinger variously bypassed, played off, flattered, inspired, cajoled, coerced, if necessary purged, and often outperformed his own staff. If inter-agency frictions became too naked, the staff man was there to absorb the blame in order to maintain the surface amenities. So Kissinger would complain to Richardson on several occasions over lunch about the aggressive anti-State Department mentality of this man and that, though both knew the fount of such rivalry was clearly the West Basement, with the NSC staff prodded constantly to discover and challenge what the rest of the régime was plotting. As a matter of intellectual technique, Kissinger could and did inspire repeated efforts from his assistants to achievements of quality and precision they were unlikely to realize otherwise. His own taste and rigor of thought gave Nixon, by several accounts, foreign policy staff work of conspicuously higher quality than that produced for either Johnson or Kennedy.

Yet that concern with quality did not extend to the toleration of dissenting views or options opposed to the preferred policy in the White House. Kissinger was never running an impartial clearinghouse for foreign policy alternatives—despite what his public image presented and beguiled reporters duly echoed. Once the NSC review had served its bureaucratic purpose, he was the most forceful advocate, the best armed and prepared protagonist in the process. And as his power grew, he became on many issues the final decision-maker, with Nixon's approval pro forma. In this rarefied atmosphere, the staff's work took on considerable gravity. The cover memos and initiatives often were literally the last word on the country's foreign policy. Accordingly, Kissinger's control here was as careful, as ruthless, yet as evasive as at any stage below. He could send an unpalatable memo, for example, to Haig or another staff man he knew was certain to criticize or oppose it, and eventually return it to its author with sympathetic noises about the disturbing objections of his colleagues. The tactic was soon transparent, but the memos seldom got through. Men who disagreed, who questioned too fundamentally, who could not easily write on instruction what they did not believe, who seemed for these or any number of lesser reasons untrustworthy, did not long survive.

The attrition of the first eighteen months was revealing. Cut out of Asian policy and reportedly distrusted, Sneider departed in favor of another career FSO. One of his aides, Daniel Davidson, was gone with a tap on his telephone and under a cloud of allegations about leaking. Halperin left under a similar shadow. Lynn and Osborn resigned for "personal" reasons, the latter having played a very minor role and apparently far less than he had been promised. Moose was brusquely moved aside within a few months amid grumblings about his past ties to Democratic Senator William Fulbright. But Moose's successor, William Watts, a former FSO and staff aide to Nelson Rockefeller, would himself resign in less than a year over the Cambodian invasion. Shocked at the bellicose bureaucratic relations in the régime, Watts had sent Kissinger a memo late in 1969 entitled "On Dealing with State," urging generally more open and less antagonistic practices, including a moderation of Kissinger's own acid commentary about other senior officers. Kissinger responded that he "appreciated the memo," proceeded to ignore it, and confided to another aide that Watts was not so bright despite being "Nelson's boy." The successor to Moose and Watts as Staff Secretary was yet another career bureaucrat like Moose from Rusk's old secretariat, but this time a woman who went on tending the paper, and safely left politics and policy to her superiors. In the first year Eagleburger too left because of sheer physical exhaustion. A few months later his successor, another young FSO and former Katzenbach aide, Anthony Lake, left over Cambodia. I also resigned at the Cambodian invasion. After this initial winnowing, however, the staff settled into the relative permanence of career officers who were compatible with both the policies and methods that had become fixed in the Nixon administration. By the end of his second year in office, Kissinger was surrounded very much by men—some talented, some mediocre— who did his bidding and knew whose policy counted, though he would never quite cease to hold most of his own assistants at the same suspicious, manipulative distance he staked out for his other Washington rivals.

Of the men who stayed, the most important would be Alexander Meigs Haig, Jr., the obscure forty-five-year-old army colonel who began in 1969, not as a senior policy aide but as a staff assistant to transmit intelligence reports and take notes at NSC meetings. Haig was noteworthy not alone because of his continuing role as Kissinger's deputy or even for his future ascendancy to Nixon's final White House chief of staff when Watergate devoured H. R. Haldeman. In Haig's profile as the consummate bureaucrat, there is much of the living reality of government, and some insight into how the Nixon-Kissinger foreign policy ruled amid its special burdens of personality. Like General Goodpaster, the arbiter of the Pierre, whose career was so similar if in the end less spectacular, Haig was clearly the special assistant triumphant. With an education at West Point and later graduate work at Georgetown and the Naval and Army War Colleges, he had served as staff officer to powerful patrons most of his career, including a tour as aide-de-camp to General Douglas MacArthur in the Korean war, followed by a steady rise through the Pentagon in the early to mid-sixties to become Deputy Special Assistant to both McNamara and Vance. It was his work for McNamara that attracted the attention of Pentagon aide (later Johnson Presidential Assistant) Joseph Califano and put Haig in the West Basement. When Kissinger asked the outgoing Califano for staff suggestions, the recommendation was impressive. Following his last Pentagon tour in 1965, Haig had led a front-line brigade in Vietnam, emerging with an extraordinary list of combat decorations. By January 1969 he had become deputy commandant at West Point. He was, on paper and in reputation with people like Califano and McNamara, an honored, educated soldier with faithful and impeccable experience in staff work. He was there to be recommended. He got the job, like nearly everyone else on the new NSC staff, because of his standing in the eyes of the administration Nixon was supposedly replacing. But behind the career officer was a human being of a decided mentality, scarring experiences, ambitions, and complexity no service record or former patron could easily reveal.

Several factors accounted for Haig's remarkable rise. The exterior of the interchangeable staff professional hid a visceral conservatism which made him ideologically at home in the Nixon White House. The convictions were seldom sophisticated. He could argue for harsher terms in secret negotiations with Hanoi, for example, by recounting a story of how his men had once entered a village where an apparently harmless old man blew himself up along with one of Haig's troopers with a concealed grenade. As opposition to the war policy mounted, such views vouchsafed Haig's tough-mindedness, as valuable a credential under Nixon as under Johnson. His effect on policy was also real. In part it was due to the skill with which he used his position. Though the special assistant nominally plays a nonsubstantive role in paper shuffling and scheduling, his insinuation of bias on his boss is frequently one of the most decisive functions in Washington. In a score of ways—the cover note on certain memos, a puncturing question at a staff meeting, a remark about this man's pet cause or that man's insensitivity to Kissinger's problems, sometimes only the choosing of time and temperament in which to put a paper in front of a busy, moody man—Haig was subtly adept at shaping the consideration of policy while only occasionally resorting to open advocacy or opposition himself.

Yet his influence was felt mainly because Henry Kissinger, for all his grasp of policy, his confidence and deftness, was also frequently indecisive. Beset by real and imagined enemies, suspicious of his own staff as of the bureaucracy, he needed a Haig to provide reassurance, as well as to act as a litmus test on the right in a government where Kissinger was unlikely to be attacked successfully from the left. For the most controversial policies Kissinger planned—initiatives in arms control and ending the war—he would be, he believed, most vulnerable to conservative criticism. Haig the decorated combat veteran, the leathery soldier of stern opinions, would help clothe those actions. Jealous of the relationship as well as of Haig's power, Sonnenfeldt would joke in acid terms that Kissinger the German-Jewish

immigrant only kept on Haig, the all-American colonel from Phila-
delphia, to testify at some imagined right-wing trial, if Henry went
too far with détente.

But if there was a political and psychological core to such ridicule
—and much of Vietnam policy would indeed be predicated on Kissinger's fear of a right-wing reaction—Haig was also much more than
front man or counterpoise. Indefatigable, formally loyal to Kissinger
yet very careful to maintain extremely cordial relations with the
other powerful men around Nixon who variously distrusted or despised the National Security adviser, he soon became, alone among
the NSC staff, a force in his own right in the White House pecking
order. Haig sometimes briefed Nixon in Kissinger's absence; but
chiefly he grew to be known because he managed the staff, the
last-to-leave, first-to-arrive organizational role that built up a reputation of devotion. "Haig's always down there while Henry's off having
dinner in Georgetown," Nixon once said to a group of assistants in
1970. The remark was obviously a portent of Nixon's own later reliance on Haig, who would be "always there" during the disintegration
of the régime. At the time, it was an impressive enough tribute to
Haig's ability to show through—by his own skill and doggedness as
much as by White House politics—a dazzling Kissinger presence that
blotted out the rest of the government. Had Henry Kissinger stum-
bled or resigned after 1970, it is quite likely that his successor would
have been Alexander Haig. As it was, Haig came out of the same
obscurity to take what Nixon must have regarded as the equally
important position as Haldeman's successor.

As he became a potential rival to Kissinger, however, he also
became very nearly indispensable. "Stalin to Henry's Lenin," I once
said to a journalist when asked to characterize Haig's position. The
analogy is, of course, too sinister and harsh if taken literally, but the
parallel also suggests much of the relationship. If Kissinger was the
theorist and politician of his coup, its outer symbol, Haig was its inner
face. He was the organizer, the not as bright but painstaking administrator with time and attention for the details Kissinger spurned. He
could also be the enforcer, making the calls and attending the meetings to deal with matters, like phone taps, which Kissinger found
impolitic or faintly distasteful or simply beneath his station to handle
directly. And with each such inheritance, Haig's power and authority
thickened. It certainly went beyond what Kissinger would have in-

tended or planned, had he perceived his own office politics as lucidly as he saw the same chemistry elsewhere. The more Haig knew, the greater was Kissinger's dependence on him, especially where so few (if any) could be trusted. Perhaps it was too obvious that Haig was no intellectual match. But then it was Professor Kissinger who had warned that intellect seldom mattered in government as much as mastering the routine.

Their alliance was no more free of suspicion and rivalry than any other at the upper reaches. Like Kissinger, Haig alternately played off his constituencies, portraying himself now as Kissinger's lone ally, now as the staff's irreverent advocate in the West Basement court. One pose required a somber, low-toned deference in the boss's presence. The other produced a running dialogue of ridicule out of earshot: the shaking head and sigh and quip that there was no use trying to see Henry now or clear the cable tonight since he was "having one of his fits" or "his mind is in his pants." As in the Johnson years, this sort of daily reality of men in government, the banal personal interplay, the rudimentary office sociology, was far different from the grave and ever serious images of national security projected to the public, and more akin to ordinary life and politics than most understood. "Deep in their souls," said one official who worked closely with both Haig and Kissinger, "they had a mutual distrust, but each was useful to the other." It was a common phenomenon in any organization; in this case, it shaped much of the means and ends of American foreign policy.

In the longer view of what the Nixon administration was and would become, however, Haig's mentality was in many ways more interesting or important than his bureaucratic skills. In fact if not in rank the most powerful and privy of career officials in the national security hierarchy, he confronted the acts and relationships of the régime with a cynical tolerance that often amounted to an abdication of judgment. "You guys don't know anything," he would say to staff men complaining about the seeming squalor of personal dealings at the highest levels of government. He then recounted his experiences with MacArthur—how he had caught pneumonia after wading ashore at Inchon holding aloft the general's sleeping bag, or how later, when the Chinese suddenly overran the U.S. forces on the Yalu, the supreme commander sent his young aide Haig back through fire to the house they had been occupying to throw a grenade in a tile bathroom "so no stinking Chinese general would get a bath that night." These things happened when you worked for great men, he had learned. As for Kissinger or Nixon or the others, of course they were crazy, but "no crazier than most." In Haig, as in many bureaucrats, intimacy with power (and his own advance by it) seemed to have instilled nothing so much as a kind of resignation to the megalomania or pettiness of superiors as occupational routine. The result was a combination of the best and the worst in the career officer, whether civilian or military. His devoted work was overlain both with personal ambition and a stoic, selfless vision of duty to those above. The tragedy for the man and the country was that neither drive left a sure sense of where to stop, of where service crossed over into compromise or became complicity against his own patriotism. Incredulous and enraged at men without his bureaucrat's private ethic, he would storm at an NSC staffer who resigned over the invasion of Cambodia, and again at William Ruckelshaus when he resigned as Deputy Attorney General after refusing to fire Special Prosecutor Archibald Cox in October 1973, arguing that they could not do it, that "your Commander-in-Chief has given you an order."

Only rarely was there the slightest hint of some inner unease, even melancholy with this taxing faith. Reading a staff briefing memo once in 1970, he visibly dropped the veneer, leaned forward, and said softly, almost wistfully, to the memo's author: "God damn, if I could write that well, I wouldn't be doing this." But "doing this" was what Haig would do very well indeed from the beginning, and some of the secrets of power of the West Basement would require every ounce of his practiced forebearance.

Ultimately, the twists of power and personality in the new administration were reduced to the single relationship between Kissinger and Nixon. On the formal, institutional level, their collaboration was unprecedented. Kissinger's access to the President in foreign policy matters was extraordinary from the first week of the régime, and continued to be generally greater than that of other senior White House aides, save only Haldeman. The President and his Assistant for National Security might typically hold a half-dozen or more conversations each day and formal briefing sessions in morning or late afternoon, interspersed with inevitable telephone calls or summons to the Oval Office or Executive Office Building suites. This communication was all animated by Nixon's constant preference for and fascination with world affairs. Meanwhile, up from the West Basement flowed briefing memos, analyses of important cables, responses to presidential queries, and the ubiquitous cover memos on all documents sent from cabinet officers. Before and after each NSC meeting and each meeting with a foreign dignitary, there were lengthy oral briefings, and often simply spontaneous discussions without schedule or limit. By the early spring of 1969 and ever after, Kissinger had acquired, through mutual interest, a near monopoly on the time, attention, and respect of the President of the United States on all matters of foreign policy. His was literally the first and final word on policy decisions, with a gathering record of personal recommendations that were tantamount to presidential decision. All the patterns foreshadowed at the Pierre became the rhythm of government. Nixon would celebrate the openness of the NSC, hear out his Secretaries of State and Defense, give Bill Rogers Africa here or a Mideastern peace gambit there, listen to Laird for his political sense, avoid an open clash, and then decide with his Harvard professor what they were going to do regardless of all the others. As a mechanism of matching minds and organizational control, it functioned better than Kissinger had ever contemplated in his scholarship.

What was perhaps even less imaginable, however, was the personal quality and tone of presidential leadership which worked to close off the system to Kissinger's advantage. At the top, born of Nixon's tortured apprenticeship, prevailed the same scorn and sense of manipulation Kissinger brought to bureaucratic relations in and beyond the West Basement. The President thus saw "fags" in the State Department, and needed little prompting from his Assistant to heed the moral. Like Kissinger, he could mistakenly introduce the new chairman of the joint chiefs to the NSC as "Admiral Morman" (Thomas Moorer) and joke later in private about the stupidity of senior naval officers—and with careful calculation call the chiefs when the Mylai scandal broke and assure them that "We're not going to let them make the military a scapegoat in this thing."

Before those fateful recording devices were installed and before he went on to become director of the Federal Aviation Agency and then to national fame as a Watergate witness, Alexander Butterfield was the assistant to Haldeman charged to sit quietly in Nixon's office and record verbatim the random presidential utterings and instructions during the reading of press and intelligence briefs. Pouring daily out of the Oval Office onto Haig's desk and then to Kissinger's (where they were usually ignored and sometimes assigned to staff), the resulting "Butterfieldgrams," two-to-three-line memos, provided a telling little archive on relationships in the régime. On a given day, Nixon would see a critical article on defense policy and Butterfield would send it along to Kissinger with the notation from "RN": "Henry, Laird is up to his old tricks. Shut the bastard up." Or if Elliot Richardson had given the wrong slant in congressional testimony: "Henry, I disagree. They're trying to undercut us again. Change the emphasis immediately"—an order Kissinger would politely file, having himself other emphases and changes in mind for Richardson. Often the orders were terse if nothing else. "Stop this!" went the instruction after reading a press report on Secretary Rogers's current negotiating tactics in the Middle East, though both Nixon and Kissinger knew the order could not be executed if Rogers questioned it directly to the President. The most frequent epitaph of the Butterfieldgram, however, was similar to the record compiled by the later tapes. Sooner or later it was asked, or stated, being both question and pronouncement, about nearly every major figure in the nation's foreign policy: "Can he (or they) be trusted?" or "He (or they) cannot be trusted."

Yet behind the petty animus and fearfulness of the President was a still more haunting problem. Not long into the administration, Kissinger began to tell with special relish a favorite story for staff and intimates. He had been at a reception during the first weeks and made a special point of telling Mrs. Nixon how much he was impressed with her husband, his grasp of issues and his command. But Pat Nixon, the story went on with pauses for effect, only drew back with a frown and said, "Haven't you seen through him yet?" The story may well have been apocryphal in itself, but it pointed to a darker reality already visible to Kissinger and some of his staff. Far more serious than his occasional impulsiveness and mean suspicions, by late 1969 NSC aide worried that Nixon seemed on several nights to be drinking, at least to the point that some of his calls to Kissinger were slurred, or he was simply not available to a nighttime telephone message from his Assistant for National Security. Like the undercurrent of racism, the question of drinking on sporadic evenings was invariably concealed from all but the closest assistants. In a sense it was all the more difficult to confront for being so, and its frequency or timing did not reduce the irresponsibility of the hours when it did take place.

In the autumn of 1969, Kissinger referred to Nixon as "my drunken friend" in a conversation with his staff. His personal aides worried that the reference would be intercepted and understood by Soviet trawlers as Kissinger spoke *en clair* over the radio from a small plane flying him to New York for a weekend.

Whatever was happening with the mercurial President, there was evidence that he could descend into sullen, almost flippant moods about the most serious of his actions. Secluded with Bebe Rebozo at Camp David the weekend before the Cambodian invasion, Nixon was overheard by an NSC aide as he taunted Kissinger on the fate of the operation. "If this doesn't work, it'll be your ass, Henry," the source vividly remembered the conversation, Nixon adding thickly, "Ain't that right, Bebe?"

There is no evidence that this occasional drinking, observed long before the stresses of Watergate, had any decisive effect on foreign policy, or that it ever directly endangered the national security. There were those moments, though, when a Soviet diplomatic note, an urgent cable from Saigon on reports of a distant coup, came to Henry Kissinger as *de facto* President of the United States. The more disturbing reality is that it went on for so long unexposed—through Nixon's landslide reelection partly on the record of his statesmanship —with no one certain how damaging it could be. People who knew about the slurred voice and the nights beyond reach seem to have had a range of contrasting motives for silence. It was, after all, they told themselves, only an occasional problem. Its revelation might invite Soviet recklessness or some other action that would not have happened otherwise. Patriotism, fear, admiration for Nixon's potential greatness, shame, personal fear, or desire for power—all had a part in a covenant of silence about the other side of Richard Nixon. Nor was the evasion only official. There were broad hints among the Washington press, particularly Kissinger's intimates, of the "martinis that launched Cambodia" or of "Henry minding the store." But the stories were never pressed, the implications of presidential disability never analyzed.

For the man perhaps most aware of the problem and its possible dangers for the country, Kissinger himself, the drinking was another symptom of a weakness that only extended and ultimately rational-ized his own power. In fact, the most direct and important product of these early episodes was to fortify still further throughout Wash-ington the necessity for "Henry." In the Butterfieldgrams, in the insiders' rumors, in the monitored phone calls from Camp David, and of course in the general Washington distaste for Nixon and infat-uation with Kissinger, there grew at various levels the picture of a President from whose excesses and worst instincts his Assistant for National Security was protecting the country and the world. In the personal dealings he would be unfailingly deferential toward Nixon. If he ever discussed the drinking problem with the President, his closest aides were apparently never told, though they were very much aware of the incidents, the jokes about that "man upstairs" and Kissinger's veiled contempt. After a year in office, Kissinger reigned almost supreme over foreign policy. What would come to be the most formidable challenge to his power was only beginning to form in the shape of what he later called with scant irony "the Gestapo"—the other senior White House assistants, Haldeman and Ehrlichman. The larger impact on Kissinger's power of the White House scheming lay ahead.

Ahead too lay the uses of the historic power Kissinger seized and inherited in the West Basement—the chance to make peace in Viet-nam, to control the arms race with the Soviet Union, to restore coherence and public faith in America's world role. Yet in a sense much of that outcome was already determined. However well con-ceived, however skillfully executed, the administration's foreign pol-icy would somehow never quite escape the character of the people and the means behind it.

IV

"And You and I Will End the War,"

1969–1973

It was there, as ever. For a generation of young Americans it had always been there. On the chill January morning in 1969 when Richard Nixon prepared for his first inaugural and Henry Kissinger moved into his White House office, it was nearly invisible in Washington. Only a few scattered demonstrators gathered along the parade route up Pennsylvania Avenue. Yet it was there, indelibly, even before the new President and his Assistant for National Security had awakened, waiting for them in the day's casualty list from Saigon. Six Americans dead, seventeen wounded. As if time and distance symbolized the relentlessness of it all, the history that no longer waited on America, their first day in power was already past in Vietnam before it had begun in Washington.

But it was there too closer to home, in a human reality beyond the demonstrators or the official announcements. If they had looked, it was there at the bottom right-hand corner of the Washington *Post*'s obituary page that very morning, where in a small box with a short verse the parents of Specialist-4 James Norcia remembered and grieved that their son had been killed on this same day, two years ago. Before it was ended, Norcia would be one of over 46,000 Americans and perhaps a half million Vietnamese killed. And on this Monday, January 20, 1969, as a new administration took power pledged to peace, more than half of those dead were still alive.

The war. No hope so followed Nixon and Kissinger into office as the national yearning to end it. No issue so haunted and consumed them during the next four years. As though it were some ugly, shameful disease, they would try somehow to deny the war, to hide it, to blame it on someone else. In their fear and furtiveness they soon made it their own, a carnage they could stop yet would not. They were to end it eventually, of course, to the rewards of reelection and a Nobel Prize. But their peacemaking was barbaric as well as subtle, often absurd, craven, and inept while historic. In the end, no other policy, no other record in his long and controversial service, so stained Henry Kissinger's claim to greatness.

On the surface, their war policy would be the most familiar story of the administration. The early NSC meetings, the troop withdrawals, the invasions of Cambodia and Laos, the ubiquitous presidential speeches, Kissinger's personal negotiations with the North Vietnamese, the blockade of North Vietnam, the famous "Peace is at hand" statement, the Christmas bombing of Hanoi, the settlement and return of the American prisoners of war—the sequence filled the news of four years in which every briefing, every utterance, every coming and going were lavishly reported. Yet for all the attention, the men and their methods remained largely an enigma. If it was often the most written- and talked-about of foreign policies, the Nixon-Kissinger record in Indochina was also in many ways the least understood. In part the reality was difficult to capture because the character of policymaking changed abruptly. What had been in the Johnson régime a tangle of bureaucratic motives in Saigon and Washington, a shifting contest of several personalities, now became very much the rule of two minds in the White House. Other figures, the bureaucracy, the sheer momentum of the war, would all continue to influence events; but the force of these two at the top would be decisive. And as the decisions narrowed and compressed in those men, the process grew no less complex. In some respects the policy was all the harder to grasp because it was no longer so much diplomacy or military strategy or institutional politics as the result of what Nixon and Kissinger brought out of their pasts to the issues of war and peace, a working out in the forests of Southeast Asia and the bargaining places of Paris of psychological and political impulses in these two men which had little to do with the underlying issues of the conflict itself, yet which nonetheless determined its later course. To understand the twisted path of U.S. policy from 1969 to 1973 was to probe

behind the developments and the public presence, into the connections between the experiences and attitudes that mold men and their
subsequent actions in office. Most observers shrank from making
those fateful connections; some seemed mercifully unaware of the
implications in any case. All went on to the end asking the poignant
questions of a country not quite able to confront how it was being led
—what are their secret plans, how are they doing it, when will they
reveal the answer that will make it all worthwhile and reasonable?
Perhaps the ultimate national tragedy in Indochina was that there
would be no answers to those questions, or at least no answers that
most would want to face.

Beyond each man's view of the world were other visions that
drove and distorted their policy toward the war: visions of American
society, of government and politics, of themselves. Their earlier experiences with national chauvinism would determine in large measure how they negotiated peace. In the shadows of their racism they
neither understood the foreign society they were dealing with, nor
were moved deeply by the bloodshed and suffering they adminis-
tered to their stereotypes. The war went on as it did also because the
policy indulged a profound weakness and indecisiveness in both
men; peace would come not by clear choice, but by the postponement of decision. But none of these influences was ever so obvious
or singular. Diplomacy, domestic politics, and personality were
tightly interwoven in the story of the war policy, the various elements now crucial, now submerged, yet always there—and it is in
that often complicated, contradictory rhythm that the story seems
best told.

Kissinger had visited South Vietnam briefly as a consultant to the
Johnson administration, and had been involved during 1967 in one
of Washington's aloof, abortive efforts to open talks with Hanoi, in
Kissinger's case an attempt to use a French scholar whom he knew
as an intermediary with Ho Chi Minh. This background was less
important, however, than sheer intellect in shaping his famous article on the Vietnam peace negotiations which appeared in *Foreign
Affairs* in January 1969, within days of his appointment. The article
distilled and refined themes he had developed for Rockefeller's campaign position on the war, but it now took on fresh gravity as the
ostensible blueprint for the new Nixon régime. In fact, though nei-

ther he nor Nixon would regard the article as any sort of commitment, few publications have so tellingly foreshadowed events. Prominent in his writing was much of the tactical shrewdness, sensitivity, and sophistication he applied in later negotiations. There, too, was the fatal conceptual flaw in his larger sense of the war, and the obliging obliviousness of his audience to some of the same bellicosity they deplored in his predecessors.

Kissinger began his analysis by recognizing the unique military and psychological reality of the guerrilla war. The United States, with its fetish for shallow pacification plans and reliance on conventional standards of winning (by which Tet had been officially counted a victory), had mistaken the limited demands for the success of the guerrillas, who needed only to keep the war going. "We fought a military war," he wrote, "our opponents fought a political one. We sought physical attrition; our opponents aimed for our psychological exhaustion. In the process, we lost sight of one of the cardinal maxims of guerrilla war: the guerrilla wins if he does not lose." He also wrote thoughtfully about the "vast gulf in cultural and bureaucratic style" between Washington and Hanoi, and of the latter's "almost morbid suspiciousness" of foreigners, the aftermath of years of defeat and exploitation and the source of a profoundly manipulative and indirect method in negotiations. Kissinger saw clearly the matching dilemma in relations between the Americans and Saigon, a régime that "cannot be given a veto over negotiations," yet could rightly "insist on a major voice in decisions affecting its own country."

But running beneath this sense of history and proportion, like an implacable fault in the foundation stone, were the same worn assumptions that had held the Johnson government at war. Though the initial American descent into Vietnam had been a "tragic blunder," he saw in the commitment of 500,000 troops no alternative but to end it "honorably." "The United States," as he defined honor, "cannot accept a military defeat," lest the loss "unloose forces that would complicate prospects for international order." It was plainly a restatement of the ever-beckoning myth that American prestige and world peace were somehow at stake in this foolish, futile embroilment in one Asian post-colonial revolution. It was not only bad history; it flew against the very realities of a lost war he had been at pains to elaborate in the article. With the same resort to official mythology, Kissinger set out the principle that negotiations should "concentrate on the subject of the mutual withdrawal of external forces," at one stroke dismissing the single most important historical fact about the conflict, that it was at root a *civil* war. This formula made American withdrawal or negotiating credibility hostage to the exit of the North Vietnamese, after more than a decade of war the single most obdurate, nonnegotiable condition in Hanoi's policy. Again, had the article represented a purely academic exercise (abandoned in power), these flawed notions would have come and gone in the harmless obscurity of the pages of *Foreign Affairs.* But now, brought alive by the fact of Kissinger's power, this argument—the refusal to see the irrelevance of the war in the context of larger U.S. interests and the ritual insistence on mutual withdrawal—would foredoom the negotiations he otherwise approached with such skill. At the end, the convoluted diplomacy rooted in these enduring misconceptions would mock even the most sensible passages in the article about dealing with Hanoi and Saigon. As the article heralded Kissinger's advent in Washington, its novelty was extravagantly praised, its essential clichés oddly and irresponsibly ignored by the press. "There is no better illustration of the new men replacing the old," pronounced the Washington *Post;* while Joseph Kraft saw in the article "the best augury to date for the incoming administration," its author "a powerful mind rising above knowledge of the details to identify the way out." It was the beginning of a long infatuation with Kissinger in which American journalism would often do its own "rising above knowledge of the details" to identify only what it wished to see in Henry Kissinger's apparent intellect and urbanity.

Nixon's intellectual approach to the war was made up of its own mixture of sophistication and blunder. If he had evaded the subject with characteristic opportunism during the 1968 campaign, in office his political instinct told him clearly that the war must somehow be eliminated, both because it was a source of domestic rancor and because it was an impediment to the grander diplomacy he at that time vaguely envisioned with the Russians and Chinese. The first Nixon conversations with Kissinger at the Pierre presupposed some withdrawal of U.S. troops. The first meeting of the NSC following Nixon's inauguration was to ratify a presidential decision to begin the pull-out, coupled with a program of intensified training and arming of the South Vietnamese forces—the process christened by Melvin Laird with that ugly, heedless term so symbolic of the American folly in the war and of what was to follow: "Vietnamization."

About the future course of policy, though, these early decisions were at best vague, uneasy, and inconclusive, threaded as they were with Nixon's convictions expressed in his verbal wanderings at the NSC meetings as well as with Kissinger alone on the importance of U.S. "credibility" in Vietnam. He saw this "credibility" not only as essential to a deal with Hanoi, but also as critical to other negotiations with the Russians and Chinese. Along with his sound political sense that the conflict was untenable persisted the phobia that had drawn each of his predecessors since Truman further into Indochina. "I don't intend to be the first President to lose a war," he frequently told aides in these early deliberations. Nixon's perception of the war would always be more distracted, less subtle, than Kissinger's. But their views on the specter of defeat were nearly identical and trapped them in a diplomatic dilemma of their own making. To disengage troops for domestic as well as foreign policy reasons was to lose, however gradually, much of the stake and power of the U.S. involvement. If so much prestige plus future international prospects depended on that involvement, if as both believed there were still possibilities to redeem it, if in any case there seemed to this President and his adviser no choice but to redeem it, the crude logic of policy was to make peace by continuing the war for whatever could be salvaged. It was to be the tautology behind one of the most savage retreats in modern history. For the moment, however, the dominant quality of Nixon's first official responses to the war was indecision. He expressed no coherent long-range strategy. This was the post-inaugural reality of his famous unrevealed "plan" from the 1968 campaign —a new President obviously still muddled between the rationality of peace and the old compulsion somehow to win a lost war.

Plagued by these contradictions, U.S. policy drifted through the opening weeks of 1969, while other influences inevitably drew Kissinger and Nixon on toward more war. As they had almost routinely but unsuccessfully put to Johnson, the joint chiefs recommended to Nixon in early March that he authorize B-52 strikes against North Vietnamese sanctuaries in eastern Cambodia. Under Prince Norodom Sihanouk, Cambodia had arrived at a delicate, in some ways ingenious bargain of neutrality on the volatile edges of the war. The North Vietnamese and Viet Cong forces marched and camped through the country's frontier regions and used the port of Sihanoukville (now Kompong Som), tolerated by the Cambodians in exchange for Hanoi's tacit agreement not to support the country's handful of indigenous Communists, the Khmer Rouge. Cambodia was therefore left to enjoy a rare peace and prosperity, though insurrection and suffering raged all around her in Laos and Vietnam. To avoid any larger direct embroilment from the other side which might destroy that immunity, Sihanouk similarly ignored the American bombing of the Communist sanctuaries.

On March 18, 1969, in his first major decision on the war and one of the most insidious of his presidency, Nixon took up the joint chiefs' option with Kissinger's recommendation and ordered B-52 strikes on Cambodia. Like so many of their foreign policy acts, the motives here were mixed, and in part irrelevant to events in Indochina. The bombing proposal was the first significant issue presented to the White House by the joint chiefs; both Nixon and Kissinger were anxious to avoid any bureaucratic clash with the military in these first months of power. Both overestimated the gravity of the Cambodian bombing proposal in the institutional politics of Washington. "One of the Joint Staff perennials, like tulips in Arlington," one high-ranking officer described the recommendation for the raids. The decision did presumably store credit for later White House encounters with the chiefs in SALT and other issues. For Kissinger it provided a ready antidote to any anticipated Pentagon sabotage of subsequent negotiations over Vietnam. There were thus strong bureaucratic incentives to be "tough" and "manly" with this first test of mettle embodied in the clipped prose of the JCS memos, the sure military intelligence, and the facile air force projections of certainty. Those calculations reinforced the already inherent truculence in their strategy, imprecise as it was at this point.

Perhaps most important, however, the Cambodian bombing decision was entirely consistent with the attitude of men who were reaching for an exclusive, often wholly secret command of American foreign policy. Defiant of previous executive restraints and congressional authority, concealed from all but the small fragment of the bureaucracy necessary to execute them, the air strikes suddenly established a direct and preemptive White House control over policy. The operation would scarcely be the only deception or defiance exercised by the Nixon régime, but it was the first of such magnitude. It aptly expressed the larger ebullience of Nixon and Kissinger as they generally walled themselves off from the public and the rest of government, and prepared to rule America's foreign relations alone. Later that spring, after hearing grousing from some of his aides that they had never even met the President, Kissinger arranged for Nixon to talk briefly to the entire NSC staff in the Cabinet Room. Nixon began the meeting with self-conscious ingratiation, commiserating with the staff for having to deal with all those "impossible fags" in the State Department, apparently oblivious that most of those in the room were FSOs on detail. At the close he told the group that they should ignore the bureaucrats and "handle the rest of the world." Turning to Kissinger, he added almost softly, perhaps as much a confidence as a boast for the audience, "And you and I will end the war."

So MENU, the cryptonym for the raids, joined those other innocuous code names of the war. In this case, it meant over 100,000 tons of bombs dropped on a neutral country with air force records illegally masked or destroyed, and, according to the best CIA and Pentagon intelligence fourteen months later, "no appreciable effect on enemy capabilities in target areas." Like every escalation, MENU spawned more involvement, and more secrecy. Accompanying the bombing would be "SALEM HOUSE," top-secret ground incursions into Cambodia during 1969 and early 1970 by U.S. Green Berets, along with CIA-trained, expatriate Cambodian units from South Vietnam, and even Chinese mercenaries recruited by the Agency's enterprising operatives from among Mekong River pirates. The later full-scale invasion of the nation by U.S. forces in May 1970 was in many ways a natural extension of this clandestine history.

The swifter and in a sense even more destructive impact of the bombing was turned back on the administration. Less than two months after they had begun, the raids were exposed by *The New York Times* in a detailed dispatch by its Pentagon correspondent, William Beecher. The bombing was largely motivated, Beecher wrote from a perceptive anonymous source, by "a desire by high Washington officials to signal Hanoi that the Nixon Administration, while pressing for peace in Paris, is willing to take some military risks avoided by the previous Administration." Beecher's revelation stirred comparatively little reaction at the time, an early symptom of the public and congressional diffidence that later overtook the anti-war opposition. Yet inside the narrowing world of the Nixon

White House, the story broke in upon a sequel of obsession and suspicion already swollen beyond reason. Once again as under Johnson the war came home.

The process had begun when the new régime quickly inherited, along with J. Edgar Hoover at the FBI, the superannuated director's unappeased dementia toward dissent on the war, particularly within the government. In the later Johnson years, Hoover had peppered the White House with reports of disloyalty in the ranks, among them unsubstantiated charges by informants against Morton Halperin and other junior Defense Department officials. When the same Halperin and other possible "risks" appeared on Kissinger's staff, Hoover had instantly objected, and continued to pursue his prey when Kissinger apparently ignored the initial warning. During the first four months of 1969, for example, Hoover sent the new National Security Adviser, presumably for his titillation as well as education, scurrilous reports gathered during the previous administration on the private life of Martin Luther King, tidbits on various NSC staff members with "Democratic" contacts, an allegation that journalist Henry Brandon, a Kissinger friend, might be associated with some East European intelligence service, and at least one formal memorandum on Halperin which only refurbished the old allegations of disagreement with Vietnam policy.

In other times, and among other politicians, this craze might have been dismissed, if not Hoover himself. In 1969 it festered for a short time as Nixon confined himself to verbal indulgence of Hoover on internal security—"Two maniacs trying to outdo each other," Kissinger is said to have told a close aide after inadvertently hearing one of those conversations. Then, amid a series of apparent leaks, including stories on possible Vietnam troop withdrawals and SALT negotiating strategy, the Nixon government's own excesses were soon joined to Hoover's. On April 25, as he later testified, Kissinger was summoned to the Oval Office, where the President was already meeting with Hoover and Attorney General John Mitchell on the question of how to stop the leaks. The participants' accounts of this meeting were to be predictably self-absolving and contradictory, with Kissinger himself giving assorted versions. The upshot was, in Kissinger's words, that wiretaps in such instances were "necessary" and "well established" (no one apparently dwelled on the term "legal"), that Kissinger was to supply names of staff people with access to the leaked information, that Hoover all but accused as security risks his *bêtes noires* Halperin and Brandon and two other NSC staff members, Dan Davidson and Helmut Sonnenfeldt. Kissinger met again with Hoover on May 5, this time alone at FBI headquarters, where he reportedly discussed with the director leaks and putative leakers with matching zeal, and established an office liaison between them in the persons of Alexander Haig and FBI Assistant Director William Sullivan.

It took the secret bombing of Cambodia and Beecher's May 9 story, however, to move the taps from bureaucratic posturing to the victims' telephones. After seeing the article that morning while standing beside Nixon, who was on vacation at Key Biscayne, Kissinger anxiously talked to Hoover four times by telephone, calling first to say that the story was "extraordinarily damaging" and request that Hoover (according to the director's memo of the conversation) "put whatever resources I need to find who did this." Later conversations that day dealt with Kissinger's concern that the investigation itself might leak, and with Hoover's dim ramblings about the possible though not proven culpability of "so-called arrogant Harvard-type Kennedy men," among whose number he counted Halperin, Beecher, and, no doubt, a host of others he simply had no time to mention at this point. For his part in these exchanges, Kissinger urged Hoover on to get the proof on Halperin or anyone else. Again in Hoover's account: "He [Kissinger] hoped I would follow it up as far as we can take it and they will destroy whoever did this if we can find him, no matter where he is."

As far as they could take it, of course, was to set off a chain reaction of events that led from the wire tapping of seventeen officials and newsmen over the period 1969 to 1971, to the White House enlistment of Howard Hunt and G. Gordon Liddy to protect (among other "White House horrors," as Mitchell called them) the shabby, perhaps criminal eavesdropping, and on to further missions of the same mold at the Watergate Apartments. Henry Kissinger's true role in the taps was still unsettled years afterward, and the subject of a million-dollar damage suit by Halperin and others; however, the charges against Kissinger were eventually dismissed. It is clear enough that the taps began in the wake of the Key Biscayne-Washington calls with Hoover; whatever the authority or intentions from the April 25 and May 5 meetings, the Cambodian story and Kissinger's outrage were decisive in unleashing the FBI. On May 10, Kissinger sent Haig to Sullivan with the names of four wiretaps—Halperin, Davidson, and Sonnenfeldt, as Hoover had suggested; but instead of Brandon, another man was suggested—the ranking Pentagon military assistant to Laird, Colonel Robert E. Pursley. The tap on Pursley almost certainly was an effort to pander to the growing Nixon distrust of Laird. At the same time, it would draw away some of the suspicion Hoover had centered so directly on Kissinger's NSC aides. As with the Cambodian raids, Haig told Sullivan on behalf of Kissinger that "no record" was to be kept of this sensitive monitoring.

On May 20, Kissinger sent Haig to Sullivan with the names of two more NSC staff members; within another two weeks, Brandon and Hedrick Smith of *The New York Times* had been tapped. Davidson was fired, although no precise charges of leaking were lodged against him. There followed a number of taps ordered directly by Nixon or others on a further reporter and members of the White House domestic affairs staff. Then again in May 1970, once more in the wake of a Beecher story in *The New York Times* on the secret bombing in North Vietnam, and yet again after the secret military action in Cambodia, Kissinger requested six new taps through Haig. All the while, the transcripts accumulated in a small safe in the Situation Room in the West Basement of the White House, within sight of the twenty-four-hour-a-day watch officers. Kissinger and Haig alone knew the combination for the safe. The contents apparently never proved to be very interesting, let alone relevant to either national security or the war in Indochina. "Just gobs and gobs of . . . gossip and bullshitting," Nixon later appraised the tapping for John Dean. On reading the first transcripts, Kissinger quipped that "Colonel Haig is obviously the only person in my office I can trust," a remark of fitting irony or sarcasm, however it was intended, since Haig would become indeed the only real threat to Kissinger's position. Later, in the most critical moments of negotiations to end the war, Kissinger could not always trust that Haig would support him.

The elaborate secrecy, the unkept records, and the little safe were availing in the search to plug the leaks. By the early summer of 1969, NSC aides were warning one another that their home and even office phones might be bugged. "Don't say anything you don't want Haldeman or Henry to read over breakfast," one Kissinger assistant warned another only weeks after the first tap. Many knew what lay in the little safe; some contemplated trying to get the transcripts and expose them; but none, including myself, quite had the courage.

Who originated the taps? Nixon told Dean it had been Kissinger. Later, he assured the Senate Foreign Relations Committee that he alone had authorized the action, and still later, after leaving office, he leaked to newspapers that it had in fact been someone else's idea. Kissinger contended through variations in detail that he was only following orders as an outsider to the Nixon circle and a newcomer to government.

Who had controlled the process and named the victims? Kissinger, said Mitchell and several FBI officials in later testimony as self-serving as Nixon's. In response, Kissinger again claimed he was "instructed" to supply names and did so only reluctantly and with distaste, a contradiction of his dutiful May 5 meeting at the FBI and the calls to Hoover on May 9 when he promised to "destroy" the leaker.

Why did they handle "the whole affair" as they did? For Kissinger it symbolized a seal of his loyalty and fervor in the White House, all the more necessary because Hoover's charges had originally been directed at the NSC staff. Kissinger could no more be hesitant to plug leaks or protect security with his own people than to bomb the Cambodians or excoriate Rogers and Laird. He was required to tolerate the taps just as he had had to tolerate Nixon's erratic behavior and racist asides, his impulsive monologues delivered at all hours on the telephone. These were the demands of power, at least in this time and place, with such men. After Nixon was gone, he confided to friends how unlucky he had been to come into history with *that* man, that régime. He had deserved better. Perhaps the other taps were designed to trap Kissinger himself, with the prospect of Haldeman, Mitchell, or Hoover triumphantly showing Nixon a transcript of "Henry" slipping a secret to the enemy, CBS News or *The New York Times*. Perhaps Kissinger leaked the secret of the Cambodian bombing himself to test the domestic waters for the Indochina policy. The early and later leaks had but one element in common: Kissinger and Haig were the only officials who knew about all of them. In the serpentine politics of the West Wing, no twist was unimaginable. And Kissinger was capable of maneuvering skillfully amid the pressures. If the taps did uncover a leaker on his staff, he had led the hunt. If, as it happened, nothing substantial turned up, he and his staff were certified safe, perhaps stronger than before. His tactics in this matter protected the flanks of his political reliability just as the bombing itself vouchsafed his toughness for the joint chiefs. Nothing more than principle was sacrificed.

In a larger sense, however, most of the commentary and controversy about Kissinger's legal liability in the wiretap episode was irrelevant, missing in particular the significant connection with foreign policy. Set against the wider backdrop of foreign affairs and his manipulation of the people and politics of foreign policy, the image Kissinger projected of himself in the wiretap episode as a professorial amateur, awed in the presence of J. Edgar Hoover and acting out of a high sense of patriotism, is far too shallow. No hesitation, no inexperience prevented him during those same months from shrewdly gathering immense bureaucratic power under his authority, as he joined purposefully, indeed often instigated, the mean-spirited climate that disarmed his rivals, divided his own staff, and fortified his position. No foreign policy official in recent history was less naïve or more cynical about the way government worked.

But there was a still more fundamental consistency behind the taps. Above all, they were the natural tools of the old imperial prerogative in matters of national security. To have the Halperin memo from the FBI on his desk months before the leaks and taps, to presume to "destroy" the offender in the Beecher Cambodian story, to solicit and read on various pretexts the transcripts of private telephone conversations, then to conceal and evade responsibility in the whole process—all were necessary and proper for a man schooled in the precepts of the foreign policy establishment. That, too, was the way government worked when the awesome duties of defining and protecting national security fell to the few men qualified to lead. That spring of 1969 had been "a particularly sensitive time," Kissinger later told the Senate Foreign Relations Committee, and the leaked stories had been "of the greatest importance to national security." As with most foreign policy leaks, though, the articles had only revealed to the American people the actions of their own government that foreign friends and enemies already knew, whether the SALT position taken toward the Soviets, the Okinawa negotiations with Japan, or the B-52 bombs falling unmistakably on Cambodia. At stake was not the capacity to keep authentic secrets, but rather the ability of the White House to continue conducting a foreign policy even more furtive and closed than its predecessors. It was of a kind, after all, with what the President told the country in April 1970, after thirteen months of MENU and SALEM HOUSE. "For five years, neither the United States nor South Vietnam has moved against these enemy sanctuaries," Nixon said in announcing the invasion of Cambodia. Kissinger's statesman could lie and wiretap because that · was the nature of foreign policy; in the end he answered only to history. Kissinger's part in the taps was irrefutable in an ethical sense, whatever the outcome of his legal defense. At root he shared too much the goals of the régime, their venomous style. For him as for Nixon, principle and legal nicety and the national interest were ultimately a matter of their private vision, a vision which included a defiance of democracy.

The wiretap scandal obviously involved issues, personalities, and consequences that reached far beyond the Cambodian bombing. When the story became public, its origins were often forgotten. Yet however far-ranging the implications, at root the wiretapping episode still belonged in a historical sense to the wider story of the war. Vietnam had afforded Hoover a fresh excuse to pursue his mania about loyalty under Johnson. He now reopened his inquisition with a new President. Nixon too could give vent here to his own feelings of fear and distrust, and Kissinger's talents for expediency could be exploited. Ultimately, each man indulged those worst instincts of himself because the war was still there. The same misrule might well have appeared later elsewhere, in the absence of a war to hide from a divided public and dissenting officials. But if it is true that the character and mentality behind the taps were very much there to begin with, it is also true that the war released them from whatever restraints or lack of opportunity had previously held them in check. In one sense, many of the tragic consequences—the official lawlessness that destroyed the President and the public's trust in its government, as well as the enormous human cost in Indochina of more war—followed from the first decisions to bomb Cambodia. Among the several ironies of the fateful Beecher leak was that it revealed only a small part of what Kissinger and Nixon contemplated for Indochina in their first year in office. Unseen, the war policy over the ensuing months would take on a still more complex and ominous shape.

At the same time that they were launching the B-52s over Cambodia and tapping Washington telephones, Nixon and Kissinger began in the spring and summer of 1969 tentative yet coercive initiatives toward peace negotiations. In May, the first formal presidential speech on Indochina expressed the position Kissinger had drafted for Rockefeller's campaign and then developed in the *Foreign Affairs* article. U.S. policy was to be centered on mutual withdrawal. In June, the first unilateral U.S. troop withdrawal of 25,000 was announced, to be followed by another withdrawal of 35,000 in September. Meanwhile, in July Nixon wrote a secret letter to Ho Chi Minh which led to Kissinger's first private meeting with the North Vietnamese in Paris in August. Accompanying all these steps, however, were none too veiled threats that the United States was also willing to intensify the war—a battlefield lull had hung over South Vietnam since Nixon's election—unless Hanoi responded. The May speech warned of confusing "flexibility with weakness," and of "other decisions" if the war continued. In private sessions with Soviet Ambassador Anatoly Dobrynin, Kissinger was more pointed, threatening a major escalation if peace talks remained deadlocked. "The train has left the station," he told Dobrynin in one summer meeting, "and it's roaring down the tracks." It seems doubtful that this rather heavy-handed intimidation frightened Hanoi. The North Vietnamese maintained their insistence on American withdrawal and the ousting of the Saigon régime of General Thieu, while denying the presence of any Northern troops in the South. When their rejection of Kissinger's terms for continuing talks became plain in the autumn yet was not followed by an American escalation, and when U.S. ground forces in South Vietnam cut back their offensive operations because of White House orders to reduce casualties, this initial diplomacy may well have seemed to Hanoi and Moscow little more than an extravagant bluff run by a new régime anxious to extract itself from the war. There was even some question whether the reported North Vietnamese build-up that followed in the winter of 1969, the build-up that helped justify the Cambodian invasion of 1970, had not been spurred by Hanoi's sense of Washington's false threat. But in the secrecy of the West Basement, it was not so clear that fall that the threats were indeed a bluff.

In early September 1969, Kissinger convened a select group of aides to study and present to Nixon detailed plans for what he described as a "savage, punishing" blow aimed at North Vietnam. At a minimum, the attack plan would include the mining of the port of Haiphong and inland waterways, a naval blockade, and intensive bombing strikes at military targets and population centers. The group was also instructed to consider the options of bombing the Red River dikes to flood the vital farm land of North Vietnam and closing the rail supply lines at the Chinese border. The study was to be undertaken in total secrecy from the rest of the government. Only a handful of officers on the joint staff were involved, those who developed with the JCS liaison to the NSC the specific military plans for the strikes. As a result of the first diplomatic stalemate of that summer Kissinger, the new adviser, was drawn to the old lure of some massive, final coercive means to end the agony. Like his predecessors, Kissinger longed for the neat "surgical" stroke to destroy, once and for all, the will of the North Vietnamese. "I can't believe," he told the September group at its opening meeting, "that a fourth-rate power like North Vietnam doesn't have a breaking point." In the Pentagon the logic was familiar; when the military plans were discreetly sent along for this new study, they were slightly updated versions of mining and bombing proposals drafted years earlier.

By the end of the month the group had produced a thick black briefing book on the several attack plans, replete with estimates of Soviet and Chinese reactions ("manageable"). The report spelled out carefully the ubiquitous "scenario" always provided in such cases for informing our allies, and fending off the Congress and the UN. Even a draft presidential speech to the nation was included, announcing the attack as a necessary step to correct Hanoi's "intransigence" and to stop "the senseless attrition of American lives." The refurbishing of the shelved mining and bombing plans was carried out with obvious relish on the part of the JCS officers in the group. Whatever the fate of the study, its very commission, added to the actual Cambodian bombing, further solidified Kissinger's early credentials with the military. But the bureaucratic or perhaps even diplomatic purposes concealed behind the commissioning of the study were remarkably tangled, even for Kissinger. Only days after the first meeting of the supposedly "Top-Secret-Sensitive" group, for instance, a brief note appeared on the front page of the *Wall Street Journal* indicating that the administration might be actively considering escalation plans.

Given the ostensible gravity of the study, not to mention the reaction to relatively lesser leaks the previous spring, even that small hint might have been expected to ignite Kissinger's anxieties. Instead, his admonition to his staff on the item was surprisingly mild, leading one aide to conjecture that Kissinger himself or perhaps Haig had leaked the existence of the study. Perhaps they intended it as a further warning to Hanoi and their Soviet patrons, or perhaps they hoped to offset the mounting ardor for new military action of the joint chiefs. It is not inconceivable either that the staff was assembled and the study proposed precisely to give the blockade-mining option a seemingly sympathetic hearing—under Kissinger's tight control—for the purpose of exposing its flaws and putting it to rest at minimum bureaucratic cost. If that were Kissinger's design, though, in 1969 it was a closely run gambit, and the plan was not convincingly killed but only set aside, to be carried out with much of its intended ferocity in the spring of 1972.

The attack plans were narrowly defeated in October of 1969 when Nixon summoned Laird, Rogers, and the chairman of the joint chiefs to discuss the proposal. Two factors may have been decisive— a scathing, detailed critique of the military operation requested by Kissinger from Larry Lynn, the former Pentagon official now running an NSC systems analysis group; and the vocal opposition of Melvin Laird, who argued heatedly with Nixon that the strikes would be a dramatic but essentially wasted gesture, only aggravating the domestic opposition while diverting resources from Laird's preferred "Vietnamization." By various accounts, through three successive discussions Kissinger himself was equivocal, apparently more concerned with the military planning imprecisions exposed by Lynn than convinced that the concept itself was dubious. Again Nixon seemed vague and indecisive in these meetings, as he had been in other discussions of the war. While the President wavered, the momentum generated by the very existence of the September group and the revival of cast-off plans began to wane too, another common phenomenon of foreign policy in this administration and others. So in later meetings, the chiefs were worried about the weather over North Vietnam, less assertive about their intelligence, suddenly reluctant to promise they could fashion a "slip-free" blockade. "I'm not sure we're ready for this," Nixon told the senior advisers in their last meeting. In the end the plans were tabled, but it was clear to most involved that the reasons for putting them aside lay mainly in Nixon's uncertainty about military efficiency, not because of any larger doubts rooted in concern for domestic or foreign consequences.

Nixon seems to have carried away from this early episode the conviction that he could, in fact should, strike North Vietnam with impunity in terms of the Soviets, the U.S. anti-war opposition, or the Vietnam war itself. His consideration of heightening the military means had been deadly serious, whatever Kissinger's intentions. Now, less than nine months after the Nixon administration took office, without provocation of a North Vietnamese offensive, still at the height of U.S. troop deployment, and with the peace movement building to its fall moratorium and march in Washington, the administration had planned and repeatedly discussed what by its own admission was a deliberately "brutal" escalation of the fighting. The speech Nixon gave on November 3 on the search for an honorable peace was thus very nearly a speech announcing a wider and more dangerous war than his predecessor had ever contemplated. Whether viewed as a reasonable gamble for peace or a reflexive resort to the toughness Kissinger and Nixon felt compelled to demonstrate as the troops withdrew, the September group was another hidden portent of the future course of the war policy. For weeks afterward, in the common NSC staff banter about Nixon's irrationality and Kissinger's taste for subduing "fourth-rate powers," aides would mockingly repeat to one another the line from the September Group presidential speech preceding the description of the attacks: "Today, pursuant to my orders . . ." But the subject was never really laughable.

Nonetheless, in that autumn of 1969 it was still possible to believe —even within the NSC, where the men and inclinations behind the public façade could be closely observed—that the new government in Washington might yet stop the war without reliving the nightmare of the Johnson years. Typical of those hopes, Anthony Lake and I (both of whom had worked on the September Group) sent Kissinger in late October a proposal to develop "another Vietnam option," beyond either the punishing military blow or a reliance on "Vietnamization," which by the close of 1969 was already being assessed realistically by the administration as a process requiring years, and offering no sure success at that. The memo argued that Saigon's military and political strength was illusory, that Hanoi would continue the civil war regardless of U.S. actions, and that the current Kissinger-Nixon position offered no incentive for North Vietnam to negotiate when they could win a total victory by simply waiting. "In the long run, Vietnamization will become unilateral withdrawal," the memo argued, contending that the difference between a settlement that could be reached now and one produced after the U.S. troops had gone lay only "in time and number of U.S. casualties." A new offer to Hanoi might include a proposal for mutual withdrawal, though not "interpreted in a rigid, narrowly American way." The essence of the proposal called for a form of "gerrymandering" in South Vietnam, leaving Hanoi and the Viet Cong in control of the territory it actually governed and envisioning the establishment of a peaceful Vietnamese political process to form a new coalition régime in Saigon. North Vietnamese troops would be expected to withdraw totally from Cambodia and Laos as a condition of the peace in Vietnam. The authors insisted that the Saigon régime could not be allowed, for purposes of its own narrow survival, to veto the agreement, and they argued that the United States should topple the Thieu government in favor of other non-Communists if this was necessary to achieve peace. Sooner or later, the memo predicted, the President would have to choose between escalation, unilateral withdrawal, or a negotiated exit close to this proposal—as indeed he did. The paper ended with a plea for urgency, "because we see the President sinking deeper into the Johnsonian bog." Kissinger pondered the memorandum and eventually sent it to Nixon "for information"; but nothing resulted from the proposal, though Kissinger's own secret meetings with the North Vietnamese in Paris soon resumed.

The incident seems notable in retrospect only because, like the September Group, it portrayed the ominous, self-defeating equivocation deeply embedded in the war policy. For the moment unready to test Hanoi's "breaking point," the President and his Assistant were unwilling as well to face the strategic blunder inherent in a policy of withdrawal at the same time expecting a better settlement as their military power shrank. Most tragically, the two seemed oblivious to the human price of the course they would soon adopt. For it was certainly true that when Kissinger forwarded the Lake-Morris "option" to the Oval Office, there was as yet no war in Cambodia, the decimation and demoralization of the South Vietnamese army in

Laos and on the DMZ had not taken place, there was no carpet bombing of Hanoi, and the numbers of American dead had not so hideously doubled. There was still time for a negotiated peace.

But apart from diplomatic or military realities, proposals like the Lake-Morris memorandum rested on a false assumption—and the point was critical in what followed. Arguments against the attrition policy of Vietnamization or against any savage new escalation were based on the premise that American domestic opposition to the war would inevitably grow. The October memo confidently warned, "We believe that the dangers of our course to domestic cohesion will begin to outweigh any foreign policy interest in Southeast Asia." In the event, however, domestic dissent briefly reached a high point in the autumn of 1969, only to fade steadily with the American troop withdrawals. This development confirmed and hardened Nixon and Kissinger in their fundamentally contemptuous attitudes toward the anti-war opposition, attitudes which, thereby vindicated, were to be a major influence on their Indochina policy.

The evidence and impact of this animus toward domestic dissenters was no less revealing that same fall than the existence of the September Group or the rejection of any new peace initiatives. It surfaced, for example, when White House adviser Daniel Patrick Moynihan returned from an Ivy League football game to write Nixon a characteristically effervescent "eyes only" memo on the new régime's opportunity to capture the "young demonstrators" and (by some osmosis) their elders, most of whom Moynihan felt might otherwise go Democratic. Moynihan's argument was an intelligent but essentially nebulous statement, which recommended that Nixon avoid any open confrontation with the younger generation. The memo was no doubt one more example of Moynihan's spontaneous enthusiasm for molding his employer into a Disraeli of American politics, a progressive conservative benignly ruling with Moynihan's ideas as a guide. But this particular effort provoked from both Nixon and Kissinger a harsh response derived from their already decided views on the question. In the margin at the point where Moynihan observed that there was potential Nixon support among the Vietnam marchers, the President scribbled an angry: "No, RN $ and votes came from West and South." It was an indication of his analysis of electoral sociology, which allowed him to dismiss and defy what he saw as the limited regional and political nature of the anti-war dissent. Interestingly, Nixon then sent the Moynihan memo to Kissinger for comment. That drew for a time a collection of acid Kissinger observations to his staff on the neurotic character of the demonstrators: "They don't know who they are," "They need fathers, not brothers." A formal West Basement response to Moynihan's memo went through several careful drafts before it was finally sent to the Oval Office. It emphasized Kissinger's personally dictated points that the "bright" and anti-establishment demonstrators were not politically significant ("you could build a broad majority however you deal with them. . . ."). Kissinger argued that Vietnam was not a special cause but only the current symptom of youthful revolt. It would be wise to avoid "a collision," he advised, although "this by no means requires appeasement."

The effect of such arguments, laced with biting Kissinger comments on the subject to a sympathetic Nixon at White House staff meetings, reinforced the caricature of the anti-war opposition which both men possessed. As seen by Nixon and Kissinger, the youthful protesters were little more than a confused, unsustained, capricious, and insubstantial force. Seldom spoken but deeply settled in both was the conviction that the Vietnam dissent was very largely a protest against the draft system by the newly expanded and educated middle class, a movement that could be weakened and ultimately stilled by means of a reduction of the draft, and by the withdrawal of troops. Perhaps most tellingly, the two men believed the protest would lose its force if their policy simply reduced the number of flag-draped coffins coming home from Vietnam to an American heartland that would otherwise abide or support Richard Nixon and Henry Kissinger however they ended the war.

As these views became plainer to those around them, there emerged other equally profound feelings about an opposite dimension of the war. Both were haunted by starkly imagined fears of the domestic consequences if they did *not* defy and defeat the demonstrators. In a sense, the specter of a politics of retribution bedeviled the very politician who had once led such forces in America, as well as the intellectual who recalled a tragic precedent in his native Germany. For Nixon, the "loss" of South Vietnam clearly evoked the "loss" of China a generation before. During his formative years as a politician, he had witnessed bitter national division, the naming of scapegoats, the McCarthy excesses which took place in the wake of that débâcle. Now, though twenty years later, his apprehension at being the victim rather than vigilante of a similar process ran through his war policy. "As we saw the consequences of what we had done," he said in his November 3 speech, describing the perils of any course other than Vietnamization, "inevitable remorse and divisive recrimination would scar our spirit as a people."

For Kissinger the similar impulses were probably more complicated though no less powerful. Behind the contemptuous dismissal of the demonstrators also lurked an uneasy scorn of what he privately called the "fascism of the streets," a double-edged fear not only that a "vocal minority" could stampede government policy, but that the same elements might then turn on the régime, blaming it for the results. It was the instinctive distrust felt by a man in the intellectual shadow of the fatal recriminations which had overtaken Weimar democracy. And he repeatedly referred to the fate of Weimar as the streets around the White House filled with marchers in late 1969. This was also the Kissinger who had stood with Nelson Rockefeller under the onslaught of the howling Goldwater galleries at the Cow Palace in 1964, and who had spent his previous "public" life largely in the genteel club room atmosphere of the Manhattan foreign policy establishment, and whose own political sociology was learned at best second-hand among his Harvard faculty rivals. There was precious little in such a narrow, insulated background to nurture trust of the new demonstrators, to accept the violent activism that had broken into the old quiescence of American politics or to understand confidently that the America of 1969 was no more like Weimar Germany than South Vietnam was like prewar Czechoslovakia. His war policy must first of all evade any influence from the rabble. There could be no "appeasing" the minority for a quick peace, nor any unloosing of a vindictive majority by seeming to "lose."

The strands all came together in the President's November 3, 1969, speech, a climactic event in the internal evolution of the Vietnam policy. It was the event that determined in so many ways that the war would go on. The address evoked the dangers of yielding to the minority, holding up a prospect of bitter recrimination in the acceptance of "defeat." It promised a gradual withdrawal (without mentioning time or U.S. or Vietnamese casualties), and made another threat to Hanoi about "strong and effective measures." The tour de force was a demagogic appeal to the "great silent majority" whose support the President and Kissinger were convinced they could purchase by ending the American participation in the war.

The national reaction to the speech was one of overwhelming popular support, and the veritable emasculation of the peace movement which left it unable ever again to mount protests similar to those organized that autumn. For its part, Congress stood mute and largely cowed in the face of its apparent preemption from policy debate. A political malaise settled so heavily over the opposition that a year later, even after the Cambodian invasion, few Democrats felt bold enough to make the continuing carnage an issue in the 1970 congressional elections. For example, campaigning that year in his home state of Minnesota, Senator Walter Mondale, an erstwhile dove and future Vice President, would refuse the requests of aides that he make even a single speech or statement opposing the régime's Vietnam policies. Within two years Vietnam had passed from the blood-letting that destroyed Johnson to a subject unmentionable among prudent politicians. That accomplishment owed much to the themes of the November 3 speech, and thus to Nixon's and Kissinger's perception of their countrymen, quite apart from what would be conventionally understood as "foreign" policy.

They were right, of course. Or at least right enough for their purposes. The effect of the troop withdrawals was to expose the core issue of the war: American ground involvement was what mattered to Americans, rather than the sheer devastation in Indochina. Most of the country would not really care, Nixon and Kissinger reasoned then and later, if their policy led to the ravaging of a helpless land by B-52 computer bombing from 35,000 feet, so long as the end seemed in sight, the troops kept coming home. Under their policy the coffins returning numbered no fewer than before. But by then it hardly seemed to matter. Although he eventually presided over more casualties than Lyndon Johnson, Nixon would be reelected by a record margin in 1972, and Kissinger celebrated for his peacemaking. In a way, all this was determined by the end of 1969. The "scenario" already present in the "eyes only" memos and secret meetings merely remained to be acted out.

Early in 1970, Kissinger resumed the clandestine Paris meetings with the North Vietnamese begun in August 1969. These early talks were futile, but they offered a vivid portrait of the man who later became a nearly legendary negotiator. His style was ardently personal, intent on individual rapport with his North Vietnamese counterparts, Xuan Thuy and the higher-ranking Le Duc Tho, just as he dealt with the journalists and other high officials he needed in Washington. He approached the process with an obvious and indefatigable relish, dictating the near verbatim talking points he would then recite with studied casualness at actual meetings. The first meetings on Kissinger's side were spent in elaborate efforts to establish the personalized atmosphere. Jokes, ingratiating remarks and compliments, self-deprecation, historical allusions, anecdotal stories about other famous negotiators, flashes of knowledge about Vietnamese history—it was not so different, apart from the gravity and secrecy, from the ingredients of a skillful series of press conferences. Some will undoubtedly read the transcripts of those meetings in the distant future and be shocked by the tone of trivia and sometimes contrived humor, but that probably accounted much less for the continuing failure of the talks than the U.S. substantive position.

The negotiations began on the premise of mutual withdrawal, and by the early spring of 1970 had progressed to the point where Kissinger had actually offered a draft schedule with specific numbers for the American reductions. But the North Vietnamese were unyielding on the question of their own forces, whose very existence they routinely denied while tacitly admitting it by discussing the political conditions for troop reductions. On both military and political questions, however, Kissinger worked, astonishingly, from a U.S. negotiating background that was nearly nonexistent. The first of these private Paris negotiations were held in strict secrecy from the U.S. bureaucracy as well as the world. Like the later talks, they were staffed by two or three Kissinger aides. Yet when those assistants discreetly examined past negotiating positions for a political settlement or withdrawal schedules, they found that the U.S. government had been carrying on formal talks in Paris for more than a year with little or no detailed notion of what a peace agreement could or should look like in detail. The whole elaborate sham continued for some time, of course. Dutiful symbols like David Bruce, the aging patrician diplomat from past Democratic administrations, presided over a makework delegation in Paris, and at the publicly scheduled sessions repeated the stale general formulas from the latest presidential speech. Meanwhile, Kissinger quietly flew in and out of Paris to do the authentic negotiating, such as it was in 1970–71, at a hidden location in complete secrecy.

This first round of Kissinger-Tho talks was locked in the mutual withdrawal trap when in March 1970 a *coup d'état* by rightist officers in Cambodia overthrew Prince Sihanouk. There is no conclusive evidence that the CIA or other U.S. intelligence agencies from the Pentagon instigated the coup, though the emergence of a new pro-Western régime reenlivened the old dream among many military and CIA partisans of closing the port of Sihanoukville, part of the endless mechanical quest to win the war by reducing tonnages in intelligence reports. It was clear in the White House that the CIA station in Phnom Penh knew the plotters well, probably knew their plans, and did nothing to alert Sihanouk. They informed Washington well in advance of the coup, and joined the chorus from the U.S. military in Saigon and from the Pentagon urging immediate aid and political patronage for the new government. Then, too, the coup coincided with the latest tide of U.S. and South Vietnamese intelligence reporting on an ostensible Communist build-up in the Cambodian sanctuaries, despite the secret B-52 strikes. The prospect of a new régime ready to deny the Communists those sanctuaries, or conversely of the Communists turning on Sihanouk's successors, clearly gave the reports—and the case for closing Sihanoukville—much heavier bureaucratic weight.

In any event, Nixon's own peculiar sense of menace was almost certainly more decisive than bureaucratic maneuvers. Atop the triumph of the November 3 speech, visibly more confident and combative, he suddenly reversed the normal flow of policy from the West Basement upward. Down from the Oval Office in March and April 1970 came a flood of memos based on the raw intelligence he had requested ever since the moment of the coup. Those papers, too, will make extraordinary reading for historians if they survive. Now stream-of-consciousness excursions into courage and aggression, now terse orders or questions, their thrust almost from the beginning was that the United States should aggressively support the new régime and strike if necessary at the North Vietnamese if they moved from the sanctuaries against the Cambodian coup. As U.S. arms went to the new régime and its army attacked suspected Communist sympathizers among ethnic Vietnamese living near Phnom Penh, Nixon began to watch repeated screenings of *Patton*. While North Vietnamese units reportedly started to move out of the sanctuaries, Rogers told a reporter that the President was "a walking ad" for *Patton* and its seeming celebration of the bellicose, decisive World War II general. The Secretary of State did not mention Cambodia, but the omission was not surprising. Neither he nor Laird learned of the planned U.S. invasion until weeks after the first memos went down to Kissinger and secret orders were thence issued to the chairman of the joint chiefs, on the eve of the attack. "The liberals are waiting to see Nixon let Cambodia go down the drain just the way Eisenhower let Cuba go down the drain," Nixon reportedly wrote Kissinger on one occasion. In response to congressional appeals for caution in the wake of the coup, he wrote: "Those senators think they can push me around but I'll show them who's tough."

On April 24 Kissinger met with dissenting members of his NSC staff (including myself). The meeting was never so stormy and impassioned as the participants later relived the drama. But Kissinger was plainly warned that there would be disastrous domestic dissent, as there would be in the murders at Kent State and Jackson State, and that the notoriously unreliable intelligence from the region, let alone the larger cause of peace, did not justify a U.S. invasion. In this encounter, as others, there was for the staff members—certainly for me—the pernicious problem of discussing outrageous, irrational official actions in the cool, bloodless language of cost effectiveness and manliness the culture of government seems to demand. Not for the first or last time, a policy in Indochina that warranted screaming was too gently opposed. Three in the room, however—Lake, Watts, and myself—later refused to work on the President's speech and the "scenario" for the invasion, and before its announcement resigned. Later, Kissinger angrily labeled the resignations "the cowardice of the Eastern establishment." Yet he may have had his own misgivings. Nixon informed the NSC of the invasion plans on April 26. As late as the afternoon of April 29, a day before the presidential speech, Kissinger had a final talk with Nixon. As Haig told the story afterward: "Henry tried to talk him out of it but it had gone too far." Perhaps. But Kissinger would be a forceful defender of the invasion. It was, after all, a logical extension of MENU and the November 3 speech as well as of the mentality that underlay his customary policy of deliberate aggressiveness interspersing negotiation and withdrawal.

The bizarre, almost manic decisionmaking involved in the invasion belonged chiefly to Nixon; the root logic of the strike was Kissinger's.

The purpose of the attack as publicly revealed was to find and destroy the legendary COSVN, "the headquarters," Nixon told the nation, "for the entire Communist military operation in South Vietnam." The rationale was similar to Nixon's assurance that the allies had never before violated Cambodian neutrality. Three days before, Laird had told him pointedly in the Cabinet Room that COSVN in that sense did not exist and had never existed. All that the combined U.S.-South Vietnamese invasion could hope to achieve was a temporary destruction of supply dumps, a bloodying of what North Vietnamese units they could find, and a diversion of any enemy forces in fact targeted against the Phnom Penh government. The larger intention was, as Nixon said of his Senate critics, "to show them who's tough." But as Lyndon Johnson could have told them, that motive in the war was always impossible to control or measure. Like the secret bombings and covert border raids before it, the invasion generated new momentum in the conflict and led to a series of unforeseen events. Over the next year, Cambodia irretrievably joined the Indochina war, its bloated army and beleaguered corrupt régime becoming another drain on U.S. aid, its previously innocuous local Communists swelling to ten times their original number with a more effective army than the government's. The descent of the country into its own national hell had begun.

Though Kissinger's contacts were reestablished with the North Vietnamese later in 1970, the positions remained completely deadlocked. Nixon's October 7, 1970, speech, by now his sixth on the war and grandly titled "A New Peace Initiative for All Indochina" (the "All" made necessary by Cambodia's engulfment in the fighting), proposed a "cease-fire in place," which the Pentagon and the Saigon field command had strongly opposed in the past. But the proposal held fast to mutual withdrawal, the source of the stalemate, and the speech was ignored by Hanoi. Before negotiations were to begin in earnest, the pull of more chastening battle intervened again, this time as much by bureaucratic force as White House initiative. Caught up in its own self-promoting zeal for "Vietnamization," believing its own rhetoric and accepting the extravagant reports on South Vietnamese units in Cambodia (where those units had either encountered little action or been screened by U.S. forces), the Pentagon and General Creighton Abrams, the U.S. field commander, had steadily urged through the latter months of 1971 a South Vietnamese strike against Hanoi's supply routes along the Ho Chi Minh Trail in neighboring Laos. The plan gradually gathered adherents in the Thieu régime, from local commanders chafing to show their mettle to politicians seeking a morale lift. Eventually Thieu himself agreed, anxious to satisfy his American patrons if only to keep aid flowing and ward off a private Washington-Hanoi agreement he seems to have chronically suspected (as it turned out, with justification).

Once more it was an operation many times broached in the Democratic administration and ever put aside for the uncertainties involved, including the specter of a major defeat. In a belated reaction to the Cambodian invasion, the Congress passed the Church-Cooper amendment in 1970, barring more U.S. ground forces in Cambodia or Laos. Troop withdrawals in any case had taken out some 260,000 Americans by the end of 1970. But in January 1971, Nixon with Kissinger's recommendation approved massive U.S. air support for Lam Son 619, a South Vietnamese attack into southern Laos. Beginning on February 8, the operation was a pathetic emblem of the war. Saigon's forces thrashed about in the Laotian jungles, fought at first a few inconclusive skirmishes, were worn down by greater enemy firepower and sacrifice, and ended in one of the great setpiece routs in twenty years of fighting. There followed the dauntless reports from Saigon claiming incredible body counts of enemy dead and tons of supplies destroyed, the arithmetic of a victory that did not exist. Even Kissinger produced a secret report for the President on the attack that was remarkably disingenuous. Saigon had shown itself, he wrote, "able to deal with the enemy threat in sanctuary areas," and had "demonstrated the ability to mount complex multi-division operations in conditions of a difficult and unfamiliar terrain, adverse weather, and against a well prepared enemy."

The American people received a more accurate picture of the battle in the television film showing South Vietnamese rangers frantically clinging to—and sometimes falling off—the skids of U.S. helicopters leaving the scene of some episode of the débâcle. The truth concealed even from Nixon was that many South Vietnamese units had suffered 60 percent casualties, virtual annihilation. The paper victory of Lam Son 619 was a psychological blow to the South Vietnamese army from which it never recovered. The defeat was, in a critical sense, the parent of the final collapse of 1975. But in the spring of 1971 the cover up of the disaster continued for all the familiar bureaucratic reasons of outward deceit and inner self-deception that accompanied the war in both Saigon and Washington. Most important in ignoring the reality was that Kissinger began that May the final, twisting diplomatic sequel that led to a settlement. And Kissinger and Nixon were to abandon Saigon much as their forerunners originally had become ensnared in the country, in a weary, expedient blindness to the truth of what they were doing.

Among the mountains of paper—the mass of cables, reports, and memoranda—heaped on history by the more than two decades of American involvement in the Indochina war, four sets of documents seem especially symbolic of the Nixon-Kissinger era. First were the September Group plans, portent of the belligerence running so deep and so long in their policy. Then there were the public or private proposals to stop the drift toward more war, such as the Lake-Morris initiative, which were ignored or spurned. Third were the reports to the President, like those from Kissinger or General Abrams on the Laotian catastrophe, which bore the imprint of the old bureaucratic unreality. The fourth would be an obscure NSC staff study of alternative peace settlements drawn up in late 1970. On the basis of all available intelligence and experience regarding Hanoi's war aims, the study concluded that the North Vietnamese, as one source put it, could be "neither forced nor persuaded" to withdraw their troops from the South. Confessing privately to aides that he was convinced on the evidence, a major participant in that study was Henry Kissinger. Yet for another eighteen months of war that same Kissinger negotiated with Hanoi in vague equivocation on this basic point—and even after conceding it, for another six months continued to evade the issue altogether with the South Vietnamese. The 1970 study represented, like most of the other documents, a government both foolish and cynical while struggling to make peace.

On May 31, 1971, Kissinger secretly presented the North Vietnamese in Paris with the first important substantive change in the U.S. negotiating position: the administration would give a specific deadline for the withdrawal of all remaining American troops in return for a cease-fire agreement and the return of all U.S. prisoners of war. A month before the meetings, Nixon had announced the pull-out of 100,000 more troops by the end of 1971, leaving roughly 160,000 covered by Kissinger's offer. From laboriously drafted talking points, Kissinger left unmentioned his earlier insistence on withdrawal of what CIA and Pentagon intelligence estimates put at some 100,000 North Vietnamese troops then in the South. Yet at the same time, with the dialogue centered on his new proposal, he did not indicate that he was dropping the condition.

Kissinger's ambiguity reflected the policymaking behind the initiative. As spring turned to summer in 1971, the administration had made encouraging progress in SALT negotiations with the Soviet Union and plans were in motion for Kissinger's historic secret flight to Peking, setting the stage for the summit meetings the following year, and perhaps for new Russian or Chinese leverage on Hanoi. Increasingly a prisoner of its own official myopia on "Vietnamization," the White House had also emerged from the Laotian invasion with the view that the Saigon régime could, in General Abrams's ironic phrase, "hack it." There was, as several officials remembered afterward, a tendency to believe that this Saigon of the bureaucratic imagination was more ready and willing than ever to face a peace settlement. On another front, however, despite the steady troop withdrawals and hints of summit diplomacy, Nixon's Gallup Poll approval ratings had plunged that spring for the first time below 50 percent, nearly twenty points less than his pinnacle of popularity after the November 3 speech, and an ominous political sign for the coming presidential election. In 1971 the President actually ran behind a possible Democratic challenger, Senator Edmund Muskie, in various polls. This political vulnerability also clearly gave impetus to a negotiating initiative which might promise some dramatic breakthrough in ending the war. But neither Kissinger nor Nixon—who had also read the 1970 withdrawal study, albeit with no apparent reaction—was willing to confront squarely a formal renunciation of the condition. Kissinger flew to Paris at the end of May with only the tentative tactic of not "pressing" the issue.

In the May 31 meeting and two others in June and July, the North Vietnamese seemed cautiously receptive to the cease-fire and U.S. withdrawal deadline, though they were noncommittal on the return of POWs, and in the June 26 session countered with their own nine-point plan, which included the familiar demand for the U.S. removal of General Thieu. The plan, like the Kissinger initiative, ignored the issue of North Vietnamese forces in the South. At another secret Paris session in mid-August—Nixon having meanwhile announced with a flourish his future trip to Peking and gained some recovery in the polls—Kissinger elaborated the earlier initiative with a nine-month U.S. troop removal schedule and the general promise to "discuss" a political settlement. Once more, participants recounted later, he was simply silent on the question of mutual withdrawal. But a month later, the Hanoi negotiators returned to Paris to reject formally the U.S. proposal and reassert their own nine points, centered on the overthrow of Thieu. Finally, in early October, Kissinger passed to the North Vietnamese by an aide yet a further moderation of the May offer, this time proposing a six-month withdrawal schedule with still no specific reference to Hanoi's troops. The more novel point in this proposal, however, was a scheme for elections in South Vietnam to be held after the resignation of General Thieu, supervised by representatives of "all political groups" in the South. In many ways the most generous U.S. offer of the war, this proposal foundered as well, broken on the complex, contradictory politics that lay behind the 1971 Paris negotiations for both sides.

According to the accounts of many official sources, it was an extraordinary tangle in which bureaucratic influences again intervened decisively in diplomacy. Hanoi's real motives over these months will probably always be shrouded in secrecy; yet it is clear enough that in the summer of 1971, the North Vietnamese were most intent on the political turmoil developing in Saigon as General Thieu prepared for his rigged election in October by variously tyrannizing his opposition. In that interest, ironically, the Communists may have been no more passionate, notwithstanding for different reasons, than the American Embassy in Saigon. There at the same time U.S. Ambassador Ellsworth Bunker and his senior aides were, as one of them remembered, "furious" at Thieu's intrigues to maintain one-man rule. Hesitantly, the mission had come to view its client (as earlier American diplomats had seen President Diem eight years before) as a dictator who represented an embarrassing liability to U.S. interests and South Vietnamese morale. They were now ready to scuttle Thieu, not in order to end the war but to prosecute it more efficiently. Bunker and his CIA station chief carried out an orchestrated bureaucratic campaign throughout the summer in a number of cables to Washington suddenly chronicling the Thieu excesses and

consequent damage to U.S. interests, which the embassy had dutifully declined to see for several years. The climax to Bunker's own
maneuvering came the first week in September when the ambassador sent to Washington a routine but highly classified telegram on
"press guidance." The secrecy and policy implications assuring distri-
bution to the White House, his cable recommended almost casually
that he be authorized to leak discreetly to Saigon newsmen an official
disapproval of the political suppression in South Vietnam—even to
the point of planting with the press a proposal by which Thieu could
resign, and a new election be called by his successor, General Ky,
under an obscure provision of the American-made South Vietnamese
constitution.

From the vantage point of the embassy, their urging was another
fateful move determining the future of Asia; to Kissinger, however,
the Bunker cable that September represented one more annoying
interference from the bureaucrats. On the eve of another secret
negotiating session with Hanoi, Kissinger seems to have been as
transfixed as anyone else by the momentum and narrowing vision of
his own preoccupation—the personal diplomatic effort to entice
North Vietnamese into a quick settlement through successive offers
of a shrinking schedule for the U.S. troop pull-out and the continuing
coy silence on their forces in the South. There is evidence, moreover,
that during this period Nixon had reacted stridently to Hanoi's failure to respond to the U.S. initiative, however vaguely put. Aides
agree that Kissinger was hard-pressed that summer to keep alive
with the White House, let alone North Vietnam, the negotiating
gambit in which by this time he had invested so much of his energy
and, more important, his intramural prestige as a presidential adviser. In the always careful politics between Kissinger and his mercurial employer, it seemed scarcely the moment in Washington or Paris
to introduce the distraction of the further and still more politically
sensitive U.S. concession of replacing Thieu. By some accounts he
was at a private party in California when his staff reached him by
phone to authorize a reply to Bunker's proposed *coup d'état* by press
plant. Enraged, railing against "those bastards around that old man"
(Bunker), clearly seeing it all more in terms of a bureaucratic challenge than a far-reaching policy choice, he ordered a reply to Saigon
that ruled out any anti-Thieu actions by the U.S. Embassy prior to the
South Vietnamese election.

But the episode may have been in some respects one of the most consequential of the war. Because Hanoi's intelligence had penetrated every level in Saigon, they very probably knew at least something of the American Embassy's simmering discontent with Thieu in 1971. Even the faintest prospect of a U.S. move against the South Vietnamese dictator—coupled with their hopes of a Saigon political crisis before the election—would have kept the North Vietnamese noncommittal on the train of Kissinger offers in Paris, offers, after all, which had casually ignored the issue of Thieu along with the premeditated silence on mutual withdrawal. Yet when Thieu rode out the elections and the United States supported him faithfully on Kissinger's orders to Saigon, the American negotiating positions may well have appeared to Hanoi an elaborate tactic to divert them while the U.S. client régime was being entrenched still deeper. Such a misreading would have been one of those failures to communicate across "morbid suspiciousness" that Kissinger the scholar had so deplored in his predecessors. Little else accounts so fully for the stubborn stalemate in Paris in spite of the U.S. initiatives.

The furtive Nixon-Kissinger style—the failure even now openly to face the mutual withdrawal issue or to deal plainly with the Thieu question by either opposing or supporting him—was in large measure responsible for that impasse. And these failures of negotiation in turn traced back to the two men in the White House, for whom other factors—reputation, power, and the appearance of toughness —were often too compelling. So the final irony of the 1971 diplomacy lay in still another twist of deception. The election in Saigon and U.S. acquiescence in it only stiffened General Thieu in his determination to hold on to power in any settlement, and strengthened perhaps his trust of the Americans. Yet even as Kissinger at his California party committed the United States to Thieu's survival at a critical point, the betrayal of the same ally was already at work in his diplomacy. At no time in 1971 did the administration make clear to South Vietnam that Kissinger was mutely abandoning the old insistence on withdrawal of North Vietnamese troops, whose presence in the South would sooner or later doom any post-settlement non-Communist régime in Saigon. As 1971 ended, Hanoi belligerently broke off the secret negotiations, Thieu confidently continued his tyranny with apparent American backing, and Henry Kissinger, with mounting disregard of both developments, proceeded toward a settlement the

North could not refuse and the South would not understand until it was too late. The stage was set for the last bloody sequel of negotiations in 1972.

The pall of classical historical tragedy hangs over much of what followed in Indochina, the actors moving on relentlessly toward the dénouement, acting and being acted upon as if all had been preordained. Politics and diplomacy are never so rigidly serial in the unfolding, of course; the events are made, and changed, by men. Yet it is a part of trying to understand Henry Kissinger and American foreign policy to wonder whether all the influences that now took over—the forces of bureaucracy, the influence of personality and of domestic politics—were not too deep, too strong for any other outcome.

In the first months of the new year, the various parties to the 1971 imbroglio seemed spurred by their separate versions of vindictiveness at the recent developments. The effect was an unprecedented resurgence of the war. Probably before the turn of the year, Hanoi had decided to launch a major new offensive in the northern region of South Vietnam. Whether it was hoped again, as at Tet in 1968, to pressure the Americans in a presidential election year, or whether the attack reflected a harder attitude among the North Vietnamese leadership after some imagined Kissinger perfidy, is unclear. Most likely it was some combination of political-diplomatic calculus and a renewed military confidence after the South Vietnamese fiasco in Laos. In any event, the North Vietnamese leaders prepared to strike savagely toward the total victory they had never wholly relinquished. Almost exultantly, U.S. intelligence warnings of the buildup poured into Washington from the Saigon Embassy. If the White House had been oblivious to the politics of replacing Thieu, certainly it could not ignore a new offensive. For a few weeks, however, Kissinger reportedly did just that. In private memos to Nixon and more caustically in talk with his staff, he accused the U.S. mission and military in Vietnam of exaggerating the intelligence for "local" bureaucratic reasons. The intelligence on Cambodia in 1969 and 1970 had been read by a White House eager to prove its fearsomeness. Now, after two years of vested interest in the success of "Vietnamization" and the skill of Kissinger's diplomacy, the same sort of reports were received with a willing disbelief.

By late January, though, the intelligence had penetrated, and the reaction was a kind of desperation. In a much-publicized speech on January 25, 1972, Nixon disclosed the secret record of Kissinger's personal negotiations with the North Vietnamese. The revelation only ignited a series of bitter and confused public exchanges with Hanoi on what precisely had been offered by either side. Washington then secretly asked North Vietnam for further talks, and Hanoi agreed as Nixon left for Peking in mid-February. At the same time, the military build-up continued, and after the China visit, the North Vietnamese stalled in naming a date for resuming talks. On March 30 the offensive began. At that, both Nixon and Kissinger resisted an acknowledgment of the weight of the blow descending on South Vietnam. Obviously the offensive made mockery of the President's triumph in Peking and his Assistant's dramatic clandestine diplomacy.

As Quangtri fell in April, Kissinger flew secretly to Moscow in a last effort to stop the attack and to avert any U.S. counteraction that might destroy the Soviet-American summit long planned for late May. This was the summit that was to be the climax of Kissinger's other negotiating feat, the signature of a strategic arms control pact. There were no more heavy allusions to those "trains leaving stations" he had made to Dobrynin three years before. In Moscow, according to official sources on the meetings, Kissinger offered in precise language to agree to the presence in the South of the roughly 100,000 North Vietnamese troops there before the current offensive, provided Hanoi halt the fighting in place and withdraw the 40–50,000 soldiers introduced since March. Unmistakably, it was the first formal U.S. renunciation of mutual withdrawal. What witnesses remembered as the "very surprised" Russian leadership then immediately sent an envoy to Hanoi as Kissinger returned to Washington.

Apparently at Soviet urging of Hanoi, there followed at last in the beginning of May another secret Paris meeting. Kissinger repeated the specific offer to accept North Vietnamese troops in South Vietnam as a basic tenet of settlement. However North Vietnam may have received the concession, it was too late for its most urgent purpose. On the crest of their battlefield victories, completely occupying and governing significant territory below the Demilitarized Zone, the North Vietnamese were undoubtedly victims of their own military momentum. The meeting ended with the Hanoi delegation repeating their old demands to unseat Thieu, all but ignoring the U.S. concession made explicit for the first time. If that concession was not enough to stop the spring 1972 offensive, however, it was now irretrievably part of negotiating ground given Hanoi. And Kissinger had apparently still not conveyed to General Thieu the substance of the offer. But before the reckoning for that was paid, the war policy shifted back toward the practiced resort to escalation.

Kissinger returned from the vain meeting with the North Vietnamese in Paris to a White House where Nixon had already called for what was essentially an updated rendition of the 1969 plans of the September Group. The response to the unchecked offensive was to bomb the North intensively and mine Haiphong, a reaction Nixon had considered and rejected as uncertain and perhaps unavailing nearly three years earlier. The decision was nearly a parody of the contradictory strains in the war policy, though now there was a clear impetus to strike in place of the doubts and critique which had marked the 1969 study. In lower-level planning meetings on the attack option, for example, the CIA was plainly in favor of the retaliation, now glossing over for its advocacy the gaps and imprecisions in raw intelligence on the impact of the same raids in 1969. Those close to him in these days describe Kissinger himself as genuinely torn by the decision, worrying that the U.S. attacks might only slow the offensive at the cost of killing the negotiations, yet still clinging to the assumption that American power could indeed punish and coerce Hanoi into a settlement. It was not only that he believed after the latest negotiating failure that North Vietnam required some final test of arms before negotiating peace, but also that their will and purpose might yet somehow be breached. Kissinger, even then, preserved an enduring belief in the "breaking point" of a "fourth-rate power."

The decision to launch the attacks and mining was already taken in effect, the military timetables begun, when the National Security Council met on Monday morning, May 8, 1972, for one of its more memorable and characteristic sessions under Richard Nixon. Secretary of State Rogers spoke first against the plan, pressing the point that enough had been done for the Thieu régime, an argument that under the circumstances of the secret negotiating concessions must have struck both Kissinger and Nixon as ironic if not amusing. Laird predictably repeated his opposition, though less forcefully than in 1969. But now, domestic dissent dead, he built his arguments more than ever on the strengths of "Vietnamization," the shell that was collapsing all too visibly under Hanoi's offensive. "They still hold Hue," Laird kept interspersing in his monologue on the virtues of the Pentagon-trained South Vietnamese, until he was stopped for a telling silence by Nixon's rejoinder: "Yes, Mel, but how long can they hold it?" It was the nature of the war, the sheer stupidity of its politics, that Laird no more than any other American official in the previous decade could escape the perplexed pause following such a question. Otherwise the chairman of the joint chiefs, Admiral Moorer, waxed confident on the crippling yield of the attacks, Vice President Agnew expressed his support with a florid statement on credibility, while Kissinger observed that the Soviets would probably cancel the summit. There were desultory questions directed to CIA Director Helms about the ability of the North Vietnamese to resupply a still viable war effort despite the bombs and mines. (The Agency wanted the NSC to know that nothing was certain.)

But by far the most dominant performance at the meeting belonged to the relatively new Secretary of the Treasury who, unlike his colleagues, had not been around these arguments before and was in any case of stronger convictions. At fifty-five, a renegade Texas Democrat come to the Nixon cabinet to retrieve a laggard career, John Bowdin Connally was at the zenith of his power in the administration. He joined the easy poise and confidence of a successful corporate lawyer with the political bluster and assurance of his early patron, Lyndon Johnson. Such gifts had made him in foreign as well as domestic affairs the most formidable force in policymaking next to Kissinger, who despised yet prudently avoided confronting him, giving Connally virtually a free hand in international monetary policy. What mattered at this May 8 NSC meeting, however, was less tangible, and more important. In his articulate advocacy of the strikes, Connally personified by several accounts precisely that private bravado, the marriage of machismo and policy, that had represented the darker side, almost the longing, of the Nixon-Kissinger policy in Indochina from the beginning. They would not be worthy of their responsibility, he told the NSC, unless they stood up to this test of national toughness. If there was ever any feeling that the meeting might be against the attacks, it seems to have disappeared under Connally's presence. That afternoon, after two more hours alone with Kissinger and Connally (a conversation never revealed), Nixon gave the final attack order to be flashed over the Pacific.

The added bombing and attempted blockade of North Vietnam followed the familiar pattern of ostensibly climactic events in the war. Months later, despite the flurry of official claims and statistics, it would never be quite certain how anything had really changed. The joint chiefs soon argued that the attacks had strangled Hanoi's supply lines, while Laird openly claimed that the quarantine would not have palpable effect for months, and that the South Vietnamese had themselves defeated the offensive in front of Hue. Politically if not militarily, however, the mining had at least halted the headlong North Vietnamese advance, and in a sense purchased time before the resumption of a similar rout and collapse occurred three years later. More restraining on Hanoi than the blockade, however, may have been the cautious indifference of its patrons in Peking and, of course, Moscow, where Nixon was welcomed within weeks by the Kremlin. The Russians had simply chosen to ignore the war's escalation and its diplomatic embarrassment for the much more direct benefits of détente.

For the North Vietnamese, the attacks would be essentially just another interlude in the long process of their revolutionary war. The May 8 decision was an interlude and defeat of sorts, too, for Kissinger. In the first hours after the presidential speech, when it seemed that both the Vietnam negotiations and détente policy were shattered, he had attempted to separate himself from Nixon in an effort at public self-exculpation. Artless leaks trickled through Washington that week that this was the decision "Henry" finally opposed; the magisterial "we" of his press briefings suddenly became "the President felt." Such sordid personal politics were soon lost in the rush to the summit, but would aptly appear again six months later as the war finally ended.

At the Moscow summit, Nixon and Kissinger reaffirmed the American acceptance of North Vietnamese troops in the South— again with seemingly no notice given to Thieu—and added still another concession in the form of a proposed tripartite electoral commission in South Vietnam which would include neutralists and the Viet Cong. Nixon also reportedly indicated to the Russians a willingness to suspend the bombing prior to the release of American prisoners, a key retreat from his May 8 public speech.

From this Moscow démarche and the ensuing Soviet mediation

of the U.S. views in Hanoi, Kissinger began the last and in some ways most familiar negotiating sequence of the war. He is described by witnesses now as a paradoxical figure, a mingling of the unprecedented public authority so apparent at the time—after Peking and Moscow he was more celebrated than ever in the press—and an even deeper private anxiety about his place in the administration and his role in the next term. In either psychology, he may well have entered the last peace negotiations with an uncertain sense of his own command with Nixon after the May crisis. That would explain both the heedless quality of his diplomacy at crucial stages, and his ultimate participation in the closing madness of the Christmas 1972 bombing of Hanoi.

Through the summer following the summit, events moved rapidly. In June, Kissinger was in Peking to brief the Chinese on the Moscow talks and convey Washington's readiness for a rapid settlement in Vietnam, requiring only the final withdrawal of the 60,000 remaining troops. In July, he was in Saigon to perform some extraordinary diplomatic maneuvering in which he explained that the administration had been compelled for domestic electoral reasons to "seem" forthcoming in its public statements, and that a reelected Nixon would support Thieu's long-advocated South Vietnamese invasion of the North as well as more intense American strategic bombing. According to the public record of those talks, as well as the recollection of some accompanying him, Kissinger did not mention to Thieu in July either the concession of North Vietnamese troops in the South or the proposal for a tripartite commission expressed to the Russians in Moscow.

Yet both these offers were obviously instrumental in bringing the North Vietnamese back to Paris in August for two meetings at which the tripartite arrangement was accepted by Hanoi. At this point, Kissinger summoned Haig to go to Saigon and try to persuade Thieu to accept the tripartite commission. Though intimately involved in the Washington staffing of the negotiations and, most important, as Nixon's liaison to Kissinger when the latter was abroad, Haig had not played a direct negotiating role before that time. The NSC staff general, channel to the military, veteran of the war, Haig was now to enter the process of screening Kissinger's evasive tactics with Saigon. His presence may have made matters worse. As a start, he was unable to convince Thieu to accept the commission and Bunker was no more successful in mid-September.

With Kissinger urging upon Nixon a unilateral U.S. adherence without Thieu, and Haig quietly advising the President that Henry was "too anxious for a deal," Nixon gave authority for final agreement to the commission at a Kissinger meeting with Le Duc Tho on September 15. By the end of the month, after further meetings, the provision for the commission was further refined and accepted by both sides. Haig was then sent on his second trip to Saigon to lobby Thieu on the point. He was unsuccessful but did not tell Thieu even then that the commission was an essentially final part of the swiftly forming settlement between the United States and North Vietnam.

The final flurry of negotiations took place between October 8 and 11. As throughout the four years of secret talks, Kissinger acted basically alone, assisted by a handful of trusted aides. In October though, for the first time the group included Haig—another precaution, for what it was worth. The settlement that emerged was a distillation of the long months of vagueness and maneuvering since May 1971. In essence, the agreement exchanged a cease-fire and return of U.S. prisoners for the acceptance of Hanoi's troops in the South and the still nebulous provision for the tripartite commission and a "National Council for Reconciliation" in Saigon.

During mid-October, Kissinger maneuvered the plan through a pro forma bureaucratic acceptance in Washington, and returned for the final negotiations in Paris on October 17, preparatory to signing the instrument of peace with a grand personal flourish in Hanoi on October 24. From October 19 to 23, he planned to stop in Saigon to get Thieu's agreement to the settlement.

His schedule, as most of the world sensed at the time, came apart during that Saigon interval. Now seeing the draft peace agreement for the first time, with its provision for the maintenance of the North Vietnamese troops in the South which he had never granted, and the tripartite commission he had repeatedly rejected, Thieu was barely civil to the Americans and wholly recalcitrant on the essential points. In an extraordinary gamble of his stock, Kissinger persuaded Nixon by cable to inform the North Vietnamese as late as October 21 that the agreement was still possible. But two days later, with Thieu unmoved and more embittered than ever at the apparent betrayal, he cabled the President again to say there could be no agreement with Saigon. The result was inevitable. Sensitive to any charge of a unilateral retreat on the eve of the 1972 election, Nixon informed Hanoi the agreement was delayed, and the October settlement disintegrated.

Kissinger had avoided confronting Thieu much, one suspects, as he had avoided confronting the worst side of Nixon, because confrontation would probably have meant early defeat. Both men, he believed, could be used and their flaws somehow outlasted and outflanked. Perhaps it was fitting that Thieu now turned against that relationship in a convincing portrayal of the righteous creature that the official American mythology of the war had made him, as the beleaguered leader of a nation fighting against great odds. And there could be little doubt, if the record became public, that those odds had been increased in part by Kissinger's extraordinary negotiating tactics. As convincing victim, General Thieu in Saigon that October of 1972 was the potential inspiration for exactly the domestic sense of remorse and recrimination Kissinger and Nixon had feared as an outcome to the war, the fear that had driven them to preside over so much further bloodshed.

There now ensued almost a repetition of the collapse of negotiations and its bloody sequel of a year before. Whether suspecting another deception or hoping to pressure Washington, the North Vietnamese disclosed the terms of the agreement on October 25. Kissinger countered with his famous "Peace is at hand" statement, in part to signal Hanoi and warn Saigon, in part (on Nixon's instruction) to preempt the Democratic presidential opponent, George McGovern, and in part also (for Kissinger at this stage most important) to involve Nixon himself publicly, and to forestall Haig's rising influence.

The diplomacy of the next month drove all parties further apart. For the third time, General Haig flew to Saigon in early November but made no progress in persuading Thieu. When Kissinger returned to meet Tho in Paris some days later, the talks dragged as the North Vietnamese raised old questions and Kissinger presented at Nixon's instruction, albeit perfunctorily, a voluminous document listing Saigon's objections to the agreement. Kissinger's own staff, including Haig, now reportedly believed that North Vietnam might be deliberately drawing back from the settlement. There was reason to believe that Hanoi saw bad faith as well as a military disadvantage in the emergency U.S. aid program which was pumping over $1 billion in arms into South Vietnam and threatening to change the battlefield balance. Contacts continued in Paris, but in Washington Nixon and Kissinger planned with the joint chiefs the ultimate exercise in military intimidation. On December 15, the North Vietnamese formally reneged on the original agreement for the release of U.S. prisoners of war, and proposed lesser changes in several other points. On December 18, Nixon ordered the execution of LINEBACKER II, the systematic terror strikes at Hanoi and other population centers known as the Christmas bombing.

For twelve days, over 100 strategic bombers and 500 fighter-bombers pounded North Vietnam around the clock. The B-52s dropped their payloads in a saturation pattern 1 mile long by 0.5 mile wide. On December 30, 1972, the Pentagon acknowledged the loss of twenty-six planes, ninety-three men missing, and thirty-one captured by the North Vietnamese. The public and editorial outrage at the raids was greater than at any time since the Cambodian invasion, but Nixon had been safely reelected to a second term by a vast margin.

Meanwhile, as the first strikes were launched, Haig made his fourth and eventually historic trip to Saigon, carrying a letter from Nixon explaining the raids as an action to "brutalize" Hanoi so as to achieve optimum conditions for a settlement. Haig also conveyed a U.S. threat to cut off all military aid to the Saigon régime if Thieu did not agree to a settlement following the bombing. Over the first three weeks of January the negotiations resumed in Paris, and on January 23, 1973, Kissinger and Tho signed the formal agreement, General Thieu having given his approval to a settlement not substantially different from the one he had angrily rejected in October.

Why had the diplomacy ended this way, in twelve days of calculated barbarism in the skies over North Vietnam? Officials admitted then and later that the final savagery of the B-52s, like the mining and bombing the May before, like the secret raids on Cambodia in 1969–70, like the millions of tons of explosives dropped on Indochina throughout the war, had made no appreciable difference in the military contest between North and South. Both Nixon and Kissinger would tell reporters privately that they had done it all in a subtle maneuver to stave off the "war party" in the Hanoi politburo, to strengthen those North Vietnamese leaders who had been in favor of the October agreement. And as in the May crisis, some favored reporters would accept the interpretation that Kissinger was once more a victim of the vicious intrigues practiced by his less likable colleagues and his chief at the White House. "Haldeman almost got me, he almost got me," he confided to one columnist, with the theory that his White House rivals had used the apparent failures of the autumn to undercut his position and even ease him out in favor of Connally in the next administration. That picture of court politics is, of course, authentic enough. The political promise and default in the peace negotiations did provide the opportunity for Kissinger's rivals to attack him, and left him little room to oppose the Christmas bombing with Nixon while still preserving his position to negotiate the peace and conduct the rest of foreign policy.

But all the motives of political coercion and bureaucratic conspiracy must trace back to the root failure of the October agreement—the deception of General Thieu in Saigon. If Kissinger had faced that problem honestly and openly, the history of the war would have been very different. In the end, the bombing was necessary because Thieu had been misled in October and before about the American agreement with the North Vietnamese on the presence of troops in the South. To buy Thieu's acquiescence and to cover Kissinger's tracks, the American planes flew at Christmas over North Vietnam—a brutal act, but the price of Henry Kissinger's statesmanship.

Like all great tragedies, the war and its diplomacy left many unanswered questions. If Washington had faced earlier the issue of North Vietnamese troops in the South, would a settlement have been possible several years and thousands of lives sooner? If the halting tragicomic maneuvers of 1971 had been somehow avoided, would America and Indochina have escaped the death and destruction of 1972? Yet most of the questions rest on one more basic—what would have happened if the men in the White House after January 20, 1969, had been truly intent on stopping the war rather than on the private fears and opportunities they saw in it?

The war ended only for the Americans in January 1973, and then only in terms of lives, for billions more dollars were to be spent in the open and still secret wars in three countries. In Cambodia the sequel to the events of 1969–70 was incredible, even in an age accustomed to disaster. In a once peaceful, prosperous land where malnutrition was virtually unknown, tens of thousands were left homeless and destitute. A new business made its appearance in the streets of Phnom Penh; a fleet of carts to haul away each morning the bodies of the starving children who had died during the night. The end was the same for both Cambodia and South Vietnam. Corrupt, alien régimes spawned by war and American money and ultimately by American foreign policy collapsed eventually of their own decay. "If we succeed," Kissinger once said of his peace negotiations and war policy in 1972, "we will have restored a degree of public confidence . . . that the country is not led by criminals, fools, but by serious people." Neither before nor after his peacemaking would those words seem justified.

V

Détente: Statesmanship and Débâcle

On September 22, 1972, as the secret negotiations on the war drew toward their cruel climax, *Life* magazine featured a column by its senior Washington correspondent, Hugh Sidey, on the subject of the most celebrated public official in recent history. "There never has been anything quite like Henry Kissinger in mythology or in fact," Sidey began. Here was a figure "full of pride and grand plans for civilizations and a taste for the priviliged life." He commanded "influence so vast . . . that he can cause the stock market to dip with a sentence or send prime ministers into fits by remaining silent." (The article did not mention his impact on presidents, either American or South Vietnamese.) In an era when governments had become "cumbersome, leaky and downright stubborn," Kissinger was the master among "modern statesmen . . . who find it easy to buzz off to each other's dachas and talk in plain language and with true security." As for the current talks to make peace in Indochina, Sidey disclosed the assurance presumably given privileged journalists "in private moments" by the President's Assistant for National Security: "When the record is known, everyone will see just how sincere these efforts were."

"Woodcutter, Woodcutter, can you hear me?" the article knowingly quoted Kissinger's secret service bodyguards calling him by his code name as he moved so dramatically around the world. "How far are you away, Woodcutter? Give us an ETA." It was all "the undercover world of power and intrigue." But for this "real" Kissinger, "the final lurid scenes of fiction are never played out," Sidey explained. "Instead of sometimes ending up spent and bruised like 007, Woodcutter always ends up back at the White House desk with new reports to file, new plans to incubate." In keeping with its theme, the article was entitled "The World Is the 'Woodcutter's' Ball."

Sidey's *Life* column was representative of the awe and sophisticated shallowness that came to surround Kissinger soon after he took office. Gorged on an admiring press and a cowed Congress, his public image grew until it dwarfed Nixon and the presidency itself, until it blotted out almost entirely the means by which the most powerful government in the world was conducting its foreign policy. Inside the administration, Kissinger had amassed power by intellect and instinct. He understood the bureaucratic realities of foreign policy, and preempted his rivals. He sensed the demands of his critical relations with Nixon, and so accepted, joined, sometimes led the frequently bitter intramural politics of the régime. Yet much of his success was always due to the particular weaknesses of the people he faced. Watching Rogers flounder in the despised State Department or Laird campaign for self-promotion in the formidable Pentagon, Nixon's haunted instinct was to hoard power and opportunity close to him in the White House, with Kissinger. It was also the nature of that power, flourishing in the President's sense of insecurity, that it was itself insecure, always vulnerable to a Connally or even a Haig, or to other figures still stronger or perhaps less threatening. This darker side of personality and its consequences for foreign policy, however, remained obscure through the first Nixon administration. To a large extent, it was hidden because in a sense Kissinger wielded equally impressive and on occasion equally decisive power *outside* the régime—in the press, in the Congress, ultimately in the public at large. And he acquired that power by a combination of skill and default similar to the influences propelling his rise inside. As journalists and politicians repeatedly asked how he did it, what secret explained his extraordinary position, what was the deeper source of his success, few seemed able to understand or admit that they and their own banal, exploitable impulses formed part of the answer. Kissinger demonstrably brought to office a theory and practice of public relations no less sophisticated than his approach to government. He understood the media and Congress as at base rather ordinary institutions, in which people were ruled, despite the pretense of higher motives, by bureaucratic, professional, and personal forces. He skillfully played to those forces. It was, after all, another élite world populated by a few hundred constantly intermingling inhabitants, run by a handful along ritual lines of authority and prestige. Kissinger had touched its edges at the Council on Foreign Relations, at Harvard, and with Rockefeller, and he was prepared to navigate its channels of influence. But just as he thrived in the peculiar climate of the Nixon administration, he became a celebrity also very much because the press and Congress of the early 1970s were themselves so ready to accept the comfortable fictions of "Woodcutter."

To the press he was unfailingly extravagant with his attention, and thus with the favor and flattery that went along. Kissinger's relations with the media were largely limited to background briefings, hidden from public view, during the first Nixon administration. But from the earliest days of the régime, reporters and columnists crowded his office schedule. A series of special assistants would recall that Kissinger spent what seemed as much as half his time courting the media, "or at least worrying about how to deal with them," as one remembered. Members of Kissinger's staff were authorized to explore secret negotiations, even to edit the ceaseless outpourings of his diary. But none of us was trusted to deal with that most sensitive and perilous phenomenon of them all—a journalist.

At work were several influences. There was, to begin with, Kissinger's considerable charm, a sharp, self-deprecating humor mixed with an intimacy which seemed to take his visitor into the confidences of power. He dealt with the press as he dealt with bureaucrats and foreign diplomats, telling each precisely what and as much as he thought they wanted to hear, if not in substance, at least in tone. Thus he reportedly told Henry Brandon, who wrote an admiring book on the administration's foreign policy, that he "never" lied to him as he did to his peers. He presumably neglected to tell Brandon that his phone was tapped or that the U.S. government suspected him of being associated with Eastern European intelligence. So, too, he was pointedly friendly to Joseph Kraft and the team of Roland Evans and Robert Novak, though almost contemptuous of all three in private. In his energetic accessibility, he was for many journalists the best single source (as well as the most powerful) in an administration which largely shut itself off from the media at the top and constantly admonished the bureaucracy against press contacts. "Kissinger was important to us," said a Washington *Post* editor. "He was one of the few in the administration who'd talk to us," confessed another. "My editors were amazed by my access," said a reporter, "but what really mesmerized them was to get a call themselves from Henry Kissinger where he'd say, 'I want you to know that . . .'" Moreover, this Kissinger was not only more available, but also generally more likable and adept at providing a story than the mediocre, often testy men elsewhere in the White House or at the upper reaches of the departments. When editors and producers pushed for "good" news amid the war and inflation, and later the visible corruption of the Nixon years, Kissinger was almost always what the correspondent needed: the peace negotiator, the architect of arms control, the professor with the longer, less mundane view, each with the time for an interview and a clever, not too complicated insight. Above all, he was soon recognized to be the most authoritative source on American diplomacy, the man who obviously had the President's ear in Washington and personally conducted the spectacular secret diplomacy that found him now in Peking, now in the Kremlin, now in a "safehouse" in Paris to end the war. The sheer mystique of national security—the hold on reporters (and politicians) of the secrets, the exotica, and the establishment élite surrounding foreign policy—would probably have been enough to choke off most penetrating journalism on the subject, as it had in the past for the much less exciting men before "Henry." But Kissinger added an extra element to all that high drama and personality in a business long beguiled by both. The "Merlin of American diplomacy," *Newsweek* pronounced him at one point; "the name that made foreign policy famous." The blurblike superlatives were typical of his press clippings in these first four years.

The effects of this relationship with the press were generally evident in the star-struck tone of reports and editorials like Sidey's paean to "Woodcutter." But there were also signs that the price paid by the press involved considerable self-censorship and even surrender of independence in reporting some historic events. Not surprisingly, the most grave cases issued from the war, where there was so much to hide, and the invocation by "Henry" of "national security" so compelling. Tad Szulc, then a *New York Times* correspondent, would claim convincingly years later that he had a solid story on the

U.S.-South Vietnamese invasion of Cambodia a day before the May 1970 attack was announced. When Szulc filed the story, however, the *Times*'s editors were uncertain about its validity. Having learned about the leak, an anxious Kissinger then had a conversation with Washington bureau chief Max Frankel, a talk recalled by sources at the paper as well as within the government. Arguing national security, Kissinger asked that the *Times* suppress the story. It was killed, and Szulc was later told that managing editor A. M. Rosenthal had made the decision.

When the incident was finally reported four years afterward, senior *Times* executives contended that they did not remember the conversation with Kissinger—or even Szulc's scoop on the invasion. "I'm not saying it didn't happen," was the representative comment of the managing editor, Rosenthal, "I just have no recollection of it." The *Times*'s decision could be debated as a question of press responsibility in national security like the paper's withholding under similar circumstances of the same Szulc's scoop prior to the 1961 invasion of the Bay of Pigs. As in Nixon's decision to invade Cambodia, the paper's decision to suppress an advance story may never be fully known or understood. But it was illustrative to at least some degree of the co-option by Kissinger already evolving in 1970—the admiration, the dependence on "Henry" for news and information in a sullen administration, and perhaps not least the press's belief in Kissinger and thus a reluctance to interfere with his policy.

Kissinger by no means succeeded in all such early appeals to his friends in the media. For example, also in 1970, he told the *Times*'s Washington bureau "it would not be right" for the paper to report that the United States had, unannounced, resumed massive bombing of North Vietnam accompanying the Cambodian invasion. But he stopped short of a flat denial of the facts—and the *Times* printed the story.

As Kissinger's reputation grew and the war wore on, it became increasingly difficult for the press to confront this awesome presence, just as bureaucratic rivals inside were chilled. On Wednesday, December 13, 1972, negotiations had broken down and Nixon and Kissinger were already approving JCS plans for the carpet bombing of Hanoi when *The New York Times* ran a front-page story by James Reston from Paris. Apparently based on a talk with Kissinger, the story said that the Vietnam peace talks were going well. Meanwhile in Washington, the same William Beecher who broke the Cambodian bombing got the first hints of quite another view—that the talks were foundering and that the administration was considering grave and immediate action to revive the negotiations, including resumption of the bombing of North Vietnam. Beecher filed what *Times* sources remembered as "quite a complete story" on the imminent resumption of the bombing on Thursday, December 14. But the story did not run in Friday's paper, and there ensued what participants remember as an editorial "tug-of-war" over perhaps one of the most important stories on the Nixon administration. The New York editors of the *Times* were reportedly reluctant to publish the Beecher story because it contradicted the earlier Reston story and because their "instincts," as one source put it, "were that things were great and the Pentagon was leaking to Beecher to upset the negotiations." In any case, Beecher was asked to go back for more confirmation, and later to "recast" the story to include the South Vietnamese role in the breakdown of the negotiations. Sources describe Beecher as "utterly convinced" by Friday that the story was solid. But even then, remembered one journalist watching the exchanges, "The desk wanted him to go further. They just didn't want to go off on something opposed to what the government was saying."

On Saturday, December 16, only a news conference statement by Kissinger about difficulties in the negotiations—predicted in the unpublished Beecher story two days earlier—finally convinced the doubting New York editors of the validity of Beecher's story. A "cut down" version was printed on the front page of the *Times* on Monday, December 18. But it was no longer an advance story. By then, Hanoi had announced the resumption of U.S. bombing, and the *Times* duly printed the news. Again there had been dubious judgments made in the paper itself, but the Beecher story languished too long principally because of one of the occupational weaknesses in the press which Kissinger had learned to exploit to his benefit—the reluctance to contradict such "authoritative sources" as either Kissinger or Reston. Incidents of other rejected or delayed reporting about the war were less precise than the Szulc and Beecher experiences, though equally important. During 1971 and 1972, according to the reporters involved, both *The New York Times* and the Washington *Post* had buried articles filed from Saigon on the massive Viet Cong penetration of the South Vietnamese government. When the stories were "checked" with the "reliable source" in Washington, Kissinger and other senior officials reportedly had intervened with the papers to dispute the articles, arguing against publication on grounds of damage to national security. No reports from the war were more accurate, of course; none bore so tellingly on the military calamities of the Saigon régime, or for that matter, on the course of diplomacy in 1971 and after. Kissinger's effort to kill investigative journalism on the topic inflicted on the public the administration's own bureaucratic blindness to Saigon's reality. And if such unpalatable though available facts were difficult even to expose, there was almost no chance that the press would probe deeper to analyze the less apparent psychological and intellectual origins of the war policy. When Kissinger "backgrounded" the media during the early anti-war demonstrations, he spoke to them darkly of the "real tough guys," who would be the "victors" if "political decisions were to be made in the streets," and about the threat of an American "Caesarism in which the most brutal forces in the society will take over." Yet few newspaper accounts drew the transparent tie between such statements and Kissinger's special European experience. Few reporters questioned why he brought this view to the White House, or asked whether it was an accurate depiction of the anti-war movement. And certainly few examined how such attitudes might be affecting a foreign policy purporting to end the war.

The alternating seduction and quiescence marking Kissinger's power over the press were present, too, in his diplomacy toward Congress. There he quickly and unerringly perceived the overriding importance of style and personal attention, the traditional lubricants of congressional accommodation. More than the substance of policy, more than exactly what was said, what mattered on Capitol Hill was that one observed the form of talking intimately to the senior members. The evening phone calls to senators and congressmen, the serious chats at cocktail parties, might be, as they most often were, utterly meaningless in making policy. But that was where the wit and superior intelligence and mystique of the subject, all the gravity at work on the press as well, were brought to bear. And the mere act of calling or meeting or socially chatting reached the deepest chord in many in Congress, playing to their sense of self-inflicted powerlessness and the desire to be somehow privy (or at least seem privy) to policy while not responsible for it. So they also had their own reasons for a genteel co-option by "Henry"—he would be the only high official in memory so widely and so proudly dropped in Washington conversations by that unmistakable first name.

The congressional abdication in the making of foreign policy was already far advanced when Kissinger took office in 1969; but his personal standing with Congress in the first Nixon administration in many ways symbolized the lowest point in that irresponsibility. Though executive privilege shielded him from formal appearances in the Senate or House, he went out of his way to stage private briefings of key members of the Foreign Affairs, Armed Services, and other significant committees in both houses. He was also the star performer at the official White House briefings for congressmen. On every occasion, however, whether with one politician or a dozen, he would be, in a fundamental sense, in control. He was the purveyor of secrets, the presence who certified their importance among their colleagues, the increasingly famous face beside them in the photographs seen by their constituents back home. His most formidable potential adversaries in the Congress he maneuvered most skillfully. To William Fulbright, the Arkansas Democrat and doyen of the Vietnam opposition, he portrayed himself as the champion of peace—the "Walt Rostow of peace negotiations," as he often put it—amid a bellicose President and bureaucracy, all the while promising a favorable postwar change of policy toward Fulbright's other cause, the Middle East. With the conservative supporters of the war, such as John Stennis of Mississippi who chaired the Senate Armed Services Committee, he was the President's lone ally for an "honorable peace" among all the wavering cabinet members and spineless bureaucrats. And so it went through the shadings between: a virtuoso performance, as with the press, which told his listeners what they hoped to hear, glossed over the differences, and sustained the whole presentation in the Washington mode, at once highly personal yet absolving them all from personal responsibility for what was happening in policy.

The result in the Congress was to help stave off for nearly four years the anti-war legislation that had begun in the Johnson years. The Church-Cooper amendment finally prohibited the use of ground troops in Cambodia and Laos in response to the Cambodian invasion, but that only returned the American war, as it were, to its original bounds. In North and South Vietnam, the administration acted with a free hand until the end. Each congressional effort to withdraw remaining troops, or to stop the bombing, or even to prohibit an invasion of North Vietnam, failed against the majority of Republicans and conservative Democrats, joined sometimes by co-opted liberals, whom Kissinger's ardent courtship kept in line.

What was seldom acknowledged in either the press or Congress was that Kissinger not only dominated them by technique, but also because on the glittering surface he was doing so much of what both institutions conventionally wanted of American foreign policy. In the final account, the mythology of an honorable withdrawal from the war, the tolerance of the increasingly unseen human costs, even the presumption of a domestic majority waiting to punish the "losers," were accepted by the Congress and the press much as by the White House. It was an agonizing choice for institutions accustomed to foregoing independent judgment, not to mention risking public wrath. Asked in effect to look at the war and country free of the old stereotypes or to cede judgment (and risk) to a policy represented so impressively by Kissinger, the decision was never really in doubt. After three more years of war, suddenly in the summer of 1971 the promise of the opening to Peking and a great arms control summit in Moscow appeared, two feats the liberal Democrats could only sheepishly applaud, having advocated both and having watched their own régime under LBJ fail at both while plunging into Indochina.

Even over the ensuing years, when Kissinger went on to become Secretary of State and his public image was eventually to be badly tarnished, it was a lasting dilemma for the Democratic opposition that they were trying to attack a foreign policy that had done so much they advocated. This larger preemption was only possible because of the shallowness with which the media and Congress viewed foreign policy. What Kissinger was accomplishing in diplomacy with such dazzle and novelty and approval was profoundly affected by how he had done it, both in Washington and abroad. The "success" would not have seemed so clear, so exculpating, had it been perceived with greater insight into how foreign policy was made, or how its future could be mortgaged by the manner of earlier decisions. The shame and outrage of the war policy clearly dissipated in this ignorance. But perhaps the more historic casualty was the détente that excused for so many the savagery in Indochina. Intent on Kissinger's visible performance, both the Congress and press neglected how much the statesmanship belonged to Richard Nixon. Further, when the transfixed witnesses saw, by definition, nothing of importance beyond "Henry's" schedule and agenda, when they could not seem to believe that anyone so brilliant, so in control as to consult them, adopt their policies, could indeed blunder and lose control, then a whole range of foreign policy disasters accompaying détente—from Moscow itself to Bangladesh to Central Africa to Latin America—would go largely unnoticed. And when much of this did later become apparent, there was a sense of puzzlement and perfidy in both the Congress and the press that ironically threatened the political survival of the best of Kissinger's achievements. Gratifying as it was for a time, Kissinger's separate peace with the press and Congress had its price, too. Like the war policy, the statesmanship and débâcle of the reach for détente in Peking and Moscow during 1971–72 was a more complex reality than the cartoon portraits of "Woodcutter." The statesmanship lay in political and bureaucratic courage worthy of emulation; the débâcle in willfulness, neglect, and a reactionary concept of world politics the country could no longer afford.

As the Sino-American détente became a commonplace of international politics after 1972, one of the least controversial and most bipartisan of U.S. policies, it was hard to evoke what an extraordinary transformation it had represented in American politics. Of the entire generation of postwar presidential politicians, Nixon had seemed most encumbered by the hostility with Communist China. His political roots were in the hysteria triggered by the Chinese Nationalists' fall in 1949. In southern California (where the issue always had a geographic immediacy not felt in the East) as well as Washington his ties to the Republican right and the China lobby were old and strong. Through eight years as Vice President and nearly eight more out of office, he had publicly characterized the Peking government as a dangerous, aggressive enemy. Yet China seems to have exercised a continuing attraction to his curiosity and political opportunism. According to some accounts, he tried in vain in 1960 to arrange a secret trip to the mainland to outflank his Democratic opponents, but in later campaign rhetoric he returned to language as strident as ever about the Chinese "threat." The subject went nearly unmentioned when he ran again in 1968, though his *Foreign Affairs* article the year before had vaguely declared, ". . . We simply cannot afford to leave China forever outside the family of nations. . . ."

Once elected, however, he moved as deliberately and consistently toward détente with China as he would toward any other policy goal, foreign or domestic. The subject was one of the many portents in the talks with Kissinger at the Pierre. "You're not going to believe this," one aide said then to another, relaying Kissinger's debriefing of an early meeting, "but Nixon wants to reorganize China." It was never that simple, but the drive was there from the beginning, before Kissinger himself had the interest or political bureaucratic inclination to raise it. China was thus one of the loftier topics of the "Butterfieldgrams" spilling out of the Oval Office. Like the other initiatives, musings, and venom in that medium, the policy was incubated in strict secrecy. In a larger context, though, its origins were contained in the most public assessments Nixon had been making about himself and America between the lines of his 1968 campaign. If he saw himself so proudly as a President concerned first with peace and diplomacy; if he sensed as a politician that the country had outgrown, in some measure at least, the cold war pugnacity of the 1950s, developing a healthy fear of the tension and isolation of the nuclear powers; if in that evolution of opinion, China and the popular image of its quilt-jacketed hordes were particularly significant, then making peace with Peking would be excellent politics, as well as an act of statesmanship. That this complicated man saw one or both of these opportunities in no way detracted from the larger meaning of what he undertook. For two terms, the supposedly shrewder, more enlightened John Kennedy and Lyndon Johnson had pursued the old China policy with occasional rhetorical hints of change; more important, they had deferred to a senior officialdom, men like Dean Rusk and Walt Rostow whose obsession with Vietnam sprang from fearful ignorance of China and the new tides in world affairs. As they had not, Nixon now saw the Chinese not only as a menace, but as an independent nation, fearful of the Russians pressing down on their northern flank, distracted by their own domestic turmoil, and ready, like any conventional power, to strike a diplomatic balance with Japan and the United States.

No impetus was more earnestly denied in later public or private explanations of the China policy, yet none was more central, than Nixon's evolving view of the Sino-Soviet rivalry. There were domestic and foreign policy reasons for coming to terms with the Chinese whatever the effects on other great power relations. But the enmity between the USSR and the People's Republic provided a rare opportunity for diplomacy. Fear of the Russians opened China to Washington. A U.S.-Chinese reconciliation would be another spur to the Soviets to negotiate their own issues with the United States. Détente with Moscow at once encouraged and balanced détente with Peking. It was a delicate calculus, involving two sets of leaders with their own volatile oligarchic politics, military pressures, domestic dissent, and not least an instinctive xenophobia bred of war and more than two decades of acrimony. Yet the calculation was there in Nixon, if only vaguely, from the first discussions of China. The international reality the previous administration could hardly admit into unread State Department intelligence notes was the premise of the new régime's approach to its most historic foreign policy. As the overtures to the Chinese began in 1969–70 and the Soviet ambassador nervously called "Henry" to ask what each one meant, as the Chinese responses quickened with the flaring of Sino–Soviet border clashes and the signs of progress in U.S.–Soviet negotiations, the full force of triangular diplomacy was confirmed.

There was still another motive drawing Nixon toward China, however, and in a psychological sense it may have been as necessary as any diplomatic or political reckoning. More than the détente with Moscow, certainly more than any other single foreign policy pursuit, the initiative to China loomed very much as the work of one man. He could still contemplate it in the context of the presidency as perhaps he had earlier in 1960—a single bold stroke accomplished not through elaborate technical agreements, but essentially through the strength of his presence. It represented the sheer symbolism of the statesman, without the bureaucrats he hated and feared, without the untidy governmental processes that slowed and subverted great plans. Aptly, it was also a policy that could be conducted in immaculate secrecy with another closed government, to burst upon the world with a dramatic announcement as they chose. The China policy reflected the abiding style as well as intellectual substance of the lonely, controlling politician in Nixon.

Kissinger himself was never as decisive in this sense of self and history that animated Nixon in the China diplomacy. Doubting the prospects, and perhaps Nixon's own commitment, he reacted only haltingly to the first Butterfieldgrams in 1969. He did not ignore them, though, as he would so many other digressions; Nixon's interest was too sustained and the subject too grave. Kissinger played an essential role by filtering bits of the presidential attitude to the bureaucracy. He orchestrated through his alliance with Elliot Richardson a government-wide acceptance of the first U.S. concessions in trade and travel—tentative steps the State Department and Pentagon were prepared to take, although no one there officially proposed or anticipated that the initiative go so far. But Kissinger's singular achievement in the opening to China was in the diplomatic style he exercised, suitably hidden from the rest of Washington. Like Nixon, of course, he savored the secretiveness, the control, the meticulously crafted notes and talking points, the hints and gestures given. Just as the China opening could not have begun or continued without Nixon's vision, it would never have been so skillfully executed without Kissinger. Certainly no one else in the administration, even with the President's confidence, approached his ability to provide what the Chinese gambit required. His predecessors were no match. McGeorge Bundy snapping out his recommendation for the first punitive raids on Hanoi, Walt Rostow stamping out guerrilla wars from the Situation Room—both men lacked Kissinger's depth of intellect and it is hard to imagine any of them talking with Chou En-Lai with equal subtlety.

The accommodation toward the Chinese involved a classic diplomatic mixture of public gesture, secret contracts, and vivid circumstance. During 1969, Washington lifted the old travel and import restrictions, publicly urged cultural exchanges, privately suggested renewal of the Warsaw talks between the two governments, and ended U.S. naval patrols in the Taiwan Straits. In the same period, Sino-Soviet armed clashes along the Ussuri River at the Manchurian border climaxed with poisonous propaganda and a massing of troops on both sides. By early autumn 1969, Kissinger had commissioned NSC contingency plans for a Russo-Chinese war—a study which showed American diplomacy at that point dangerously devoid of possibilities to deter either antagonist in a war that could involve nuclear weapons, a preventive Soviet move in Europe, and the ultimate catastrophe. Meanwhile, the Chinese noticeably moderated their anti-American propaganda, and agreed to reopen the Warsaw talks, moving them to their embassy there. They also indicated early

in the talks, as the minutes of one meeting recounted, that "a representative of the President would be welcome in Peking."

But ultimately the most instrumental diplomacy—and in another
sense the most tragic—began that late summer and autumn when in
an exchange of visits Nixon tried to enlist Pakistani President Yahya
Khan as a go-between with Peking. On the face of it, the involvement
of Pakistan was logical enough. The Yahya régime had been tacitly
allied with the Chinese in the South Asian subcontinental rivalry
with India and her Russian patron. Pakistan was also an old, well-
armed American client, supposedly (now ironically) a buffer against
the Soviets and the Chinese. A succession of U.S. presidents had long
preferred its swaggering, British-mannered military government as
more congenial and comfortably manly than the unctuous nonaligned civilians who ruled India. Nixon was no exception, and his
personal rapport with Yahya, who was somewhat more florid and
rough-hewn than his predecessors, was strong. For the Pakistanis the
mediation bound their sponsors together in the South Asian jockeying, and promised its generals a fresh flow of weapons from the
grateful Americans, who had curtailed shipments under congressional pressures after the Indo-Pakistani war of 1967. The bargain, ex-
changing guns for mediation, was sealed with Yahya in Washington
in October 1970. Only weeks later the Pakistani dictator was in
Peking bearing a secret letter from Nixon, the first of a series of
messages obligingly carried back and forth by the Pakistanis over the
next several months. At the same moment, seemingly ignored by all
the maneuvering governments, a cyclone and tidal wave left 300,000
dead and 4 million injured or destitute in East Pakistan—the Bengali
province separated from Punjabi, West Pakistan, by 1,000 miles of
India and deep ethnic and cultural differences. When the Yahya
régime responded sluggishly to that disaster, the effect was incendi-
ary on the already strong forces of separatism in East Pakistan. Ahead
lay one of the great human calamities of the century, and one of the
débâcles of American foreign policy that marred the statesmanship
of détente in Peking and Moscow.

Interrupted by the Cambodian invasion in the spring of 1970 and
the South Vietnamese attack into Laos the following January, the
secret contacts with China suddenly resumed in March 1971. At that
point the Pakistani ambassador delivered to Kissinger's White House
office the Chinese message inviting Nixon to send an envoy to Pe-

king. In April came the famous Chinese invitation to the American table tennis team, then in Japan. By May the White House told Peking the secret representative would be Kissinger. By June a small group on the NSC staff had prepared briefings for Kissinger, again in total secrecy from the rest of government, save Rogers, whom Nixon eventually told after the U.S. reply accepting the Chinese invitation. Arrangements were promptly made with Pakistan to fly Kissinger clandestinely to China during a visit to South Asia in July. There followed his disappearance with a diplomatic "illness" in Islamabad, the flight over the Himalayas, Nixon's stunning television announcement of the mission and his own future journey to China.

Kissinger conducted the technical negotiations during the February summit in Peking as he had the earlier notes and the July talks. But the essential brilliance of the diplomacy inside China—the communiqué which accommodated sharply conflicting views by the device of separate U.S. and Chinese paragraphs on controversial topics, the moderate tone of the discussions with the Chinese leaders— belonged again to Nixon. It was he who decided, without the hesitation that reportedly plagued both Kissinger and Rogers, to soften the U.S. language on Taiwan without changing the genuine substance of Washington's commitment to the Nationalists. It was he who absorbed, along with the popular acclaim, the bitter criticism of the Republican right and the backdoor sniping at the policy by Vice President Agnew in preparation for some future presidential campaign. The same President who struck impulsively at North Vietnam in the grip of other myths could also break through similar barriers of race, history, and ideology to take the boldest, perhaps most sensible U.S. initiative of the postwar era. To have disengaged from Vietnam without this opening to China would have left America's Asian policy in the same isolation and rancor that had sowed the seeds of the Indochina disaster. At last able (and expected) to treat with Peking as an independent power possessed of some mutual interests, Nixon's successors and their constituents would never again be prey to the ignorant rationale that had cost so much in the Vietnamese war. Similarly, to negotiate a détente with the Russians alone would have left festering—and perhaps even provoked—the Sino-Soviet hostility that had become the single gravest threat to world peace in the early 1970s. There would be no proof that Nixon's three-cornered strategy helped deter a Soviet preemptive nuclear strike on

China, or that fear of some U.S.-Soviet condominium was a decisive motive in restraining a Chinese attack. But in the twists of *Real-politik* in 1972 and afterward—as Chinese children drilled to repel an expected Russian invasion and Soviet troops remained massed in Siberia and Central Asia—those influences were clearly felt. The uneasy truce along the far eastern frontier of China and Russia over the ensuing years owed something to American diplomacy, which, before Richard Nixon, had been impotent to surmount its own mindless posture of belligerence in Asia.

The détente with the Soviet Union promulgated at the Moscow summit of 1972 grew out of a more familiar diplomatic history, and another intense personal commitment from the President as both politician and Chief Executive. Nixon's past, of course, had been as impeccably militant against the Russians as the Chinese. His first summit diplomacy took place in the snarling kitchen debate with Premier Khrushchev in Moscow in 1959. There were scant revelations in his 1968 campaign rhetoric, still filled with the usual incantations of military strength, announcing his intentions in office. But here, too, he had made a private passage from zealous young prosecutor to mature negotiator, a passage undoubtedly made easier by the expectation that it would win him votes because of the public mood of the time. If China was a wholly novel and only potentially winning issue, summitry with the Russians was sure-fire presidential politics. The history of popular approval stretched back for at least a decade, from Johnson's last gasp in the polls at Glassboro through the public disappointment at Eisenhower's abortive Paris meeting with Khrushchev in 1960. What was extraordinary about Nixon's reach for détente was not that he did it—by 1972 that much as a political and diplomatic preoccupation was almost conventional—but rather, how he did it.

In sheer number and importance of agreements reached between the two powers, the Moscow summit was unprecedented. The effort was not only to cushion the rivalry through a new sense of dialogue, the ostensible purpose of past summits, but also to knit together the mutual interests of Washington and Moscow in a web of specific pacts. A series of trade, cultural, scientific, and maritime agreements were negotiated in 1970–72 and signed during the first days of the week-long Nixon stay. At the heart of détente, however, was the strategic arms control pact, named SALT I, concluded only in the final hours. It included the long-sought limitation on ABMs which amounted to a mutual renunciation of defense against nuclear weapons, a freeze on strategic missiles, and a limitation on ballistic missile submarines. The agreements gave the USSR roughly a three-to-two superiority in numbers of offensive missiles and perhaps three times the megatonnage of the American nuclear force. Still, the United States retained more than twice as many nuclear warheads. Though specific aspects of the agreement would later come under attack—not least the vigilance of the U.S. monitoring of Soviet compliance—its essence was historic. The nuclear superpowers had acknowledged a kind of parity and agreed on a plateau to slow what McNamara had called so aptly the "mad momentum" of the strategic arms race. The treaty did not alter the larger reality that both nations possessed the nuclear power to lay waste to themselves and the world many times over. Refinement and development of offensive weapons would go on, feeding the political irrationality and the insatiable military-industrial establishments on both sides. Nonetheless, in relative terms it was a major achievement, and like the approach to China, it was a permanent attribute of Nixon's presidential leadership, whatever followed.

But much of what made it so, the secret of Nixon's command and of Kissinger's essential genius played out in the SALT process, lay largely beyond public view and beneath the surface of most journalistic accounts. In many respects, the most decisive diplomacy on the arms control which formed the underpinning for détente took place well before the presidential party went to Peking or Moscow. It was achieved not in shrewd bargaining with the Russians on numbers or a more subtle evocation of the Chinese peril in some gilded conference hall, but rather within the bureaucracy of the U.S. government itself, usually over the plastic veneer and metal furniture of a conference room in the White House West Basement. There, by a unique disregard and discipline of the bureaucrats, Nixon and Kissinger largely defeated the inertia and disarray that had paralyzed American arms control diplomacy for years under their predecessors.

The first adversary the administration faced in the SALT talks was itself. On no other foreign policy subject was the White House so politically vulnerable to the bureaucracy. During or after the fact, the strong opposition of the joint chiefs or the intelligence agencies, echoing in Congress and the press, might easily wipe out almost any negotiation with the Russians. Yet there was also a sizable civilian officialdom in the State Department and the Arms Control and Disarmament Agency (ACDA) capable of raising the opposite and similarly damaging cry of missed chances for negotiations. Nor could the White House prudently ignore the rest of the government in a subject of such technical complexity. Under Johnson, SALT had been a welter of confused and conflicting intelligence estimates, technical assessments, and negotiating points. Successful negotiation required careful coordination of those splintered views, separating accuracy from bureaucratic advocacy, in order to produce a coherent American position. It was Kissinger's major and mostly unseen influence which managed to subdue this bureaucratic anarchy. Though his success again rested ultimately on the larger presidential commitment and personal backing, he was in that sense a much more primary and moving force behind détente with the Soviets than he had been in the China policy.

Kissinger's general diplomatic vision of détente was as clear and premeditated as Nixon's political instincts on the subject. The shape and negotiating techniques of a post-cold war settlement between America and Russia were central themes in his later writings on U.S. policy and already implicit in 1957 in *A World Restored*. Détente, with all its operational contradictions and fundamental logic after 1972, reflected his concept of a great two-power condominium, joined together by a framework of personal contacts and formal agreements, which might mitigate rivalries and lead even to collaboration on common problems. But that vision would have remained an academic theory without his matching appreciation of the real bureaucratic obstacles and opportunities.

In the early months of the Nixon administration, Kissinger deliberately left SALT in its state of chronic malaise, putting responsibility for the first presidential directives on negotiations with the Arms Control and Disarmament Agency. When the old habits soon became apparent—the endless, incestuous tinkering with processes and papers, the bland refusal of the Pentagon to provide data or positions, and ACDA's timorous resignation to the military's familiar defiance—Kissinger moved decisively. His principal weapons were themselves two common bureaucratic instruments: secrecy and control of the agenda. In 1969 he arranged with Soviet Ambassador

Dobrynin an exclusive, ultra-secret "back channel" communication system, a cable traffic exchanged between the two men by which the White House and the Kremlin could communicate directly without the knowledge of the rest of the U.S. government. The back channel was to be the scourge of the bureaucrats, and a legitimate object of later heated controversy over alleged mishandling of the SALT talks. But at critical moments between 1970 and the 1972 summit, it allowed Nixon and Kissinger to "anticipate" Soviet positions and test their own, free of the bickering and bureaucratic preemption that customarily overtook issues within Washington when both sides' positions seeped through the inter-agency mesh. The back channel, in fact, would make the difference between a May 1972 treaty and deadlock. In the closing days before the summit, only Kissinger, Nixon, and a few NSC aides would know of the precise Soviet offer to limit submarine launched missiles. It was a question the bureaucracy had long struggled over—with the joint chiefs cryptically withholding their backing of SALT in return for White House support of the planned Trident submarine program. And in these tangled internal politics, supposedly fateful numbers on Russian strength were often no more than expendable fuel for bureaucratic budgets. Consequently, using the back channel, Kissinger was able to place the actual Soviet offer of submarine missile limits in the center of a "hypothetical" range of options, and thus maneuver the joint chiefs' acceptance of the treaty. In a sense oblivious to the actual numbers, the military settled in traditional bureaucratic style on the middle choice without realizing its diplomatic significance and without holding the administration hostage to a firm commitment on Trident.

Along with the back channel, Kissinger controlled the institutional chaos of SALT by bringing it into the discipline of the NSC system. His vehicle was the Verification Panel. Originally founded to study issues of Soviet compliance in a future treaty, the Panel would also be embroiled in controversy for its performance after SALT I. But its part in securing the agreement, if not in later policing it, was crucial. As he did with the other bodies of the NSC network, here Kissinger could—by dint of his intellect, his independent staff, and the palpable authority of the President hovering there in the West Basement—force to the surface the evasions and equivocations of the policy process on arms control. Senior officials of State, Defense, the joint chiefs, the CIA, and other concerned agencies all sat at the table. Under Kissinger's orchestration, the agenda at once drew them out on positions and, equally important, politically drew the separate agencies *into* the shaping of a negotiating posture. Given the volatile domestic politics of defense and the convoluted bureaucratic maneuvering, that joint participation was the essential condition for the U.S. agreement to SALT. For more than two years, by means of excrutiating haggling, cajoling, and deceptive ploys, through victories and defeats in which a Russian never entered the room, SALT was born of Kissinger's diplomatic virtuosity with his own colleagues. To the end, of course, the specter of the supreme bureaucratic veto, the defection of the joint chiefs, hung above the negotiations. In a frantic last day and night of negotiations in Moscow, the prospect of that veto stopped Nixon and Kissinger short of further concessions they might have made to break the deadlock, concessions on what was in any case the flexible issue of submarine missiles. But the Soviets, subduing their own bureaucratic inertia, agreed to the final terms.

The SALT treaty was undeniably the product of devoted diplomacy with the Soviets at the working level of the negotiations in Helsinki and elsewhere. It reflected the hard work and insight of intelligence analysts laboring honestly in the bowels of the CIA and Pentagon to see the shape, size, and future silhouette of the Soviet nuclear force. Almost certainly the most important external factor was the triangular *Realpolitik* with China. Only a day after the critical negotiating round on ABM had begun in July 1971, Kissinger first landed in Peking; and the progress in SALT over the ensuing months gathered speed as the Sino-American détente became a decisive new international reality. But everything traced back in the end to the two men in the White House and their extraordinary, often risky, usually effective assault on their own government. Even as Kissinger flew to China, the May 20, 1971, public statement by Nixon announcing that last critical round on ABM—which broke the bureaucratic stalemate on both sides and freed the negotiations to proceed as they did—was made possible by the intense, secret negotiations between Kissinger and Dobrynin conducted in the back channel.

Yet the Nixon-Kissinger statesmanship in Peking and Moscow carried a price, and a paradox. And that darker side of the record would be recognized only slowly.

In December 1970—as the White House resumed its secret contacts with China, as the maneuvering on SALT went on in the West Basement as well as with the Russians, as the first plans were made for the summits that would crown the feverish, historic diplomacy—an obscure young official named Joel Woldman was writing an intelligence report that foreshadowed part of the tragedy. Woldman was a highly trained specialist on South Asia who had been languishing in the makework of the U.S. Information Agency in Washington. By the random fortunes of personnel switches, a "slot" had come open for a few months on the Pakistani desk of State's Bureau of Intelligence and Research, and he wangled a temporary detail to fill it. If more lively than the USIA position, the intelligence job was still very much part of the vast waste and featherbedding of the Department. From a linoleum-floored, gray metal cubicle in the back hallways of Foggy Bottom, its occupant went to the endless rounds of vague meetings, wrote the bland reports unlikely to rouse the bias or wrath of more powerful officers in the mission abroad and the regional bureau in Washington, and much of the time simply lasted out the day, the month, the year of his apprenticeship. It was no different in those last months of 1970, except that beyond the deadening routine there was the evidence of an ominous crisis mounting over the South Asian subcontinent. And Woldman, the temporary, fill-in expert from USIA, was perhaps the first man in the U.S. government to sense the magnitude of what was happening. He wrote his analysis in time to forewarn the administration, but was largely ignored.

Following the disastrous November cyclone in East Pakistan and the indifferent relief efforts of the central régime, events moved swiftly. In early December, the East held their long-postponed elections for a constitutional assembly. The results, a popular referendum on years of exploitation as well as the angry sequel to the recent calamity, gave the Awami League party, led by Sheik Mujibur Rahman, a stunning victory, and a 53 percent majority over the representatives of West Pakistan in the assembly scheduled for March 1971. In the East, the Awami triumph was taken as a mandate for nearly complete autonomy. In the West, it struck a complacent government as a sudden menace to vital interests. For the Punjabis, the confederation with the still colonized East housed both the symbol of national power and a source of substantial profit for the oligarchy standing behind the generals and politicians in Islamabad. Woldman's memorandum traced the background to that point, and was then grimly prophetic. The West might concede the granting of some constitutional process of self-determination. More probably, he predicted, the Yahya régime would move to suppress the unruly politics by sheer military force—after its model of a British colonial army that had preferred to deal with Bengali agitation in that manner. The schism between East and West had gone too deep, Woldman warned. An attempt to subjugate a nation of 70 million would lead to much bloodshed, eventual civil war, and sooner or later the emergence of an independent Bengali state. Moreover, the paper argued, the crisis would inevitably embroil neighboring India, her patron Russia, and Pakistan's ally China. The developments in South Asia would soon have "major" consequences for the history of the subcontinent, and, not least, for American interests there.

Slowly, haltingly, Woldman's paper wound its way through the usual maze of clearances in the State Department, to be sent forward to senior officials on the seventh floor and in the White House as one more intelligence note in the daily shower of paper. Months afterward, when its prophecy and neglect were maybe too painful to acknowledge, the responsible NSC staff officers would recall only vaguely having seen it, and ranking State Department diplomats could not remember it at all. The memo was thus not only prophetic of the crisis, but of the distraction of the U.S. government over the year to come. From bottom to top, the administration in part could not see, in part did not wish to see, the human and diplomatic ruin in South Asia until it was too late. As 1971 began, Woldman returned to the USIA, his memo was filed, and the predictable sequence unfolded.

Through most of March, Yahya and Mujib conducted fitful and increasingly acrid negotiations. Their positions were duly reported to Washington by the U.S. Embassy in Pakistan, which perceived a client's natural virtues in the Western case. Out of much the same bureaucratic chemistry, the American Consulate-General in Dacca, East Pakistan, sympathized with the Awami League. By mid-March, CIA, Pentagon, and electronic intelligence sources all reported back to Washington the telltale Pakistani military preparations, warnings that were never relayed to the Dacca Consulate, let alone to the then unarmed Bengalis. Near midnight on March 25, the blow fell on Dacca. As army tanks moved through the streets and artillery raked the university and other residential sections, there began one of the more savage episodes of military reprisal against a civilian population. Over the first three days the rampaging troops may have killed more than 10,000, most by indiscriminate fire, though hundreds of students, teachers, and professionals of the small political élite of East Bengal were systematically executed. Mujib was arrested and taken to West Pakistan. The killing continued for several weeks in Dacca and the countryside, adding thousands more to the carnage.

In many respects, the next nine months were to be as the Woldman paper had suggested. The repression drove the Bengalis into guerrilla warfare; across a 1,000-mile supply line, the hold of the Pakistani army gradually weakened; an independent Bangladesh emerged. But no one had gauged the enormous human costs in that evolution. As the repression went on in unrelieved brutality, as many as 1 million people perished. By July 1971, an impartial World Bank team of observers reported that the civil strife had created a major "catastrophe" in the already destitute economy of the East. And by that autumn, the flood of Bengali refugees fleeing into India had swollen to 10 million, the greatest single mass exodus of its kind in modern history. For the political sympathy it provoked in West Bengal, for the opportunity it offered to dismember and weaken an old enemy, the secession struggle made likely the intervention of India. The crushing presence of the refugees made an Indo-Pakistani war all but certain.

It was one of those dramatic, pregnant conjunctions in the history of diplomacy: during the last week in March, probably at the very hour the Pakistani army was carrying out one of its day-and-night executions of Bengalis, the Pakistani ambassador in Washington entered the White House to deliver to Henry Kissinger the secret message from China formally inviting a presidential envoy to Peking. From the beginning, of course, American policy toward the humanitarian crisis in East Pakistan was hostage to its China diplomacy. The two men who so largely controlled U.S. foreign relations were to be found in the Lincoln Sitting Room or the Executive Office Building, not reading the cables from Dacca or New Delhi but absorbed in the nuances of the latest Chinese note, planning their reply, contemplating the historic stroke ahead. When the bloodbath in East Pakistan intruded on all that, it was a distant rumbling of vague origins and still vaguer outcome. There was no question of denouncing or turning on a Pakistani régime that was right in the middle of the delicate negotiations with China, on whose plane, from whose territory, under whose cover of secrecy, Kissinger would fly to Peking that July. And later, when the horror became undeniable, the China trip was already there and the heady triangular strategy toward Moscow already at work. Then it would be important to show the Chinese that this White House meant business, that it would stand by an ally even amid a public outcry or other diplomatic pressure. Besides, the ally was Pakistan, whom this President favored as much as his predecessors had before him. And standing to gain at Pakistan's expense were the Indians, for whom he shared the same old matching distaste. All those calculations were present in 1971 as the United States continued to support the faltering military dictatorship in West Pakistan. The débâcle of the policy belonged amply to the White House, the price Nixon and Kissinger were willing to pay in their distorted zeal to reach Peking with all its political and diplomatic prizes. At the same time, there were also other influences shrouding the policy. Other men as well misread the portents, protected their interests, accepted the foolish callousness of the stand. Like their successes at the summit meetings, the policy Nixon and Kissinger conducted toward the tragedy in East Pakistan was only possible because of the peculiar weaknesses and vacillation in much of the rest of government.

Watching the slaughter of the Bengalis, the U.S. Consulate in Dacca sent to Washington a remarkable series of secret dispatches in which sensibility and decisive judgment suddenly breached the customary numbness of foreign service prose. "We here in Dacca," began a March 28 telegram, "are mute and horrified witnesses to a reign of terror by the Pakistan military . . ." The régime was practicing nothing less than "selective genocide," the cable reported, in a term that would come to symbolize the repression. It concluded that the murders would now finally destroy the last prospects for the unity of the two wings, that "the breakup of Pakistan as we have known it [is] now inevitable." The telegrams urged an immediate high-level statement in Washington to deplore the genocide and express concern for Mujib's safety. But what seemed clear outrage within earshot of the gunfire in Dacca was less urgent in the State Department in Washington. Along with the dispatches from the East had come the predictable cables from the U.S. Embassy in Islamabad, finding the "reported" actions "regrettable," and recommending against any "premature" judgment about this "internal affair" of a "staunch ally." The embassy also argued against an early evacuation of the Americans in Dacca lest the departure imply an official slap at Pakistan. These conflicting telegrams in hand, the White House lost in a distracted silence, none of the officials in South Asia or Foggy Bottom aware of the momentous cables arriving from China to Kissinger via Pakistan, for the first two weeks of the repression the State Department simply observed its most common habit whatever the administration—it equivocated. Back to Dacca went the careful, understated, questioning telegrams of a foreign ministry trying somehow to blunt the reality with rhetoric and routine. When, at the insistence of the Dacca consul-general, the evacuation of Americans began on March 30, the Department described it as a "thinning out" of women and children. Even then the shocked and appalled evacuees were placed aboard Pakistani military aircraft rather than U.S. planes, in a characteristic half-gesture toward both the Yahya régime and the worried U.S. mission in Islamabad.

In a tone of almost poignant disbelief, the Dacca Consulate reacted on April 6, 1971, with the most moving of its extraordinary cables, and one destined for the melancholy folklore of the American foreign service. Signed by nineteen officers from the consulate staff, the AID mission, and USIA, the telegram registered "strong dissent with fundamental aspects of this policy," which "serves neither our moral interests broadly defined, nor our national interests narrowly defined." In failing to denounce the suppression and atrocities, it went on, "our government has evidenced what many will call moral bankruptcy." The dissenters pointed out the "irony" that even the Soviets had sent a strong protest to Yayha, and that, "In our most recent policy paper for Pakistan, our interests in Pakistan were defined as primarily humanitarian rather than strategic." The telegram concluded by repeating once again that the crisis in East Pakistan was one "in which unfortunately the overworked term genocide is applicable," and urging "as professional public servants" that "our policies be redirected in order to salvage our nation's position as a moral leader of the free world."

The dissent was formally transmitted and endorsed by the consul-general in Dacca, a forty-eight-year-old career officer named Archer Blood who was at the peak of nearly a quarter-century climb through posts in the Near East and Asia. Smooth, discreet, conventionally promotable, Blood seemed to many before and after the events of 1971 a pattern of the service ideal. At this historic moment in Dacca that spring, he was spared the dilemma that gagged so many of his colleagues from Saigon to Biafra to South Asia, the choice between clients and principles. Through the horror at the murder of a people they had known and in a sense represented, Blood and his mission found a rare bureaucratic courage and clarity of national interest. Yet in the larger context of American foreign policy, their insight now was too little, too late. It was very much because the foreign service was so often otherwise, so frequently in Washington and abroad provincial, muddled, and meek, that it was now so wholly excluded and ignored by Nixon and Kissinger, who knew very well—if Blood and his colleagues did not—that there were indeed certain new "strategic" interests in Pakistan which no State Department policy paper could be trusted to explain. And even without the iron control of the White House and its clandestine priorities, there was a naïve quality in the appeal of the Dacca cable to the authority of policy papers and "national interests narrowly defined." Whether Blood and diplomats like him, their careers spent mainly in the field, understood or not, their cables fell among capricious personal politics in the State Department as well as at the White House.

The dissent telegram arrived in Washington at 2:00 A.M. on April 6, and by the opening of State Department business had set off a potential bureaucratic rebellion. Emboldened by the cable, junior officers on the Pakistani desk by noon had written a memorandum to Secretary Rogers recommending a U.S. statement condemning the genocide and an embargo on arms and economic aid for the Yahya government. The draft memorandum went to the office of Joseph Sisco, then Assistant Secretary for Near East and South Asian Affairs, and thus the superior through whom the Bureau's officers communicated with the seventh floor of the Department and beyond. At fifty-two and also the high point so far of his own career, Sisco was in many respects the organizational obverse of Blood in Dacca. He had spent his twenty years of service entirely in the Department in Washington. He was one of a scattering of such shrewd and durable bureaucrats (Kissinger's old army friend and NSC aide for European affairs, Helmut Sonnenfeldt, was another) who reached the top ranks of the career without the usually essential unction of a foreign posting. In his case, Sisco distinguished himself in the small, happily forgotten appendage of State acting as the Washington desk for the U.S. Mission to the United Nations in New York. There for years he handled the verbose, meaningless UN effluence most FSOs thought unrewarding. There, too, he cultivated both a pugnacious style that set him apart from the oily culture of Foggy Bottom and a coterie of protégés and bureaucratic debtors elsewhere in State and other agencies. When by the natural institutional accretion the UN desk puffed into a full-fledged Bureau for International Organization Affairs, Sisco was the ranking bureaucrat and in 1965 became Assistant Secretary under Dean Rusk. So he had met and impressed Rogers among the honorary members of the U.S. Delegation, and in 1969 was named the new régime's Assistant Secretary for the Near East and the South Asian subcontinent—less for his knowledge of the area or his intellect or independence than because he was simply there and was a senior bureaucratic survivor the new Secretary of State happened to know. Rogers and his aides—again, men from UN affairs who had worked for and with Sisco—apparently believed that Sisco's affected toughness might hold off a grasping Kissinger from a new U.S. peace effort in the Mideast, perhaps the one sustained interest Rogers brought to office, and anyway one of the few issues seemingly left him by the White House.

In the event, the attempts to mediate between the Israelis and Arabs soon sputtered away in the old incompetence and inertia that traditionally marked Washington's diplomacy in the region. With practiced instincts, Sisco dutifully staffed the futile negotiations for Rogers, while quietly nurturing close relations with Kissinger. For most U.S. diplomats, the chief client was the foreign régime they dealt with. For home office civil servants, it was also and more immediately the men who came and went in ruling the foreign policy régime in Washington. Earlier from Rusk, then from Rogers, now in discreet but real ways from Kissinger and Nixon, Sisco received the acceptance, the favor, the authority, the implicit bureaucratic alliance that was vital. That special cliency lifted career officials into high office, and kept them there, if they were careful. This was the organizational reality which awaited Blood's impassioned cable from Dacca and the memorandum it provoked from the junior desk officers.

Sisco was alerted to the drafting of the memorandum soon after work began that morning of April 6. White House sources say he then called Kissinger to discuss both the Blood cable and the memorandum being written, saying, "My people seem to be leaving the reservation." By this account, Kissinger told Sisco that there was "no possibility" the administration would change its policy toward Pakistan, and that the dissenting FSOs should be held "in line." "After all, Joe," one witness remembers the telephone record of Kissinger joking with Sisco, "you must be capable of intimidation of subordinates as well as of superiors." On receiving the memo, Sisco called in the desk officers for what most participants remembered later as a vague yet decisive meeting. Their proposed condemnation of the genocide was "premature," Sisco reportedly told them. He suggested that Blood and his staff might be "overreacting" in Dacca, and that in any case a formal policy memo should await a meeting of the Interdepartmental Group that afternoon. The junior officials left Sisco's office with the clear "signal," as one of them put it later, that he was not "buying." At the interdepartmental meeting the discussion rambled in the customary ambiguity, the hedging of intelligence and cautious rhetoric, as the middle-level representatives of the various agencies waited for their own "signal" of the reaction to the Blood telegram.

By the spring of 1971, White House dominance of these groups and of the policy process in general, including Kissinger's alliance with men like Sisco, was plainly recognized throughout the government if not outside it. The crucial roles in the meeting belonged to Kissinger's NSC aide for South Asia, Harold Saunders, and Richardson's staff officer for the area, William Cargo. As Sisco sat silently, Saunders, a former CIA analyst, argued at length that the Bengalis would yield to the Pakistani repression, and that even a guerrilla movement would fail against the occupying army. The President, Saunders apparently told the group, would not change policy to be on "the losing side." Cargo, a middle-aged FSO who had served in West Pakistan, echoed Saunders's confidence in the Yahya régime's forces, the residue of Cargo's own four years with the clients in the mid-1960s. The meeting ended with the agreement that the bureaucracy would send on to the Secretary of State and President a "Situation Report" on the events in East Pakistan, which turned out to be an obliquely worded description of the "disorders" in Dacca, on the model of similar intelligence reports sent before the Blood telegram.

Neither the Blood cable nor the dissenting memorandum, which had repeated the cable's language about "moral bankruptcy" and predicted "possibly ruinous consequences" for U.S. policy on the subcontinent, survived the meetings of April 6. The senior officials continued largely to ignore the savagery and to rely on the Pakistani army to quell the problem; the junior men returned to their desks to produce the routine reports, resigned to their defeat. None of the men involved, including Sisco, knew the details of the China diplomacy. All had served in responsible posts in the Johnson administration, where Sisco, Saunders, and Cargo had all been in positions to make much the same decision had the issue risen years earlier. Nor was it simply that these officials were unintelligent or utterly insensible to the outrage in East Pakistan. Around other tables, at other sessions, Saunders and Sisco urged humanitarian assistance to Arab refugees in the Middle East. Cargo was a bland, genial man ever in favor of more generous economic aid to poor nations. Yet in this Pakistani crisis—as too often in a system that spawned such decent men capable of such indecent decisions—judgment and sensibility were challenged in an unequal struggle by the habits and inner ethic of career survival. For men who by 1971 had accommodated themselves to the autocratic control of Kissinger and Nixon, for people like Saunders and Sisco who occasionally glimpsed the squalid, frightful politics at the top of the administration and treated it in effect as one more swing in the rhythm of government, there obviously had already been bargains struck between doubts and careers. Those bargains may have been in part a calculation, but they also made it easier to *believe* that Blood, the dissenting officers, and the Bengali rebellion would all blow over. In East Pakistan in 1971, as in Biafra, or Vietnam, or other issues pitting principle against bureaucratic politics, American foreign policy was all the more complex, and all the more tragic, because it mingled cynicism with that almost desperate kind of conviction.

As it happened for a while, of course, the situation did "blow over." There were other bargains down the line. The dissenting desk officers contented themselves with a few leaks which triggered a brief congressional storm. There were no readier resignations or public protests than in any other foreign service episode. Blood returned to the Department at midsummer to be given a token award and a harmless sinecure in the personnel bureau. The "Situation

Reports" continued for a few weeks, then trailed off into oral briefings among junior aides in State and the NSC staff. Only reality resisted the bureaucratic process. In East Pakistan the Bengalis slowly gathered a formidable guerrilla force that began to drive the occupying army into fortified enclaves; in India the massive catastrophe of the millions of refugees drove the government toward war.

Over the summer of 1971, the White House remained absorbed in the intricate China diplomacy and the tangled negotiations with North Vietnam. The natural tendency to ignore the events in East Pakistan for reasons of state was now reinforced by the mounting demands on Kissinger's time. The sole negotiating agent to open China and end the war, he was now increasingly the victim of the over-extension he had deplored often in his predecessors. Still, there was no will to alter the South Asian policy in the White House, and no more dissent from below to give pause or create a political problem. The abdication by the State Department was complete, symbolized in the artless efforts by its official spokesmen to cover the continued shipment of arms to Pakistan. On three occasions during the latter half of April, for example, State had assured questioning reporters that "No arms have been delivered and none are in the pipelines." As the statements were made, military items were in fact on the high seas bound for Pakistan. Some $35 million in munitions were licensed before March 25, and would be free of embargo despite the public assurances. Millions in ammunition and crucial airplane spare parts were shipped furtively between March and September, including the release of some Pentagon weapons even after a Defense Department directive ostensibly put a hold on such items in late April 1971. Only in November, after congressional exposure of the shipments and the deception, and following a Government Accounting Office investigation of the secret contravention of the declared policy of an arms embargo, did the shipments and the cover up stop.

On November 12, the U.S. Embassy in New Delhi sent its first unequivocal warning of an Indian attack on East Pakistan, the climax of months of halting aid by the United States and other wealthy powers as the refugees filled one camp after another. Earlier in the autumn, similarly ineffectual diplomatic efforts had begun to bring together the leadership of the Bengalis in exile and the West Pakistanis. Kissinger approved the mediation, in a dawning awareness that the Pakistani position was rapidly becoming untenable; but the diplomacy was left to State Department officers in Calcutta and Islamabad, where it foundered in the delay and instinctive reticence of negotiators unsure of their policy or authority. The warnings from New Delhi went unheeded in Washington, and war broke over the borders of Bengal on December 3.

The next week was to be almost a tragicomic parody of a régime trying somehow to retrieve a foreign policy disaster of its own making. Symbolic of the disarray, the minutes of the top-secret Washington Special Actions Group (the crisis control committee of the NSC system) were promptly leaked to columnist Jack Anderson. And though the leaked record was not a verbatim transcript of the meetings, in tone and content the minutes were authentic Kissinger in bureaucratic action, with an equally authentic Nixon hovering in the background. Not long after the first intelligence flashes on the war had been sent to the President, verbal and written orders streamed back to Kissinger to condemn the Indians. This reaction reflected the spasmodic defensiveness of a failed policy as well as the old animus for New Delhi, and it consumed American diplomacy during the war. "I'm getting hell every half hour from the President that we are not being tough enough on India," Kissinger told the WSAG at its first meeting on December 3. "He just called me again. He does not believe we are carrying out his wishes. He wants to tilt in favor of Pakistan. He feels everything we do comes out otherwise." In the furor and sensation that attended the leak of the minutes, the emphasis would be on the term "tilt" and its contradiction with public declarations of neutrality. Few observers saw the deeper and more abiding problem of the man in the presidency. When Henry Kissinger spoke that morning about mistrust and suspicion, about "carrying out his wishes" and "everything we do," the U.S. government had not yet reacted officially to the war at all! Like so much else that haunted foreign affairs (and long eluded otherwise shrewd witnesses), the WSAG began its meeting with a phenomenom that existed for the moment only in the mind of Richard Nixon.

But the minutes were redolent as well of other characteristics of policymaking in the régime. Throughout the record, it became clear that the WSAG was no more a collegial body screening information for the National Security Council. Everywhere in the text, "Dr. Kissinger instructed" . . . "ordered" . . . "requested". . . "asked that"—

the euphemisms of authority clearly acknowledged by all the participants, with no mention of the Secretaries of State or Defense. Visible more starkly than usual was the bland hypocrisy greasing the relations between government and the media. On December 6, the White House obligingly staged a mock meeting of the WSAG for the benefit of NBC television cameras. The film would depict the President solemnly ordering his minions to "get the facts out . . . [on] what we have done for the refugees and so forth and so on." At the real WSAG meeting a few hours later, Kissinger cajoled his colleagues to treat the Indian ambassador with "a certain coolness." And in his much-quoted response to the prediction by a State Department official that the new Bengali state would be an "international basket case," he observed that "It will not necessarily be our basket case."

To appease mounting pressure from the press, Kissinger gave an extensive background briefing on December 7, insisting that reports of any bias in American policy were "inaccurate." The next day, according to the leaked WSAG notes, he ordered no more refugee relief released to India without White House approval, discussed what "the next turn of the screw" on the Indians might be, instructed that no AID funds for India be placed in the next federal budget, and reminded the Group that "We are not trying to be even handed . . . there can be no doubt what the President wants. . . . The lady [Mme Gandhi] is cold blooded and tough and will not turn into a Soviet satellite merely because of pique." The irritated, exhorting tenor of his dialogue reflected in part the natural lethargy of the bureaucracy when asked to respond promptly to any direction; in part it indicated the resistance of the State and AID officials to retaliatory acts against India that would threaten current programs; and in part, also, it railed against the general bureaucratic sense—perhaps in this case more measured than any political reaction—that a bad policy should not be made worse by exaggerating its mistakes to the end. In any event, the WSAG meetings on the Indo-Pakistani war in December 1971 provided the opportunity for an unusual emergence in the rest of government of the sort of pressures and impulsiveness Kissinger had long endured, almost alone, at the White House since 1969. The WSAG meetings, unlike the China démarche, the Vietnam negotiations, or even most of the preparations for détente with the Soviets, marked an instance in which Kissinger worked with the government at large rather than as a lone, secret negotiator. The peremptory and impatient quality of the minutes bore the marks of all of that—though, again, few noticed any details beyond the sensation of the leak itself. At the same time, the bureaucratic-diplomatic skill that had produced so much of this unalloyed power was displayed, characterized by the tone of ingratiation and cynicism that showed Kissinger at once as Nixon's man browbeating the bureaucrats and as the intrepid adviser trying to steer the mad politician past the shoals of policy known only to the men at the table. "We have to take action," he says to one of the WSAG gatherings. "The President is blaming me, but you people are in the clear." And his discreet ally, Sisco, comes back, "That's ideal." The exchange captures so much of the layered dissimulation of the government toward its own reality as well as the outside world.

Reading Kissinger's backgrounder in New Delhi, Ambassador Kenneth Keating, a former Republican senator from New York dedicated to the politics of vindicating his new clients, swiftly sent a cable back to Washington listing the discrepancies. U.S. efforts to mediate the Bengali-Pakistani dispute had been halfhearted and futile, he documented, and Washington had been pro-Pakistan to the end. The telegram itself was leaked within hours of delivery and became more notable as another immediate political embarrassment to the administration than as a primer on the anatomy of policy over the months leading to war. At any rate this flap was quickly blotted out by more ominous events. From the beginning of the war, CIA and Pentagon intelligence had pointedly alluded to an Indian strike into West Pakistan to regain old irredenta in the Punjab. By December 5–6 the almost predictable reports had begun to come in from Moscow, Hong Kong, and Katmandu, Nepal, of the bellicose but always inconclusive maneuvering of the Soviets and Chinese to posture on behalf of their client-states fighting in South Asia. On December 7, in reply to a specific Kissinger request, the CIA could make no precise estimate of any Russian or Chinese intention to intervene in the war. Yet as the Pakistani defeat became plainer with each day, as the public folly of the policy deepened the sullen, defensive mood already pervading the White House at the outbreak of the fighting, only scattered shards of raw espionage would be enough to justify a menacing gesture by Nixon and Kissinger to save face.

Vague electronic intelligence from the Sino-Indian frontier raised the possibility that Chinese forces might be in some stage of alert. At the same time, however, no other evidence gathered from the usual extensive monitoring of mainland China suggested that Peking was preparing a military intervention on the losing Pakistani side—an action that might offer a pretext for some Soviet move against China proper, and conceivably jeopardize the Sino-American summit announced that summer. From Nepal came similarly questionable reports from the U.S. military attachés that Russian officers had stridently warned Chinese diplomats at a local reception that the USSR "would not stand by" if Peking interfered in the Indo-Pakistani war. Still more provocative than these shadows, though, was a CIA cable from the New Delhi station which arrived at the White House on December 8. The source was a prominent Indian politician who had been a venerable CIA informant of varying reliability and motives. At this point he was recounting a decision supposedly taken by the Gandhi cabinet that week to go beyond the developing victory in the East to attack and dismember part of the Punjab in West Pakistan, thus permanently crippling the country as a power on the subcontinent.

As with the intercepted signals from the Sino-Indian border, there would be no more precise military or political intelligence to confirm the alleged Indian decision. Keating in New Delhi and Sisco and the India desk in Washington contended throughout the war that the Gandhi régime's war aims were limited to the detachment of East Pakistan and return of the 10 million refugees. But the specter of Indian aggression in the West was what the White House wanted to see, much as everyone had wanted to see a swift end to the rebellion nine months before. Among the familiar little memos of Nixon suspicions, epithets, and edicts which deluged Kissinger at the beginning of the war had been top-secret orders to the joint chiefs to prepare Indian contingency plans, as one instruction put it, for "a show of force, if we need it." Now, both men aroused by the hints of Russian and Chinese saber-rattling, both willing to believe they could and should bluff the Indians, Kissinger recommended and Nixon ordered on December 9 that a naval task force of 8 vessels, led by the carrier *Enterprise* and carrying 2,000 marines, sail from station off Vietnam into the Bay of Bengal. It was a fitting final sequel. Reckless and futile, the gunboat display arrived on the scene too late to affect the war either in the East, which ended within a week in a total Pakistani collapse, or in the

West, where both sides had accepted the line of their old stalemate.

By any measure the policy had been a profound mistake. In the name of preserving Pakistan's territorial unity, U.S. weapons had armed, and Washington's silence condoned, a reign of terror that made secession inevitable. In the name of preserving stability and American influence on the subcontinent, the support for the Yahya régime hastened war and drove an already alienated India closer to the Russians. Even the calculations of *Realpolitik* which supposedly lay behind the policy were simplistic and contradictory. To bring together its two patrons, the United States and China, was more than ever in the interest of an increasingly isolated Pakistan facing the Bengali rebellion that spring and summer of 1971. In the coldest diplomatic terms, Kissinger's flight over the Himalayas did not ransom American influence in Pakistan; it was a mark of Washington's ultimate force with the precarious Yahya régime. And if the still deeper logic of the policy was to appease the Chinese, to prove that the Nixon régime could somehow hold unpopular ground with a mutual ally, that too was in a sense bogus. The Sino-American détente rested on the bedrock of the Sino-Soviet hostility, and depended on the submersion and acceptance of conflicting interests between Washington and Peking, whether over Taiwan, Vietnam, or parallel American détente with Moscow. The secret Cambodian bombing and the 1970 invasion, the South Vietnamese attack into Laos in 1971 in the midst of Kissinger's exchanges with the Chinese, the blockade of North Vietnam, the Christmas bombing, the planning, meetings, and hidden personal compulsions that drove that sequence of war from Washington—all of these events had proceeded on the assumption, in part the insistence, that the administration could and should have détente only as it fearlessly pursued what it saw as its own interests. Now the Pakistani policy had defied that principle by drawing the administration into a relative weakening of influence in the world and political controversy at home. Ironically, it was even a failure as a petulant foil to the Indians. Had the White House genuinely understood and played the actual twists of *Realpolitik* in South Asia, it would have seen the reality that emerged within months of the war—that an independent, poor, and basically ungovernable Bengali state on her border was much more a problem for India than the East Pakistani province, and so also even perhaps an asset to the Chinese. But their policy had not been based on either

those cold-blooded insights or on a principled revulsion at the outrage of human rights. As Kissinger and Nixon maneuvered subtly
with the Russians, the Chinese, and their own government to super-
sede the myths of the cold war, they drifted through the Pakistani
tragedy demonstrating a shallow, parochial, and cruel perspective on
world politics.

Kissinger's first notable blunder before the press and Congress
was revealed in this moment at the close of 1971, when the WSAG
minutes, the December 7 backgrounder, and Keating's responding
cable were all leaked and published. The cloud soon passed in the
normal rapid dissipation of congressional or media interest, and was
nearly forgotten altogether amid the summit spectacles and revelations of Kissinger's secret Vietnam negotiations over the next few
months of 1972. The tendency in the admiring press to exculpate
"Henry" from the régime was still evident. When two prominent
Washington journalists, Joseph Kraft and John Osborne of *The New
Republic*, reflected on the disclosures, they stressed the motive for
the leak. Kraft diagnosed it as "a vulgar bureaucratic row aimed at
getting the President's chief Assistant for National Security affairs,
Henry Kissinger." "A high-ranking rat" had been "shooting at
Henry," agreed Osborne, and the culprit "should be dug out of his
hole and fired." Kissinger had indeed been shown to have lied,
though "in the President's behalf and at his direction," wrote Osborne, adding: "but the Administration lie was never an effective
lie." For too many journalists for a long time to come, any discrepancies would be assigned to the "Administration."

Yet the Pakistani episode was a brief foretaste of the disillusion
ahead, leading to the reluctant public accusations of deception, hypocrisy, and sheer ignorance in Kissinger's diplomacy alongside the
candor and brilliance. It gave a glimpse of the disregard of political
forces and the disarray within the government that existed alongside
the sophisticated diplomacy and careful bureaucratic discipline. Kissinger himself sensed the omen if few others did. As he would do later
in explaining the blockade of North Vietnam and the Christmas
bombing, he portrayed himself as the victim of bureaucratic vengeance. By several accounts, he saw the WSAG leaks and the subsequent release of his backgrounder by Senator Barry Goldwater (R.
Ariz.) as inspired, or at least exploited, by his White House rivals
Haldeman and Ehrlichman. Again, in the essential politics of foreign

policy as he practiced them, the substance of the policy was less important than how it affected his public image or bureaucratic standing. It had been a bad moment and he considered quitting, he later told two sympathetic biographers, Marvin and Bernard Kalb. His anguish was not over the failed policy, but over the fear that he was "losing Presidential favor."

In fairness, the bureaucratic warfare was always there, though in this case it was more complex and ironic than in Kissinger's simplified version for friendly reporters. A frenzied internal White House search for the WSAG leaker led, if not precisely to the origin of those breaches, to a naval yeoman in the office of the joint chiefs' liaison with the NSC staff, who was alleged to be rifling briefcases and even classified wastebags to pass back to the Pentagon whatever tidbits could be gathered on the policies and intentions of the President's Assistant for National Security. Behind the yeoman was reportedly an admiral seconded to the NSC staff, and beyond him the shadow of bureaucratic espionage aimed at the presidency by the highest military officers of the country. Even in a régime where the shocking became commonplace, it was a bizarre exposure of the sordid side of foreign and military policy, and it was swiftly buried beyond the timid reach of journalists or Congress. What was clear, however, was that the issue went far deeper than the Pakistani policy. Among the documents stolen in the bureaucratic war were accounts of Kissinger's July 1971 talks with the Chinese and internal NSC memoranda on SALT. Suddenly visible, then quickly pulled back out of easy sight, was a fragment of the reality of this administration, in which Kissinger and an angry excluded bureaucracy frequently treated one another as separate, alien governments, to be subdued, manipulated, if necessary spied upon.

But the immediate effect of the case inside the White House was only to sharpen Nixon's own distrust of the rest of government and therefore strengthen his alliance with Kissinger. Implicit in the interoffice spying was not just a circumvention of White House secrecy on grounds of internal prerogatives or policymaking, but also the old threat of the joint chiefs sabotaging presidential initiatives on Capitol Hill or in the press. There would be no direct confrontation with the chiefs, no firings or rebukes, any more than Nixon would face the less sinister insubordination or incompetence of the State Department. As always the effect on this man of challenge, within or without, was to bury the White House further in the very rancor and furtiveness that had created the problem to begin with. As the contrived or random leaks embarrassed Kissinger, as the South Asian policy crumbled while the issue turned from substance to the "rat . . . shooting at Henry," the men who fashioned the débâcle were again brought together by personality and politics.

The South Asian policy slowly came to the surface, flushed there by the enormity of the human suffering involved and the crisis of a war, as well as by the leaks from a deeply divided bureaucracy. Yet for the most part other, ugly aspects of American foreign policy remained hidden as the administration paraded forth the statesmanship of the summits. Nowhere was the paradox so harsh, or so shrouded by official secrecy and public indifference, as in Chile.

On September 15, 1970—some ten days after the free election in Chile of President Salvador Allende Gossens as the head of the first popularly chosen Socialist-Communist coalition government in the western hemisphere—CIA Director Richard Helms was summoned to the Oval Office. Waiting for Helms were Attorney General John Mitchell, Kissinger, and the President, who promptly instructed him to prevent the legal accession of Allende by immediate and unlimited covert intervention in Chile. Helms's handwritten notes of the meeting, which were later given to a Senate committee investigating the CIA, were tersely expressive of the climate and tone:

> 1 in 10 chance perhaps, but save Chile
> worth spending
> not concerned risks involved
> no involvement of [US] Embassy
> $10,000,000 available, more if necessary
> full-time job—best men we have
> game-plan
> make the economy scream
> 48 hours for plan of action

As he left the White House that day—as Helms would later reportedly tell an associate sarcastically—he felt as though he "had been given a field marshal's baton without an army to wave it at." The analogy was not quite precise. In the first weeks of October prior to Allende's confirmation by the Chilean Congress on the twenty-fourth, CIA operatives in Santiago swiftly approached a score of right-wing contacts in the Chilean police and military with offers of U.S. money and official backing for a coup. On Helms's approval, U.S. agents on October 22 passed three submachine guns to military conspirators who planned the kidnap and murder of General Rene Schneider. This would remove the highest-ranking officer opposed to a military takeover and would serve as the provocation for a coup. But General Schneider was abducted and murdered later that day by other plotters, apparently not directly armed by the United States. No coup materialized despite the killing, Allende was installed in office, and the machine guns were duly returned to the CIA —for the time being, at least, like Helms's imagined baton, unused.

Of its kind, the September 15 White House meeting was remarkable only in degree. Covert CIA subversion of politics in Chile, one of the last remnants of democracy in Latin America, had been a bipartisan tradition in U.S. foreign policy. In 1958, under Eisenhower, the CIA bribed newspapers, political parties, and legislators. In the early 1960s, the Kennedy administration passed hundreds of thousands in covert money to back the country's Christian Democratic party, and spent $3 million in Chile's 1964 elections to pay for polls, propaganda, and other secret aid to the U.S. clients. Another half million in covert funds went into Chile during the Johnson period. But the Nixon intervention during the Allende period 1970–73 was to be the heaviest. Over $8 million was spent covertly in nearly every sector of Chilean politics from financing newspapers to fomenting riots—all of it a premium investment of the CIA dollars, since they were funneled through the currency black market in Latin America, where the conversion into Chilean money was five times the legal rate. The CIA subsidies had begun to flow early in 1969 to defeat Allende in the September 1970 election, and amounted to nearly a half million dollars before the vote. In meetings chaired by Kissinger immediately after the election, the 40 Committee approved still another quarter million to sway the October 24 congressional confirmation. That covert funding was to carry out a strategy advocated by the U.S. ambassador to Chile, Edward M. Korry, who urged on Washington an effort to back the congressional election of another candidate, who would then, according to the American "scenario," step aside for the long-time CIA client heading the Christian Democrats.

At this juncture, almost routine by standards of CIA meddling in Chile, Korry's approach would later be distinguished as "Track I." The September 15 meeting in the Oval Office provided "Track II," on the premise, as Nixon explained to Helms, that neither the 40 Committee nor what he would later call that "soft-headed Korry" could be trusted to execute the necessary policy: an immediate military coup to stop the electoral process altogether in Chile. To an abiding contempt for Allende and the democratic system in Chile, Nixon now brought even greater fervor and a matching distrust of his own government in its most secret councils. It was an impulse which, for its own bureaucratic reasons, the CIA was able in part to accommodate, however, and a tangled dual policy process started in which the United States began the subversion of another government by subverting the policies of its own.

Half in ridicule, half in respect, aides remembered Ed Korry in Santiago in 1969–70 as the "Kingmaker." Voluble and energetic, he was then forty-eight, a former journalist who had covered the postwar Communist takeover in eastern Europe. That experience fixed in him a lasting, often undifferentiated fear of the specter of Communist subversion everywhere. Korry had been drawn to government under John Kennedy, by admiration of the young President as well as by ambition. Early in 1963 he became ambassador to Ethiopia, where his client was the autocratic government of Haile Selassie, for which he enthusiastically prescribed a diet of weapons and economic aid in exchange for renting an obsolete U.S. electronic intelligence base in the rebellious province of Eritrea. By the time he was named envoy to Chile in August 1967, Korry combined the vestiges of his anti-Communist zeal with the conventional cold war demonology of the bureaucracy he had melted into. Like so many from lowly desk officers to Rusk and Rostow, Nixon and Kissinger, he would appear to act in Chile largely in the grip of an irrelevant experience. The alien ghosts of Prague and Budapest loomed over Korry's Santiago. The analogy rubbed out a century of Chilean history and the singular phenomenon of Allende himself, however benign or evil. This sort of thinking at the highest levels of U.S. foreign policymaking ultimately rationalized the authority vested in ambassadors like Korry to dispense the money and to fashion the discreet deals with dependable politicians that would make America's "kings" in Latin "democracies" ritually extolled by U.S. presidents as examples of freedom and dignity in the hemisphere. From 1967 to 1970, Korry advised his Christian Democratic clients like "a campaign manager," one aide recalled; he lobbied and maneuvered and spent sums to "win" the election. Meanwhile, he regularly cabled Washington dire warnings of the threat of an Allende success—warnings written with characteristic zeal and color. At stake, he repeated, were not only millions in U.S. corporate investments, mainly in copper, but also "the survival of Chilean democracy." In Korry's preelection view, Allende could be reasonably expected to tyrannize the country and perhaps provide a new base for Communist, anti-U.S. revolution in the rest of the continent. "For many, many years," Korry later told a Senate committee, "Allende had personally been financed from foreign Communist enemies." Like the marines in Vietnam who burned the village in order to save it, Korry and his colleagues were obliged to emulate those "enemies." To save Latin freedom, they would have to buy a free election in Chile.

What Allende represented then or afterward, of course, would never fit the caricature drawn by either U.S. officials or journalists variously transfixed by the red menace. Behind Allende's self-proclaimed, often strident radicalism and anti-American rhetoric, history and politics were more varied, and far more ambiguous. Even discounting Allende's frequent pledges to maintain the constitutional liberties of the "Chilean way," there were tangible limits on the totalitarian urges of his new government. The governing coalition would be made up not only of Communists, but also of several other mutually suspicious parties and organizations, including Allende's own Democratic Socialists. That coalition took office with a history of bitter, often violent divisions—among the Communists, within the non-Communist left, and between Socialists and Communists. In the opposition-controlled Congress that confirmed Allende's popular election despite all the covert U.S. efforts, Communists held only 6 of 50 seats in the Senate, and only 22 of 150 in the Chamber of Deputies. Moreover, Chilean politics also had an ambitious right, well-organized and generously financed elements who matched their leftist counterparts in their barely disguised impatience with the democratic system.

Allende later negotiated fast and loose with Korry on the seizure of U.S. corporate holdings, and the act was done with predictable rhetorical flourishes in a nation long exploited. Yet both Allende and the Christian Democratic opponent he narrowly defeated had campaigned for the nationalization of copper, including the enormous mining interests of Anaconda and Kennecott corporations. Together, the two candidates had received more than 60 percent of the presidential vote. Nationalization was to be approved in 1971 by a unanimous vote of the opposition-controlled Congress. It was a law, wrote one British scholar, "against which no Chilean politician would go on public record any more than he would publicly vote for polygamy." In nationalizing copper, Chile followed several other Latin American countries of various political character, from elected nationalists to right-wing juntas, in similarly "seizing," buying out, or otherwise expelling U.S. interests—including, since 1968, Peru, Ecuador, Bolivia, Colombia, Argentina, and Venezuela.

Allende similarly "seized" farms. But in a Chile where 5 percent of the families owned some 35 percent of the land in huge estates and a quarter million rural families were landless, he ran his agrarian reform under a statute which had been passed earlier by a conservative Congress. The preceding régime, in fact, had already redistributed land to some 30,000 peasant families in the same way. Allende, the "Marxist" menace, was elected to power in a constitutional government that already provided 70 percent of the country's investment, employed large numbers of the population, and was already interfering extensively in the private economy. Later there was no doubt among either supporters or critics that the new régime often mismanaged both the design and the pace of its economic efforts. Its policies were anathema to a large number of Chileans. The régime was engaged in radical redistributive economics unique in Latin America. Some elements were squeezed, particularly the privileged minority, and they reacted with highly visible opposition. The same reforms, however, also benefitted others whose response was less visible. The government's rhetoric and style, militant from the outset, hardened almost in proportion to its blunders and opposition. On neither side of the ledger, though, were the politics simple or readily apparent.

But far too little of the jumbled, contradictory reality of Chilean affairs penetrated the U.S. Embassy, let alone other anxious onlookers in the White House. Again, as in Vietnam or Pakistan, Africa or the Middle East, the U.S. government saw only the Allende it found familiar and comfortable, another justification for what it had been so long fearing and believing and doing. Out of its disparate ignorance and obsessions, in Santiago and Washington, the United States produced another unrelieved blunder.

Though unabashedly interventionist and covert, Korry's "Track I" during the autumn of 1970 depended upon the willing puppetry of his own client Chilean politicians. Convinced that a military coup would fail and only entrench both Allende and anti-U.S. sentiment —that, as he put it in testimony later, "the Chilean military was no policy alternative"—Korry had taken a number of steps dating back to 1968 supposedly to bar CIA or other U.S. contacts with likely assassins or coup plotters. The policy distinction was often a fine one, even in Korry's subsequent self-defense before Senate investigators. He had told the lame-duck régime of Eduardo Frei that autumn that "the United States had not supported, had not encouraged, would not support any action by the Chilean military taken outside the constitution, independent of President Frei." Left to the senators' imagination, as no doubt to Frei's, was what the ambassador would have done had his clients conveniently given their sanction to the military and some fabricated constitutional pretext for the action. In any event, when pressed by Washington in early September to develop "possible scenarios" for what he termed "independent Chilean military intervention" (presumably "independent" of Frei, if not the CIA), Korry dismissed the prospects. On September 25, he cabled the warning that a military coup would risk "another Bay of Pigs," and that, "Hence, I have instructed our military and CAS [the bureaucratic nomenclature for CIA stations abroad] not to engage in the encouragement" of such a coup.

Again on October 9, he sent an "eyes only" telegram to Kissinger and Deputy Under Secretary of State U. Alexis Johnson, the Department's representative on the 40 Committee. It repeated that a military coup apart from Korry's Chilean politicians "could lead us to a Bay of Pigs failure . . . an unrelieved disaster for the United States and the President." The cables only reinforced the already settled and perhaps mistaken view in the White House that this holdover from the Democratic régimes—however certified his animosity for Allende—lacked the stomach for dealing with the problem. Thus, as Korry tried in vain to spend his covert money for a more delicate "political" overthrow of Allende, Nixon ordered Helms on September 15 to stage a military coup with "no involvement of Embassy."

Helms in turn ordered the CIA station, by the separate cable traffic the Agency has to every embassy, to begin coup contacts without the ambassador's knowledge. CIA operatives proceeded to instigate the action which Korry had solemnly promised would never take place without the permission of the moderate politicians. For Chileans watching the two "tracks" snake out of the U.S. Embassy, the double cross undermined Korry's attempts to spur the politicians. It also further divided the civilian and military opposition to Allende, strengthening extremists of both left and right. The effect was to foredoom the coup to the adventure of a few Fascist officers, whose only allies would be, ironically, a few leftist radicals behind Allende who wanted General Schneider murdered for their own reasons.

The politics inside the U.S. mission and later in the Oval Office were hardly less convoluted or seamy. Having before September 15 berated Korry openly for not supporting a coup and having under the ambassador's rebuke on that occasion promised to drop the subject or leave the country, the CIA station chief blandly lied to Korry after the clandestine September 15 orders from Washington. Helms had indulged Nixon's passion for a coup because the White House so fully controlled policy, because the Agency had already been shown up once too often in NSC episodes such as that in southern Africa, and because Helms and his colleagues were under rising pressure to come up with the right, tough answers to maintain their own ebbing institutional power. The Santiago station now similarly proved its worth and virtuosity. It could contact the potential plotters through relationships it had purchased years before Korry arrived. Like their headquarters back on the Potomac, stations endured as the political appointees and career diplomats came and went. So in Santiago the CIA could, as Korry put it afterward, "disengenuously" assure him that it had no liaison with plotters—when in fact it was handing over money and machine guns to others certain to reach the conspirators. The CIA was, Korry admitted to senators five years later, indeed an "invisible" government.

Korry sensed for a moment that autumn that "our" CIA people were "up to something behind my back," as he described it to his foreign service deputy, who investigated and found nothing. His October 9 cable struck a quaint, almost plaintive tone in advising against the "abortive coup" he suspected to be "what is here under discussion, not more beknownst to me." The cute, archaic phraseology masked a man suddenly and cruelly cut off from his own government and work. Yet when Korry came to Washington in mid-October—forbidden to see anyone in Congress, coolly treated by colleagues who knew he had lost "credibility" in the White House—he met with Nixon and Kissinger without pressing the awkward issue of a coup or White House subvention of his Mission. Instead, according to secret White House records and Korry's own testimony, he advocated a policy of "understanding" with Allende, combined with more discreet CIA funding of media and politicians. (Both the Chilean beneficiaries and the Agency providently discovered the need for added subsidies under the dangerous new régime.) As Kissinger described the encounter to aides, Nixon pronounced some well-chosen expletives over Korry after he left, more persuaded than ever that he was another of "them." Lost then and later to each man, the self-besieged President and the fugitive Kennedy admirer, was an awareness that the essential difference between "Track I" and "Track II" boiled down to the fact that the former required the acquiescence of Frei—a notable difference of method and tactic perhaps, but not of kind in the larger sense. They shared the fundamental bipartisan arrogance of American power that blighted U.S. foreign policy from Korry's embassies to the Oval Office. When both tracks failed and Allende took office, policy fell back to one of economic harassment and covert political action intended to destroy the stability of Chile. Nixon had told Helms to "make the economy scream." Korry, talking to a Frei aide a week later, found his own words for the same idea. "Not a nut or bolt would be allowed to reach Chile under Allende," he reported telling the Chilean with apparently as much bravado as Nixon had summoned. Korry survived another year in Santiago before he was reassigned and the White House would be rid of him. The personnel system reserved for Korry an apt and black irony, no doubt inadvertent, given the thick secrecy of all this. Before he left government in angry frustration, Korry came home from his Chile service to a remote Washington job in the Overseas Private Investment Corporation.

Throughout the three years of Allende's régime, U.S. pressure was relentless. Once the highest per capita U.S. aid recipient in the hemisphere—a showcase for the "Alliance for Progress" into which Washington had poured $1 billion between 1962 and 1969—Chile was now largely cut off from development assistance. Bilateral aid went from $35 million in 1969 to $1.5 million two years later. Export-import bank credits fell from $234 million in 1967 to nothing in 1971. Under quiet U.S. vetoes, loans to Chile in the Inter-American Development Bank dropped from $46 million in 1970 to $2 million in 1972, including refusal of an emergency earthquake relief loan in 1971. Loans in the World Bank ceased altogether in 1970–73 with similar vetoes. There seems no sure way to estimate the exact impact of these actions on Chile. The need for food imports, purchased only by the foreign exchange that vanished as copper production sagged, was obviously acute amid growing shortages in the country in 1972–73. The United States cut food aid and financial assistance at a moment when both were crucial to Allende's survival. According to Department of Commerce statistics, from 1969 to 1972 U.S. exports to Chile fell from $315 million to $186 million, imports from $151 million to $83 million. To the material economic effects, moreover, was added the political and psychological impact of ostracism.

Meanwhile—though the CIA on Track II had threatened in the autumn of 1970 to cut off arms aid if the military did not stage a coup —the Pentagon cultivated the Chilean officer corps. The courtship in fact became embarrassing almost immediately when U.S. flag officers displayed unseemly haste in attempting official visits to their Chilean peers and Allende's would-be opponents soon after his election. "I don't know how it looked in Santiago," one former NSC aide sighed about the incident, "but we had to reprimand the Joint Chiefs for getting out in front. Totally unsubtle, as usual." As the economic quarantine grew, equally unsubtle arms aid during 1970–73 would total $47 million, including increased training of Chileans in Panama and jet fighters for the air force that was to lead the September coup in bombing and strafing the presidential palace.

For its major part, the CIA recovered swiftly from the failure of the preelection coup maneuvers. Within a year, the Santiago station had spun a new web of agents in the military and government from whom it received virtually daily intelligence on Allende's policies. This intelligence included his own covert bribery, blackmail, and fraud in Chile's politics, his wary relations with Cuba and Russia (by CIA accounts "distant" and "restrained"), and not least the progress of new coup plotting. The Agency schemed to provoke Chilean officers with forged evidence of Cuban infiltration of the régime. It orchestrated a "march of the empty pots," a protest of middle-class housewives against higher (fairer) farm prices, which had been staged successfully by the CIA years earlier in building a coup in Brazil. It also helpfully (and hopefully) collected arrest and target lists handy for a military rising. And it drew ever closer to the group planning the successful September 1973 overthrow. Later Senate investigations unearthed no conclusive evidence of direct CIA involvement in the coup in which Allende was murdered. But again the margin between knowledge, encouragement, sanction, and complicity was a bad bureaucratic joke in policy terms. There was no doubt the Agency—and thus at least part of the U.S. government—knew of the coup in advance and wholly supported it.

As the Chilean Junta then imprisoned thousands and set up what a UN report called "torture centers," the CIA reportedly paid economists to help compose the new régime's economic plan, used its old media clients to propagandize for the Junta inside Chile, and hired agents to help with a White Book to justify abroad (including the United States) the overthrow of Allende. No 40 Committee meetings mourned the extinction of Chile's constitution and politics. No covert action would be mounted to stop the savage violations of human rights. No money would be passed to a now endangered left to preserve the "democracy" that was supposed to be the object of U.S. national interest under Allende's rule. No women's marches were organized, laborers bribed to strike, journalists subsidized to harry the régime, though its policies swiftly proved more brutal than Allende's. "The scale of CIA involvement in Chile," observed a Senate report, "was unusual but by no means unprecedented." The tragedy in Chile stripped off the pretense of principle and revealed with rare clarity the naked reactionary character of so much of U.S. policy in Latin America.

When it was over, there would be another of those mocking "policy papers" sitting in the files. NSSM 97, the formal 1970 NSC study of Chile, judged that Allende did not threaten the peace of Latin America or the military balance in the world. His election was a "psychological disadvantage" to the United States and a "promotion of the Marxist idea," it concluded; but "the United States has no vital interests in Chile." As in East Pakistan, of course, the men and actions behind the words were never that simple. Even four successive National Intelligence Estimates, written by CIA analysts each summer from 1970 to 1973, stressed that, whatever his original intentions, Allende was observing constitutional forms. He was compromising with opponents as well as realizing genuine popular support for his reform measures. By 1973, thought the analysts, a "political stalemate seemed the most likely prospect for Chile. But then the CIA's analysts, segregated by secrecy and bureaucratic *élan* from their fellow employees in clandestine services, did not know about the burgeoning coup or the role of covert U.S. money against Allende, nor therefore if the visible opposition would even have been strong enough to produce the "stalemate" without the U.S. intervention. It did not matter. Policy was not based on intelligence estimates or NSSM papers in any case. When in December 1969, the 40 Committee discussed subsidies for the coming election, a State Department official argued that Allende's triumph would not be, after all, the same as a Communist victory. The officer was colossally wrong, thundered Korry, at the meeting while in Washington for consultation. It was not only the same; it would be worse than Castro. He, Ed Korry, had seen it all before, from Belgrade. On March 25, 1970, the 40 Committee approved $125,000 for a "spoiling operation," and Under Secretary of State Johnson told the group some in State had "reservations" about "too much" interference. Yet Johnson and his skeptical fellow FSOs deferred to Kissinger and the CIA, with the unbreakable habit of submission. Again at the 40 Committee on September 29, 1970, State meekly questioned the policy of economic warfare. This time the spokesman was Charles Meyer, a former Sears-Roebuck merchandiser in Latin America become by his Republican loyalties Assistant Secretary of State for the hemisphere. Meyer did not understand, said Helms and his aides, according to minutes of the meeting. Allende was a "real Marxist" and the United States could not "throw in the sponge." Meyer backed away, to join Johnson and Korry, Blood, Sisco, and Saunders, and scores of nameless others who made folly possible, and so shared it. Helms, of course, had a sizable advantage on his colleagues at that 40 Committee session September 29—an advantage on all, that is, save Kissinger there at the head. They alone knew that two weeks before, Nixon had ordered that Allende be overthrown and Chile's economy made to "scream."

While they skillfully fenced with the Soviets and Chinese in order to break free of the past, Nixon and Kissinger reacted to Allende with all the cold war mindlessness of their predecessors and more. "I don't

see why we have to let a country go Marxist," Kissinger told a 40
Committee meeting about Chile on June 27, 1970, "just because its
people are irresponsible." At the heart of their view was all the old
arrogance and simplistic fear of falling dominos in America's status
quo. Allende would pose "massive problems for us . . . in Latin
America," Kissinger told the press in a background briefing the day
after the 1970 election. "It was the 'who-lost-Chile' syndrome,"
remembered an NSC aide. "Henry thought Allende might lead an
anti-U.S. move in Latin America more effectively than Castro, just
because it *was* the democratic route to power." Witnesses recall
Kissinger's recurring remarks that Allende would "infect" the hemisphere. Underlying the mentality, too, was the familiar contempt for
American clients and an ironically realistic appreciation of the vulnerable, repressive order on which U.S. policy rested in the continent. Thus Kissinger would also tell his staff how much he "admired"
Allende, how this "little Marxist" was "smart enough to bamboozle
those weak-kneed Christian Democrats and ineffectual generals."
But it was in the greater national interest that Allende not succeed
—or at least the interests of stability as Kissinger had imbibed them
in Cambridge and Washington and the midtown Manhattan of the
Council and the Rockefellers. "We set the limits of diversity," Kissinger once told a Review Group meeting on Chile. The reality of
Kissinger's convictions was even stronger than the stereotyped
image that emerged later in leftist criticism of the débâcle, the image
of Kissinger representing Kennecott or Anaconda. "He never gave
a shit about the business community," said an official who followed
Kissinger throughout the Chile policy. "What really underlay it was
ideology."

When Korry returned to Chile after Allende's inauguration, he
began negotiations to mediate between the new régime and the
companies. Having variously subsidized Allende's predecessors, the
companies were ready to make a deal. Even John Connally at Treasury supported some arrangement for a quiet U.S. government bail-
out of the corporations and an "expropriation peace" with Allende.
Let everyone get on with business. As it developed, Allende himself
backed away from such a settlement. But Kissinger was always opposed to concessions of that sort anyway. "Our interests aren't necessarily the same," he told a corporate executive who came to urge the
Korry-Connally plans. "We have the larger national interest to think

of." He would be tougher than the corporations, and see further than Korry or Connally, ready to go with their clients. "Copper just gave us an opportunity to take the harder line we wanted to anyway," said a high official afterward. Kissinger's own primary client remained, after all, the man in the presidency—whose primitive brooding fear of Allende, another foreign "enemy" to add to the list, mirrored all these views.

For Nixon, Chile was another testing. He would make peace, arrive at détente, on his own terms. This administration would not "cave in at the edges," he told Helms and Mitchell and Kissinger at the September 15 meeting. It was the awful dichotomy in the man that he could come to terms with the post-imperial world in Peking and Moscow, but that he also continued to see "the edges" of his own power and authority in Chile or Cambodia or East Bengal. In one effort he had risen out of his basest prejudices to become a statesman; in the other he remained the political everyman of parochial U.S. politics, ordinary, bigoted, the lowest common denominator. So it was too for Kissinger and the sad, trapped men below in the régime they dominated. In détente, Kissinger and Nixon defeated the worst instincts of that government. In these débâcles in Chile and Pakistan, they only fed them.

The story of the Chile policy went unreported in the press from sordid beginning to end. "There has been and there will be no resistance by the U.S.," announced Howard K. Smith on ABC Television as Allende was inaugurated. Diplomatic correspondents in Washington lunched with "Henry" and attended the backgrounders, but never explored the dry Commerce or AID statistics which held the outline of the economic warfare. And the dutiful men of the 40 Committee never leaked. Seasoned journalists hurried to Santiago; Allende's "Castroism" was hot copy. For over three years the reporters variously believed, invented, and perpetuated the stereotype while never noticing the CIA do what it had done in Brazil, Ecuador, and a dozen other places in Africa and Asia. Several U.S. reporters took their cues from the American Embassy, some from ITT—a corporation so anxious to depose Allende that it offered its own money to the CIA. Many noticed the empty shops and protesting housewives from the affluent districts of Santiago, and thoughtlessly filed stories on the "devastation" of the "middle class," as if a true middle class existed in Chile. Few reporters explained that Chile was a country where closed urban shops affected only a tiny fraction of the population, where empty pots had been common for the majority before Allende took power, and where to be "middle-class" was the distant dream of the impoverished masses. Fewer still wandered from the city streets and avenues into the slums and countryside, away from the familiar dialects and sources. Cultural bias, ideology, sloth, co-option by government and business, self-censorship to get play back home, stupidity, and naïveté—all the worst weaknesses of American journalism abroad stunted the coverage from Chile with cliché and banality, and thus abetted the cover up of the CIA intervention.

The Congress joined as well in the customary quiescence. Its CIA oversight subcommittees routinely gave their blanket approval for the Chile operations as they were dimly reported by the Agency. The Foreign Affairs committees were indifferent as usual. In 1974–75, when revelations on Chile seeped out at last along with other tales from the Watergate-stricken régime, the same Congress would be eager for facile answers and scapegoats. Korry was called before the Senate Select Committee on Intelligence chaired by Frank Church (D. Idaho). The former ambassador wrote the committee a letter in much the same style he had employed from Chile. It was defensive and too revealing, yet poignant; and, like his experience, it testified movingly to the pervasiveness of the habits of thought behind the policy blunder. "Your wash must be pinned on the same sunlit line with mine," Korry wrote Church, reminding the Senator that the latter had been chairman of the Subcommittee on Inter-American Affairs during 1969–70, when Church and his staff had been wearily uninterested in Chile or American policy there. "Is it unfair to compare your looking-the-other-way in 1969–70 to a sentry asleep on duty on the eve of battle?" Korry asked. "Is it not right to inquire how such a negligent guard turns up as presiding judge in the resultant court-martial?" The questions, whatever Korry's substantial complicity in Chile, went to the marrow of congressional irresponsibility. Like his colleagues, Church had had no time for Chile before it became a public sensation, before the damage had been done. His select committee produced a telling record of the Chile policy eventually. But after a heady excursion into that, the FBI, and other intelligence scandals, the senators quickly sensed the issues fading in notoriety, and politely disbanded, giving the CIA final authority to censor from the committee's summary report awkward discoveries —such as the revelation that the Agency had subsidized as many as 200 U.S. newspapers and news services.

Church and his colleagues themselves usually found it easier, more expedient perhaps, to deal with men at Korry's level, and to avoid more formidable encounters. The day Salvador Allende was overthrown and murdered in Santiago, Henry Kissinger was in affable hearings before the Senate Foreign Relations Committee to be confirmed as Secretary of State.

VI

Uncertain Greatness, 1973–1976

Wednesday, October 24, 1973. Four days earlier the President had fired Watergate Special Prosecutor Archibald Cox, triggering the resignation of Attorney General Elliot Richardson and his deputy William Ruckelshaus, in what came to be known as the "Saturday Night Massacre." On Monday, an uneasy cease-fire sponsored by the United States and the Soviet Union settled over Israeli and Egyptian troops in the Sinai after sixteen days of bloody fighting. On Tuesday, following a wave of national fury over the firing of Cox, a presidential counsel agreed, in the U.S. District Court of Judge John J. Sirica in Washington, to surrender subpoenaed tape recordings of White House conversations bearing on Watergate. The same day, on the east bank of the Suez Canal, Israeli forces moved through the cease-fire to encircle and thus threaten with annihilation the 20,000 man III Corps which was the cream of the Egyptian army. Early Wednesday morning, the National Security Agency intercepted Russian military messages to the Soviet Southern Command indicating the imminence of special orders from Moscow, the alert of seven airborne divisions in the Ukraine and Caucasus, a new naval deployment in the Mediterranean, and the flight to Cairo of several large Antonov 22 troop and cargo transports. About ten-thirty that night, Soviet Ambassador Anatoly Dobrynin delivered to Henry Kissinger at the White House an urgent message for Nixon from Brezhnev.

Kissinger and Dobrynin had sparred throughout the day on the issue of a great power peacekeeping force to police the cease-fire. Alarmed at the Israeli encirclement, at three in the afternoon Egyptian President Anwar Sadat sent both Washington and Moscow an urgent appeal for such a force. The political survival of Sadat's régime depended on the III Corps, and on the marginal but symbolically vital Egyptian recapture of territory in the Sinai. Much of Soviet prestige and influence among its Arab clients in the Middle East also lay with the encircled army. The United States had strongly opposed a Soviet-American presence, on grounds that it would only aggravate tensions and entrench the Russians deeper in the region. While he alternately joked with and threatened the Israeli ambassador, Kissinger promised Dobrynin that the cease-fire would hold. By evening he seemed successful in deflecting the Soviet and Arab pressure. But now the Brezhnev message brought diplomacy to an ominous impasse. Charging that Israel was "drastically violating" the cease-fire and "brazenly challenging both the Soviet Union and the United States," insisting that the cease-fire be observed "without delay," the message concluded:

> . . . let us together . . . urgently dispatch Soviet and American contingents to Egypt. . . . I will say it straight, that if you find it impossible to act together with us in this matter, we should be faced with the necessity urgently to consider the question of taking appropriate steps unilaterally. Israel cannot be allowed to get away with violations.

Within minutes of reading the message, Kissinger contacted Dobrynin to reconfirm its contents. It was almost eleven. He then called Nixon in the living quarters of the White House, to inform the President of the Soviet threat of unilateral action and the possible consequences. In the accounts of that conversation later leaked to journalists, Nixon at this point "empowered" him to "take charge of the American response." By one version he did not see or speak to Nixon again that night; by another he went to the presidential bedroom at three the next morning to tell Nixon of the actions that had been taken.

There followed in the Situation Room what the two participants afterward described as an "abbreviated" meeting of the National Security Council. Present were Kissinger, then both Secretary of State and Assistant to the President for National Security, and Secretary of Defense James Schlesinger, now at the Pentagon by way of the Rand Corporation, the Atomic Energy Commission, and brief tenure as Helms's successor at the CIA. They were joined by Admiral Thomas Moorer of the joint chiefs, William Colby, a career bureaucrat who had succeeded Schlesinger and Helms at the CIA, and General Haig, become White House chief of staff after Haldeman. NSC and State Department aides, working under Sonnenfeldt and Sisco, appraised the Soviet note and the day's earlier electronic intelligence. They concluded, as they reported to Kissinger, that the evidence was "ambiguous," that it could be an elaborate bluff, but that the Soviet moves might also presage the introduction of a sizable force which might in turn prompt some desperate new Israeli escalation. As one witness recounted, the senior policymakers then agreed that the intelligence was "inconclusive" but "menacing."

Before midnight Kissinger ordered a worldwide alert of U.S. military forces. The Strategic Air Command and one fleet of nuclear missile Polaris submarines were deployed one stage short of their prewar readiness. The Sixth Fleet in the Mediterranean was put on prewar alert, reinforced by the attack carrier *John F. Kennedy*. Fifteen thousand men of the 82nd Airborne Division were alerted at Fort Bragg, North Carolina. Within hours, the American actions were being monitored by Soviet electronic intelligence, and the chilling shape of a nuclear counter-threat was visible to the Politburo in Moscow. Whether because of intimidation or by original intention, the next day the Soviets and Egyptians accepted a UN peacekeeping force, the Israelis held back, and the crisis seemed to melt away almost as quickly as it had loomed.

In the aftermath of these events, there was widespread public suspicion that Nixon had exaggerated the crisis and cynically seized upon the alert to deter, not the Russians, but the domestic forces of impeachment mobilizing after the Cox episode. Asked at his press conference the following afternoon if the alert might have been "prompted as much perhaps by American domestic requirements," Kissinger's tone was extraordinarily indignant yet strangely melancholy. His words are worth recalling in some length:

> We are attempting to conduct the foreign policy of the United States with regard for what we owe not just to the electorate but to future generations, and it is a symptom of what is happening to our country

that it could even be suggested that the United States would alert its forces for domestic reasons. . . . I am absolutely confident that it will be seen that the President had no other choice as a responsible national leader. . . . We will be prepared . . . I am certain, within a week to put the facts before you . . . after that you will be able to judge whether the decisions were taken hastily or improperly.

At one point the studied charm and earnestness of his usual press conference demeanor turned almost bitter and didactic. "We are attempting to preserve the peace in very difficult circumstances," he told the reporters. "It is up to you ladies and gentlemen to determine whether this is the moment to try to create a crisis of confidence in the field of foreign policy as well."

At his own news conference two days later, Nixon abandoned what had been Kissinger's relative restraint in describing the gravity of the incident or the real certainty of Soviet intentions. It had been, the beleaguered President told the nation, "the most difficult crisis we've had since the Cuban confrontation of 1962." He had been in charge. "When I received that information, I ordered shortly after midnight on Thursday morning an alert for all American forces around the world." As for the doubts about his rule, "Even in this week, when many thought the President was shell-shocked, unable to act, the President acted decisively in the interest of the country . . . I have a quality which is—I guess I must have inherited it from my midwestern mother and father—which is that the tougher it gets, the cooler I get."

The speculation in the press about domestic motives continued for a time, soon to fade from public notice as one more slightly shady interlude in the continuing legal and political reckoning of Watergate. Kissinger never released "the facts" of the alert. Disclosure would only embarrass the Soviets and damage current diplomacy, he privately explained to sympathetic diplomatic reporters.

So the incident passed into the old obliging obscurity—if not the worst international crisis in recent experience, it had been quite probably the most somber constitutional crisis in the conduct of recent American foreign policy. For behind the official versions and misinformed journalism, the issue had never been really that Nixon had ordered the alert to offset domestic scandal, but that he had deliberated, decided, ordered at all. According to authoritative official sources, that Wednesday night the nation had been unknowingly plunged into a possible nuclear confrontation with the Soviet Union while the President of the United States sat upstairs in the White House unwilling or incapable of confronting the crisis. By this account, he had barely roused when Kissinger first reached him by phone at eleven o'clock to report Brezhnev's threat. Other efforts by Kissinger and Haig to draw him into a full deliberation on the crisis had been largely unavailing. It was not so different from other White House evenings, when Nixon was consumed by private torments, except for the life-and-death magnitude of these particular events. With Haig and the assortment of senior bureaucrats acting as his rump NSC, Henry Kissinger became for the night an unelected, unconfirmed, unacknowledged President, by default ordering American forces to the uncertain edges of war with an authority the Constitution has specifically reserved only for the elected Chief Executive.

The October alert symbolized in many ways the political and personal decay that had eaten into the making of foreign policy soon after the 1972 reelection. To begin with, there was little public understanding of the generic relationship between foreign affairs and the evil folly that now brought down the administration. The forming of the "plumbers" group—those men who ended in handcuffs at the Watergate Apartments—stemmed from a rancorous, suspicious White House largely because there were ugly secrets to be kept, many of them pertaining to foreign policy, and because the men in the White House thought the established intelligence agencies could not be trusted. Much of the mistrust that Nixon and Kissinger felt arose from bureaucratic experiences as well as from the methods and goals of foreign policy. When the *Pentagon Papers* dramatically appeared in the summer of 1971, it was Kissinger who inflamed an initially complacent Nixon to take action. Nixon himself saw the documents chiefly (and rightly) as a rebuke to the previous Democratic administrations. In what former White House aide Charles Colson remembered as "panic sessions," Kissinger argued that the publication of the *Pentagon Papers* cast doubt on the capacity of the government to keep secret even its most sensitive and current policy negotiations—the Pakistani mediation with China, the détente with Peking, SALT and other dealings with the Soviets, and, not least, the delicate negotiations with North Vietnam. Each of those foreign policies rested on varying layers of subterfuge, practiced within the régime and without. Each negotiation was peculiarly vulnerable to public disclosure, as was Kissinger's command and success—or so it seemed to the man manipulating all the lines. Then there was Daniel Ellsberg, the most famous leaker of all. Kissinger had known Ellsberg, had even worked with him on Vietnam policy options at the Pierre when Kissinger invited the Rand Corporation to submit a pre-inaugural study of alternatives. Like the NSC staff with their tapped telephones, Ellsberg became another test of Kissinger's patriotic zeal and loyalty to the administration. Ellsberg was a former official who perhaps possessed other, potentially embarrassing information, a veritable representative of, and likely example to, the mutinous bureaucracy below. Ellsberg, after all, had leaked the documents *because* the war was continuing, as a blow, however indirect, at the administration's war policy.

So Kissinger pressed within the administration to stop the leaks "at all costs," portraying Ellsberg as a "fanatic" much as he had portrayed the peace demonstrators months before as childish and disoriented. Even allowing for the distorted recollections of rivals like Colson or Ehrlichman who reported his zeal, the character of his reaction was unmistakable. "At all costs": it was the same imperial habit of threat that told Hoover they would "destroy" the leakers of the Cambodian bombing. Beneath it is visible not only his instinct for self-preservation and his intense ambition, but also the familiar establishment view of the exclusivity of foreign policy. That conviction justified extraordinary actions, with impunity expected, given, and deserved. Such a mentality shaped Kissinger's and Nixon's approach to détente, their fear of the Vietnam backlash, their imperious course in Pakistan and Chile, accompanied by the natural presumption that everything be hidden. Wedded to the remarkable weaknesses of the President and the rowdy reactionary impulses in his men, this *hauteur* of those concerned with national security was to prove fatal to the Nixon government. From the first discussions of the Ellsberg matter, the fear and self-invested authority fed on themselves until the Special Investigations Unit inauspiciously appeared in Room 16 in a remote basement corner of the Executive Office Building. Kissinger was never to be involved directly, of course, though his former appointments secretary, David Young, was on the original "plumbers" staff. But Kissinger and his foreign policy were very much a moving force of the furtiveness which characterized it all.

The "plumbers" and their illegal purposes, the dirty money and the campaign sabotage, the Watergate burglaries and others, followed by the reflexive cover up of everything, were all foreign policy come home in deception, secrecy, even in techniques employed. Generals and politicians from Brazil and Chile, through Indochina to Africa and Europe, would have recognized the hallmarks of U.S. policy making, however shocking and alien these episodes seemed to most Americans watching the poison run through their own politics. The similarities were close in every respect but one—abroad the Watergates were rarely exposed. Foreign policy in many ways remained the impenetrable sanctum.

In October 1973, at the time of the Mideast crisis and consequent alert, while Nixon was already numbed by his long fall toward impeachment and resignation, Kissinger remained at the height of his power and celebrity. What happened in the alert was both effect and cause of that sordid state of affairs. Nixon had come to that moment in October 1973 in effect unable to meet his responsibilities of office. He had been reelected in 1972 in considerable measure because his policies and personal weaknesses had been shielded by Kissinger, Haig, and others below them with more fleeting views of the squalor. Replacing the old establishment élite, these men nevertheless governed foreign affairs in the traditional vacuum of accountability. Kissinger had not had to deal with open public scrutiny of Nixon's reeling impulses in Cambodia or of the machinations in Chile. Nor did he now deal with the grave issue of presidential disability. The October alert might have been an occasion for a serious confrontation between the two men. Kissinger might have made some provision to cope with the problem of Presidential disability. Instead, the disgrace and the danger were buried—rationalized, as so often before, as "Henry" quietly, stoically, wisely held together national security while the politician tottered. This kind of cover up was virtually a tradition among the élite, though seldom as momentous as Nixon's condition made it now. Again, democracy was denied even the chance to see—let alone remedy—the price of its ignorance and error.

The October alert marked as well the beginning of Kissinger's dramatic and, for a time, almost exclusive involvement in Middle East diplomacy over the next year and a half. What followed clearly owed much to Watergate and the desperate weakness of the administration. The domestic scandal distracted Nixon all the more and conferred on Kissinger immense power, both publicly and inside the administration, as nearly the sole figure who legitimized or redeemed the government. That emergence and his appointment to the State Department also may have unlocked some more personal aversion to the subject of the Middle East. For all his power and repute at this stage, some of those close to him saw as late as the summer of 1973 a calculated reluctance on the part of the self-consciously German Jewish immigrant, still the outsider in the American foreign policy establishment, to become too identified with the Middle East, for the perils of credibility it might pose in domestic politics as well as diplomacy. When a friend urged him that summer to concentrate on the region and its explosive tensions, he shot back, "Not until I am Secretary of State and more my own man." Yet when he turned to the problem after the war, the visible result was an extraordinary diplomatic *tour de force*. His indefatigable shuttling between the belligerents produced military disengagement, a lifting of the Arab oil embargo, the first cession of the volatile Israeli-occupied territory since the 1967 war; and it created an apparently major new American influence in the Arab world at the expense of the Soviet Union. Predictably, it also produced still more extravagant press notices and an even more formidable political standing with an accompanying mythology. The Middle East diplomacy seemed to rival the openings in Peking and Moscow as a historic achievement. And as the image of the President sank into the muck, the triumph transparently belonged to Kissinger alone. Eventually, the glitter and the myth waned. His Middle East policy was to suffer some of the broader disillusionment that set in around Kissinger in 1974 and 1975. Israeli and American Jewish critics in particular came to see a concerted deception afoot to compromise Israel's interests in order to protect détente, oil supplies, and new Arab clients. But if the diplomacy was often remarkable, and to a degree historic, it was never so magical or miraculous as the original public likeness suggested. Nor were the results so simple or one-sided as the later critics believed.

The new American embroilment in the Middle East began badly enough. Kissinger and most of the rest of the government had misread or simply ignored the numerous intelligence signs of Arab preparations for the October 1973 war, and of the Soviet shipments of sophisticated anti-tank and anti-aircraft missiles that made the Egyptian and Syrian attack so punishing when it came. Not since the Nazi invasion of Russia or the Japanese attack on Pearl Harbor had governments so widely and recklessly blinded themselves. The myopia was mutually reinforcing in a classic bureaucratic conundrum. The CIA and the Pentagon had cultivated a long and dependent client relationship with Israeli intelligence. The two countries were thus literally reading each other's estimates, which were both drawn mainly from the Israeli service. For the usual bureaucratic reasons, both sides were loath to question their own, their client's, their patron's view—all largely one and the same. The worst common flaw in the reading of the intelligence was an abiding cultural, perhaps racial, contempt in Washington and Jerusalem for the political posturing and fighting skill of the Arabs. Born, like much military folly, of past wars, this disdain led Kissinger no less than the Israeli cabinet to scorn the otherwise ominous indications of Arab warnings and military deployments. That weakness was compounded because both Israel and her advocates in the U.S. government—most particularly the special, nearly autonomous Israeli section of the CIA—so often used threatening intelligence to plump up the arms aid requests that were constantly in some stage of maneuver between the two *de facto* allies. The complex intimacy between the two countries had the effect of denying Washington an independent intelligence view, while at the same time fostering a cynical discrediting of what it did get.

Added to all these ingrained problems, however, was now Kissinger's own more general outlook on the region. He remained convinced in the autumn of 1973—as he had been five years before when he so willingly and confidently abandoned the issues to Rogers —that the Arabs would never negotiate from a sense of military weakness, at least of the kind that had followed the 1967 rout. On several occasions during the first administration, he told NSC aides and bureaucratic gatherings that the two sides needed "a brutal episode of battle" before authentic diplomacy could begin. In Vietnam he had seen the same sort of "brutality" as some final spending of Hanoi's belligerence. In the Middle East he saw it as the means to Arab confidence, and thus to negotiating concessions. In both cases, Kissinger seemed to consider a new war as an almost indispensable, mystical midwife to peace. It was the lasting conviction, after all, of a diplomat who modeled the conception of his policies on the great postwar settlement of nineteenth-century Europe, the professor who made his scholarly reputation and his later political success on the acceptance of the post-World War II reality and who saw diplomacy's strength mainly in its capacity to ratify and order change already imposed by arms.

Flowing from this basic concept were the corollary propositions that made a Mideast war palatable. Détente with the Soviets would make the new fighting manageable. The ensuing settlement could secure U.S. oil supplies and perhaps even supplant Russian influence. It was because others in Washington shared or imitated much or at least part of these views—including, most importantly, James Schlesinger, the new Defense Secretary, and Kissinger's most potent rival since Connally—that U.S. policy during the war would be so labyrinthine. Finally, the impact on all sides of the Watergate scandal was an incalculable element. It may have distracted the Americans more than ever from foreign policy decisions. It probably emboldened the Soviets to equip the Arabs. It almost certainly misled the Israelis on how easily the shaky Nixon régime might equivocate on arms supply as part of a new mediation diplomacy. At any rate, when war broke out over outmanned Israeli lines on October 6, Yom Kippur, the American government was partly oblivious to the event, partly reconciled to its coming, and as personified by Henry Kissinger at least, eager to seize the opportunity for fresh diplomacy.

The shock of the Arab blow made itself felt in Washington, however, within twenty-four hours of the attack. On October 7 the Israeli ambassador to the United States, Simcha Dinitz, a bureaucratic protégé of Prime Minister Golda Meir, rewarded with the vital and prestigious Washington Embassy, called on Kissinger to press for delivery of the Phantom fighters promised Israel during Mrs. Meir's visit to the White House the previous spring. There began a characteristic Kissinger gambit to hold the Israeli requests at bay as later leverage for use against the Arabs, alternately conspiring with and then blaming (in part deservedly) the Pentagon for the arms supply delays. Typically, not the least of his intentions was to cut off Schlesinger from an inattentive, irascible Nixon.

Kissinger told Dinitz the Phantoms would be coming, though the White House did not want to be "provocative" about resupply of the planes. The very same day, by several accounts, he proposed to Schlesinger that arms resupply to the Israelis should be "slow and deliberate." He advised that to avoid pressures on the irresolute President, the delays should be ascribed to "normal" bureaucratic red tape in the Pentagon while the White House maintained it was faithfully urging action. When Dinitz pressed Kissinger again on the eighth, as the Israeli forces were still reeling back in the Sinai Desert and holding thinly against Syria on the Golan Heights, Kissinger replied that he was having "bureaucratic problems with the Pentagon" but would do his best. Yet, in a later phone conversation with Dobrynin, Kissinger told the Russian ambassador that he was all but alone in holding back the "Israeli shadow government" in Washington from ordering a massive resupply to enable the Israelis to launch a crushing counteroffensive.

Once again on October 9, Kissinger complained to Dinitz about the Pentagon, while that afternoon he privately recommended and obtained a blanket Nixon approval "in principle" for resupply in answer to the now mounting Israeli requests. Nixon's approval provided him with insurance against the Israelis and their domestic allies, and a tool to trap Schlesinger, who was reportedly told by a Kissinger aide that there was a "general" October 9 presidential instruction "to do all we can" to help the Israelis, but that the order failed to specify what or how much or when, which of course was its deliberate ambiguity. Early on October 10, U.S. electronic intelligence detected a major Soviet resupply of the Arabs, and revealed a first alert of Russian paratroop units. Meanwhile, Schlesinger—to some extent by prearrangement with Kissinger, and no doubt in part by conviction even if he sensed the game—continued to stall an almost frantic Dinitz, while the White House was absorbed in the resignation and disgrace of Vice President Agnew.

By Thursday, October 11, Kissinger had decided that the Soviet resupply made a U.S. response as necessary to his posture as the earlier delay had been, and he proceeded to exercise that carefully reserved option. At this juncture, however, the partially contrived Pentagon delays had become real enough to resist their sudden reversal. Though Kissinger remonstrated bitterly with Schlesinger that the "situation" had now changed, the Defense Secretary continued to move hesitantly, quibbling over the Israeli use of charter commercial aircraft rather than U.S. military planes. By the next morning,

Kissinger was telling Dinitz the White House would be "tough" on the Pentagon, while at the same time telling Dobrynin that he could no longer forestall a resupply—expressing both attitudes with more truth than during any earlier conversations. That same Friday, Schlesinger again avoided a firm commitment to Dinitz, and near midnight, the Israeli ambassador presented Kissinger with the ultimate threat of his government in its singular cliency with the United States: unless the arms flowed immediately, the Israelis would "go public" with documented charges of perfidy, bringing down on the vulnerable Nixon régime the considerable weight of pro-Israeli sentiment in American politics, perhaps even toppling it. The following Saturday morning, having been briefed by Kissinger on the Pentagon's "foot-dragging," Nixon furiously called Schlesinger, Admiral Moorer, and other senior men to the White House in an unusual personal confrontation to order that U.S. military transports begin to fly arms directly to Israel.

With the American weapons, the Israelis went on the offensive, smashed back across the Suez Canal to begin the envelopment of the Egyptian III Corps that preceded the October 24 "crisis," and overall salvaged the "manageable" stalemate, including a plausible Arab claim of victory, that Kissinger had hoped would emerge from new fighting. But in large measure it was luck and raw courage on both sides that had shaped the outcome—not the muddy battles in Washington. Kissinger's own device had given the Pentagon the mandate it wanted at the upper levels anyway to hold up arms to Israel and court the Arabs after the war. His manipulation of the gullible Dinitz, though never really exposed at the moment, planted the first doubts of American support among the Israelis, doubts that were to grow in the postwar negotiations and in the end to poison them.

The new negotiations began immediately after the war in November 1973 and produced a stunning series of headline successes. On Kissinger's first visit to Egypt, Egyptian President Sadat agreed, chiefly on his own initiative, to negotiate in the wider context of a general disengagement of the two armies rather than arranging a piecemeal withdrawal along the cease-fire line. In December, Kissinger got Israeli and Egyptian agreement to negotiate at Geneva on roughly the same terms, the first prospect of such genuine and potentially broad negotiations between the sides in nearly a quarter century. Later, with the Geneva talks seemingly headed for a prolonged diplomatic deadlock, Kissinger flew to the area again in early January 1974 to spur the process, to "grease the wheels at Geneva," as he told the press traveling with him. Instead, he found Sadat ready to negoti- ate immediately and directly on disengagement with Kissinger him- self acting as intermediary. Between January 10 and 18, 1974, in three hectic round trips between Aswan and Jerusalem, he emerged with the first disengagement agreement. It called for pushing back Israel's troops still west of the Suez Canal and separating the Israeli and Egyptian forces by a UN buffer zone in the Sinai. At a critical midpoint in the shuttles, Kissinger had agreed to make the bargained territorial changes an "American" proposal. Though he continued in effect to carry back and forth, and present interpretations of, the proposals of the two sides, the change bridged the old Arab aversion to "direct" talks with Israel, and transformed Kissinger in name as well as in fact from interlocuter to the arbiter he had hoped to become from the outset.

After a similar, if even more taxing shuttle between Damascus and Jerusalem, an Israeli-Syrian disengagement along that bloodied frontier was concluded on May 31. The agreement with Syria cleared the way for Nixon's triumphant visit to the Mideast in June 1974. The trip was essentially an escape from Watergate, but it also represented the beginning of a new and abortive round in the negotiations, the effort to produce some comparable disengagement between Israel and Jordan on the sensitive West Bank. That summer, as Nixon slouched from office, Kissinger slowed down military assistance to Israel and even orchestrated public hints by Sisco and others that Washington contemplated a more benign policy toward Israel's hated nemesis on the West Bank, the Palestine Liberation Organiza- tion (PLO). But his diplomacy broke on the deep fears and contro- versy the PLO issue aroused in Israeli politics. Another shuttle trip in March 1975 to widen the Sinai disengagement collapsed as well, with Kissinger leaving Israel in a tearful public farewell blaming no one for the impasse, while later aboard his plane he bitterly ridiculed the Jerusalem régime. But the need of the strained Israeli economy for major American aid rekindled the negotiations over the summer. A final successful shuttle brought an agreement on September 1, 1975, withdrawing the Israelis eastward beyond the strategic Mitla and Gidi passes in the Sinai, ceding the Egyptians significant ter- ritory, and policing the separation with an early warning electronic network manned by American technicians.

Throughout the entire sequence there was a continuing sense of public marvel over how he had done it, feeding first the image of a superhuman diplomat, but eventually also the figure of an ambitious schemer. As in much else Kissinger did over the eight years he dominated American foreign policy, his performance was remarkable in both the skill and the manipulative means he employed as compared to any of his predecessors. Nevertheless, many of the secrets to his success were unmysterious. His capacity to conduct the free-wheeling shuttle diplomacy can be traced in the first instance to the peculiar environment in Nixon's Washington. Vaguely anti-Semitic in domestic politics, Nixon looked on the Israelis from the dual aspect of admirer of their obvious military machismo and proud patron of their survival. Presidential monologues on Vietnam seldom failed to make some reference to the fact that the "Israelis could do it" (meaning win a war) even if the Americans could not. Nor did discussions of the Mideast pass without some reference to how "I've saved their ass, and they know it." But the mixture of feelings had produced a tendency to be stern and inflexible with the Israelis before 1973, and to slow up seriously any U.S. diplomacy. Watergate softened the situation, for it took Nixon out of foreign affairs in many respects, and gave him a vast stake in Kissinger's success. In turn, this gave Kissinger the nearly free hand every diplomat covets. In that respect, Watergate made the Mideast diplomacy instantly both possible and necessary. Moreover, the move toward the Arabs satisfied an old and broad stratum of bureaucratic sentiment in the State Department and Pentagon, if not in the CIA. Kissinger was thus able to operate thousands of miles from his bureaucratic base with an exceptional immunity from sabotage. At the top was a President being deposed and at bottom was a bureaucracy at last being appeased after years of neglect. To that secure flank was added the warm support and acquiescence of William Fulbright, the powerful Arkansas chairman of the Senate Foreign Relations Committee, who had long advocated a more pro-Arab diplomacy, and whose serious probings of Kissinger's diplomatic techniques or his role in wiretaps or other White House scandals might have emasculated the shuttle at any point. But Fulbright held off, like the bureaucrats flattered and vindicated by Kissinger's very presence in the Arab states.

His presence was decisive, too, with the Arabs. He was, quite simply, the first American Secretary of State to treat with them seriously in the twenty years since Dulles. His readiness to go to Egypt or Saudi Arabia or Syria, just as to Peking, was part of the success. More vital, of course, was the equally simple reality underlying the negotiations—that the United States possessed what the Soviet Union or any other patron lacked: leverage with Israel. "The Arabs can get guns from the Russians," Kissinger repeated to aides, "but they can get their territory back only from us." The oil embargo was a historic shift in Arab policy toward forcing that singular leverage; and another U.S. régime led by its foreign minister might have responded with serious internal and foreign trade reforms to mitigate the pressure. But Kissinger virtually ignored the embargo as little more than a domestic irritant. His diplomacy envisioned its own historic shift toward the Arabs for purposes of negotiating a settlement, whatever the price of oil. He saw the Middle East not as a problem in economics or resources but as a political problem, to be resolved by political and diplomatic means. Moreover, the careful, expedient but real turn away from Israel met the new currents running deeply in American politics—the fear of foreign military entanglements after Vietnam and a new popular appreciation of how much gasoline consumers were hostage to Washington's Middle East policy.

None of this backdrop was more important, though, than the personal context in which Kissinger operated in the Middle East. It was essentially the same combination of factors that had won him such power in Washington. Armed with unique authority and control vested in him by Nixon, he dealt with the Israelis and Arabs very much as he dealt with the NSC, the press, the WSAG, the Congress, with Nixon or his own staff. He succeeded in nearly direct proportion to each one's peculiar weaknesses, divisions, vulnerabilities. The war did shake Israel and created an unprecedented Israeli mood for settlement; it did restore pride in and political stability for a leader like Sadat, who also understood Kissinger's drive for a settlement. Similarly, Kissinger played shrewdly on each of the separate personalities involved. With the strong old guard in Israel, Meir and General Dayan, he was firm but respectful; when they passed from power in mid-1974, victims of the obvious débâcle of the war, he treated their mediocre successors with alternating face-to-face cajolery and behind-the-back contempt. It was not so different from handling Schlesinger, Laird, Rogers, or a dozen lesser FSOs—and no less effective. All the tried and true stratagems were employed, not of some abstract *Realpolitik,* but the same board-room humor, the ingratiating intimacy, charm, self-deprecation, and intellectual ease that invariably wowed the press in the back of the Secretary's plane.

With the Israelis he reminisced with melancholy about how their intelligence services had botched the early warnings and thought Sadat a "clown." He drew in the cabinet in Jerusalem as he had Dinitz in Washington, with confidential complaints about Schlesinger, and later even demeaning stories about Nixon. No one else was competent, could be trusted, went the dialogue between allies. The Japanese were "congenitally treacherous," he told the Israelis on one occasion. On another he could indulge their distrust for the UN, a cause he was supposedly advocating, by joking about Secretary-General Kurt Waldheim. Back in New York, however, his attitude toward Waldheim was friendly and intimate, with jokes about the Israelis that soon made the rounds at the UN. To Sadat he described his efforts to save the III Corps; to Dayan and Dinitz he spoke of how he had saved the Israelis from a Russian invasion. In Aswan, the Soviets were bound to the United States in the *de facto* alliance of détente, unable and unwilling to undercut his diplomacy or help Sadat because their greater interests lay elsewhere. In Jerusalem, the Russians were "inept" and "laughable," and he regaled the Israelis with tales of absurdities in the SALT negotiations, lest they believe he might take too seriously the Soviet threat and scuttle Israel if necessary.

And so it continued. He orchestrated leaks, planted doubts that widened divisions among his adversaries on this point and that. With the Israelis he used military aid to purchase their cooperation in blunting Democratic Senator Henry Jackson's amendment to ease migration of Soviet Jews. With the Syrians he openly threatened their isolation in an Arab world in which his diplomacy had breached the fragile unity of the Saudis and Egyptians. More vital than his mastery of the substance of the military or political problems—always adequate and sometimes brilliant as it was—was the mastery and exploitation of the banal human relations, the fear, ambition, pettiness, and vanities that shape high-level politics often more than the press or public ever imagine.

In the end, he succeeded in the Middle East, as he did in Washington, because he operated in a context ready to be exploited, and because his interests in most respects could be shared by the protagonists. The Middle East is one of the last of the great post-imperial problems of frontiers and sovereignty. It is thus one of the last international issues subject to control by the will and personalities of government élites, and one of the last susceptible to Henry Kissinger's willful and intensely personal diplomacy. When that diplomacy encountered more diffuse and less manipulable factors, like the West Bank question in Israel's lively democratic politics, it foundered. On the opposite side, it was not Kissinger's charm or persuasion that drew the Israelis back to disengagement negotiations in the summer of 1975, but rather the war-torn Israeli economy, a weakness Kissinger had never even invoked in earlier talks or pressuring.

Ironically, however, it was the most ruthless exploitation of internal weakness that crowned Kissinger's Middle East policy in 1975–76 —and this time (his Jewish detractors silent) on the side of Israel. As Lebanon plunged into a bloody civil war, the CIA, with the connivance of the intrepid if short-sighted Israeli intelligence service, was accused by some officials of supporting covertly the fighting that inflicted an awful, temporarily crippling attrition of the PLO. Allegedly conducted by the special Israeli bureau of the CIA, the Lebanese operation proceeded, according to these sources, while unknowing American diplomats (like Korry in Chile) tried to arrange a cease-fire, and while congressional and executive oversight groups were consistently misled on the scope and purpose of our covert involvement in Lebanon. Perhaps the final irony was that the same officials who were shocked at the CIA role and apparently leaked it could not be quite sure if Kissinger himself even knew the full details or motives of the Agency's operations. Having watched the shuttle diplomacy extract concessions from their clients, having weathered a congressional and public storm intact, the CIA by 1976 still possessed the bureaucratic capacity and self-defined mission to carry out its own Mideast policy.

Whether or not he had any knowledge of such a gruesome intervention by the CIA in Lebanon, Kissinger would leave the Middle East in an uneasy balance, the fundamental issue of Israel's security unresolved by the diplomacy that ate at the country's conquered borders and fortified Arab confidence, yet achieved little else. In a Democratic administration he would pass on diplomacy to men of the old establishment with no more knowledge of the region and generally much less virtuosity or flexibility in dealing with it. Kissinger's purpose was to fashion out of the trauma of a last battle in October 1973 a final orderly settlement reflecting the realities of power. But the profound religious and ethnic tensions of the Middle East were its realities of power, and they took it far away from easy historical analogy. The new resource power of the Arabs, a new generation of leaders in both Israel and the Arab states, the carnage in Lebanon and the changes it wrought in the military and political balance by removing the PLO as an effective force for a time—none were affected by Watergate or Kissinger's ambition and style. Laudable and dramatic in intent though not technique, his Middle East diplomacy left an area in which no settlement was final, and the last battle not yet fought.

The Middle East shuttle diplomacy was the scene of Kissinger's ultimate seduction of a consenting press. The sleek blue and silver 707 flew in and out of the ancient exotic places with the accompanying reporters less a fourth estate than a fourth branch of "Henry's" mobile government—or, as one of them put it, "the biggest permanent floating foreign policy establishment in our history." As Secretary of State with regular news conferences and his own press corps, Kissinger and his relations with the media had become more visible than when he was National Security Affairs adviser. Both NBC and CBS often showed brief film clips of a casual Kissinger standing in the aisle of his plane, chatting cheerfully with smiling journalists. But the visibility of the relationship did not seem to deter what was happening. "Probably no Secretary of State in history has had a closer relationship with the newsmen who cover him," wrote *The New York Times*'s Bernard Gwertzman about one foray through the Middle East and Europe. "Particularly on these trips, newsmen are continually in communication with Mr. Kissinger," he went on. "He likes to wander to the back of the aircraft where newsmen sit to crack jokes and exchange impressions."

Murrey Marder, the respected diplomatic reporter of the Washington *Post*, noted the same congeniality during Kissinger's first trip to the Middle East in November 1973, but saw some drawbacks: "Dr. Kissinger would tease the press about 'cutting off the caboose,' meaning the press end of the aircraft, if anyone wrote anything unfavorable about him. The aircraft remained intact. There was so much news generated during the journey, and the trip was so physically exhausting, that there was little time or energy for drawing critical balance sheets." Marder confessed that Kissinger's visits to the press section, along with the jokes, gave him "the advantage of supplying newsmen with his own interpretation of the news he made in each capital." And if Marder and others saw such news as "hard and interpretive," it also "supplied the Nixon administration, at a time of urgent need, with a public display of action in world affairs to set against the miasma of Watergate." "He briefs them to death," said one journalist of the group covering the Middle East trips. It was not only that Kissinger made himself available. He was also careful to protect his credibility. He would begin a trip to the Middle East, for example, with a list of Israeli POWs held by Syria already in his hands, rather than, as much of the press believed and reported, flying to Damascus to receive it. Behind the secret possession of the list was a tangled diplomatic gambit, but, after "fibbing" about the list (both journalists and officials used the same word), Kissinger called the press back to his cabin to admit—off the record—that he had it.

If some diplomatic journalists were aware of the danger of being exploited by government, Kissinger clearly added special dimensions to the old problem. There on the plane, his wit was more than ever disarming, his brilliance intimidating. Intimacy with his extraordinary success and power in the negotiations not only affected the reporters' self-esteem, but began to confer a special sense of professional accomplishment and even participation in the historic events they were describing. Gwertzman's published diary of one trip is telling:

> ... wherever the Kissinger plane has gone, the newsmen aboard have been the envy of their colleagues on the ground. An article in the Israeli press called the airborne press "the best informed in the world." Correspondents in Syria and Egypt, who have virtually no access to officials of Mr. Kissinger's rank, swarmed over the American correspondents when the plane landed trying to find out what was going on.

"We know more than most U.S. Ambassadors in the places we visit," added another frequent passenger on the plane. It was often as if the State Department press contingent was holding its own backgrounder on the tarmac at Damascus—and choosing its words with customary diplomatic caution.

The seduction went so far as to create a mutually protective Kissinger lobby within the media. "Have you got anything coming up that'll embarrass us?" one reporter recalled being asked by a worried diplomatic correspondent from the same newspaper who was about to depart on a Kissinger trip. "It was the 'us' that really killed me," the reporter added.

When Seymour Hersh wrote a two-part story on the "plumbers" in *The New York Times* on December 9 and 10, 1973—although there was only fleeting reference to Kissinger's feeding presidential fears of the dangers to national security posed by Ellsberg—there was visible distress at both ends of the Kissinger press plane then shuttling in the Mideast. The angry Secretary of State promptly issued a statement (reported by the accompanying press) rebutting the story. He fended off questions from foreign correspondents. But at least one reporter present later confessed that the traveling American press contingent "implicitly" agreed "not to ask questions about the subject in front of the international press." "They took a dive," said another journalist who heard about the episode later, "for the good of the mission."

Traveling with Kissinger to the Mideast compressed and intensified the pressures that were present in Washington as well. There too he was witty, ingratiating, and intimate in State Department press conferences, where the transcripts reflected the "clubby" atmosphere of first names, flatteringly personal references to "former students," and laughter strategically placed to break the tension of a tough question. The subtle compromising in these encounters was unmistakable if unacknowledged. Journalists called by first names, their graduate work at Harvard casually mentioned in the banter, found it all the harder to summon the grit—not to say outrage—it would have taken to pry out reality. And looming over everything for reporters, editors, columnists was the incalulable privilege of access. Without the right access in this *de facto* administration where one man and a small circle of staff aides directed American foreign policy, a diplomatic correspondent was professionally and personally threatened. "If a reporter loses access to Henry because he's tough," admitted one former journalist, "his editors won't ask whether he's right; the first question they'll ask is, 'How do we cover Kissinger?' "

"Henry's shown the media remarkable candor," said one of his close aides at the time, "and he outmaneuvered them."

If that docile press glimpsed the foolish and callous sides of Kissinger's statesmanship, it was usually because someone else made the issue plain and newsworthy. Even then, the continuing tendency was to exonerate "Henry" and move swiftly with him on to more vital matters, which was to say whatever that "higher-level official" on the Secretary's plane happened to be confiding at the moment. The most critical reporting around the 1972 summits had been of the obvious astonishment and resentment in the Japanese government when it turned out that Washington had not consulted Tokyo in advance of Nixon's Peking visit. The incident was serious enough in diplomatic terms, emblematic of the petty, back-biting alienation between the two régimes that had begun with the Nixon-Sato anteroom fiasco three years before. But that background was scarcely probed; nor was Kissinger's clear role in an embarrassing incident which the press generally ascribed to Nixon alone. Even at that, the Japanese "shock" reverberating from Japan and the rest of the world press received much more press attention than the policies in Pakistan or Chile.

In much the same fashion, the journalistic passengers on the Mideast shuttles and their envious colleagues back home seldom looked beyond the palpable and heady diplomacy in Jerusalem, Aswan, or Damascus. The reality of the negotiations—the cajolery, the ceaseless posturing, the seamy jokes and threats, and thus the limits and frailty of what Kissinger accomplished with his personal diplomacy —remained hidden behind Kissinger's banter with Sadat or Rabin in front of the microphones, and were never mentioned in those candid briefings on the plane before the next stop. Worse perhaps, there seemed almost no awareness in the reporters or their pleased editors that this was *not* foreign policy. The press coverage of Kissinger represented at once the élitism, the erosion of democratic instincts, and the isolation from reality that had infected the media as well as the government in the America of the 1970s.

Lost in the naïveté and self-indulgence of the press was not only Kissinger's diplomacy, but also any chance for public understanding of the large submerged reality of foreign policy that went on without him. As Nixon plummeted from reelection to resignation, as the "biggest, permanent floating . . . establishment" cruised through the Middle East, other human and bureaucratic dramas were being played out, no less revealing about the character of America's relations with the world. Burundi, a small central African country, was one of the more gruesome cases in point during 1972–74. Frightened by an attempted *coup d'état* in 1972, the ruling Tutsi minority in Burundi began the systematic killing of the Hutu, the ethnic group which made up 85 percent of the country's 3.5 million people but had been denied economic or political power for centuries. The slaughter reached the rate of 1,000 deaths a day in 1972. When Burundian army units ran out of ammunition, they used hammers and nails to continue the slaughter. By 1973, as many as 250,000 were dead, and 100,000 more in exile.

Late into many nights that spring of 1972, open trucks loaded with corpses rumbled past the American Embassy bound for bulldozed mass graves outside the capital. And inside the embassy sat Thomas Patrick Melady, the U.S. ambassador to Burundi, temporizing in sending the first reports of genocide to Washington, concerned that the State Department would somehow "over-react" and destroy his carefully nurtured relationship with the Burundian régime. Melady was a forty-five-year-old academic, a prominent Catholic layman who had written on Africa. He had lobbied hard for a Nixon ambassadorial appointment, and finally got Burundi in 1970. He had been concerned from the beginning of his mission about Tutsi fears that the United States would take sides with the suppressed Hutu. "He told them [the Burundis] every chance he got," remembered an official who read Melady's telegrams, "that the United States was absolutely impartial as between Tutsi and Hutu, that their relations were their own affair, and he apparently got through to them." So Melady maneuvered nimbly around the slaughter. He conveyed to the régime, according to his official cables, "the necessity of avoiding *undue* bloodshed" (as distinct, presumably, from bloodshed *due*). And as the loaded trucks rolled past the U.S. Embassy and Melady pondered his diplomatic relationships, back in Washington the Department of State's African Bureau was equally worried about its own clients among the other African states. The Organization of African Unity, its members haunted by tribalism and sensitive to any precedent for outside interference in the continent, had refused from the outset to take action. Once the Africans looked the other way, the

Department was free to pursue its policy in Burundi as it had a few years before in Biafra. On May 25, 1972, in the face of undeniable evidence of the continuing genocide, Melady routinely left the country for a new assignment. He departed with a decoration from the Burundian government, he and his home office in Foggy Bottom maintaining total silence about the horror.

The administration, it turned out, had various interests in Burundi. Americans purchased the bulk of Burundi's coffee—an extraordinary 65 percent of the small country's commercial earnings and a potentially powerful economic weapon against the Tutsi régime, which was supported almost entirely by the open proceeds and graft of the coffee trade. But the African Bureau bureaucrats dismissed out of hand a secret proposal in the summer of 1972 to suspend the coffee trade, if only to dissociate the United States from the murders. "If we'd involved ourselves in this," one FSO explained, "we'd be creamed by every country in Africa for butting into an African state's internal affairs. We just don't have an interest in Burundi that justifies taking that kind of flack." With the same reasoning, officials dismissed a State Department legal memorandum pointing out that the United States had solemn obligations under international law and treaties to deal in some manner with such human rights abuses. The coffee trade continued and Washington never spoke out—"frustrated," as a memorandum later put it, "by the absence of a suitable opportunity." By October 1972, after the slaughter had diminished somewhat, Washington did tell the Burundian régime confidentially that it could not expect "normal official relations" until a "genuine national reconciliation" had taken place. A $100,000 aid program was suspended, but the cutoff was only announced publicly a year later.

Then, in January 1974, despite a thick file of cables confirming that the ethnic genocide continued to claim "thousands," the State Department secretly decided to resume aid to Burundi, including the $100,000 and a new $52,500 for three Burundian-run maternity clinics. The resumption of aid was rationalized in a secret policy recommendation to the White House as encouraging "pro-Western moderates" in the Tutsi élite. It was probably better explained by a quiet UN discovery in the summer of 1973 of a $14 billion deposit of nickel in Burundi, a find which sent agents of Kennecott, Bethlehem Steel, and American Metals Climax rushing to Africa and to lobby the State Department. The new U.S. aid, according to the paper on the policy shift, was to "increase US influence over the final disposition of the nickel." Beyond political or economic designs, however, there was also a bureaucratic factor, articulated in this case with rare honesty. The new U.S. aid to Burundi might be small and unavailing, admitted the policy paper, but it was "both useful and necessary because it is difficult over time to maintain a large diplomatic establishment in Burundi without any apparent substantive raison d'etre, in the midst of an autistic and suspicious society." As for the maternity clinics, officials saw them as "a model of what can be done in over-populated predominantly Catholic countries." Nowhere in the policy paper were questions raised about the propriety of U.S. funding for population control measures by a régime pursuing a deliberate policy of ethnic killing and terror.

Like the official silence on the earlier genocide, the new aid was not a matter sufficiently important for high-level attention. Replete with its maternity clinics and $14 billion in nickel, the January 1974 recommendation went from Foggy Bottom to the White House in a routine form memo Kissinger did not even sign. It was addressed to General Brent Scowcroft, an amiable air force officer of modest foreign policy expertise who had become Kissinger's deputy succeeding Haig. "The US has proved its point [i.e., its repugnance toward what had happened in Burundi] for both domestic and foreign consumption," concluded the paper. The memo blatantly lied in saying that the Tutsi régime "had refrained from taking reprisals" against Hutus. Scowcroft in any case gave the recommendation his rubber stamp approval reportedly without showing it to Nixon, an authority both he and Kissinger seized more and more in the closing six months of the administration. On January 29, in the name of the President, the general authorized a modest allocation of money "predicated on continued evidence" (which the State Department knew did not exist) "that Burundi is following a national policy of respect for human rights." By July 1, 1974, the American subsidies for the maternity clinics were on the way.

Only a month before, Kissinger had returned from Syria expecting a hero's welcome for the disengagement agreement negotiated between Damascus and Jerusalem. Instead he encountered an unusually prickly June 6 news conference which featured questions about his role in the wiretaps; he was visibly stunned. It was true that he "went along" with the wiretaps. But he had been cleared by the Senate Foreign Relations Committee. Ultimate responsibility lay with others, and it was impertinent to link the Secretary of State, fresh from another Mideast triumph, to the tawdry domestic scandal. "I consider this a press conference and not a cross-examination," he retorted. The shrill, perplexed pitch of the answers was another exceptional moment in his public relations. For similar reasons, it was reminiscent of the dismissal of questions about the October alert seven months before. Over the next few days, however, the speculation about the taps grew. FBI documents emerging in the impeachment investigation of the House Judiciary Committee began to supply a picture of the discreet vendetta of 1969 that was not even supposed to exist in the normal secret channels, much less be made public. In a bold, chastening stroke to quash the threat, Kissinger then threatened to resign in his famous June 11, 1974, press conference in Salzburg, Austria, where the presidential party was pausing before a two-week junket to the Mideast and the USSR. The tone in Salzburg was emotional. "When the record is written, one may remember that perhaps some lives were saved and that perhaps some mothers can rest more at ease, but I leave that to history. What I will not leave to history is a discussion of my public honor," he said with a choked voice. "I do not believe it is possible to conduct the foreign policy of the United States under these circumstances when the character and credibility of the Secretary of State is at issue," he concluded. "And if it is not cleared up, I will resign."

Transfixed by Nixon's fall, many observers saw in Salzburg an effort to put Kissinger's still vast and uncommitted prestige on the scales against further pursuit of Watergate in general. Again, as with the October alert, the reality was otherwise. "I cannot let my policies or myself be dragged down with that man," Kissinger is said to have told aides in the anxious hours before he decided to call the press conference. The intent was first and foremost to separate Kissinger from the collapse of Nixon he had come to see as inevitable. No one seemed to recognize that better than Nixon himself. "Informed" the night before of Kissinger's plans, the President tepidly "suggested" to Haig that Kissinger's statement might be "inappropriate" since it would steal attention from the continued presidential journey. Yet Nixon was at this late moment politically powerless to prevent Kissinger from doing almost anything. Between the lines at Salzburg can be seen a last public sign of the root expedience and shabbiness in their relationship. More important than the separation from Nixon, however, was what Salzburg showed of the private Kissinger. The brief flurry of questions and attacks—not unusual by Washington standards and almost mild by comparison to the rest of the reporting on Watergate—exposed the insecure, anxious, indecisive, sometimes tormented man who was masked and so ardently protected by the poised, charming statesman in the briefing situation or the *tête-à-tête* meeting. This was the same man who had struggled in 1969 in much the same calculated way to secure himself with a then all-powerful Nixon, and thus left himself ethically and legally open to the very attacks he now fended off. In Salzburg his sense of outrage, anguish, and victimization was genuine enough, despite the pervasive cynicism—genuine because he believed too in that *droit de seigneur* of the statesman that allowed him to hunt down leaks, to shade the truth, and now to supplant and survive a corrupt politician. And, as always, others believed in the *droit* as well. His tactic produced quick results. In two days fifty-two senators signed a resolution of confidence that Kissinger's "integrity and veracity are above reproach." The leaks, questions, articles, and editorials dwindled.

When they returned from the Mideast and Moscow on July 3, Nixon would have thirty-six days left in the presidency and Kissinger would be seen as the single most respected, legitimizing force in the new régime of Gerald Ford. For a time, he was once again viewed as he had been so long, as *Newsweek* had portrayed him on the cover of its June 10 issue, before the awkward questions. Muscles rippling beneath the familiar comic-book blue suit and cape, his sleek caricature now recognizable without caption throughout the world, the miraculous "Super K" soared in upward flight.

Less than a year after Salzburg, however, the aura was gone again, this time some of it permanently. The cover of the same magazine was once more symbolic. "Super K" had become a pudgy Gulliver, watching helplessly as Lilliputian figures of Viet Cong, U.S. congressmen, Arabs and Israelis, Greeks and Turks, and other assorted international protagonists tied him down. For at least some of the public and press by the spring of 1975, Henry Kissinger had been brought abruptly back to earth. The curdling in coverage was the result of a dramatic series of setbacks. In rapid succession occurred the Greek-Turkish clash over Cyprus, with a resulting acrid congressional fight over U.S. diplomacy in the crisis, to be followed by further congressional doubts about conventional arms sales and détente. Next, a temporary collapse of the Mideast shuttle diplomacy took place and new and often sordid revelations of covert interventions from Iraq to Chile became public. Not least in this series of setbacks was that spring's final débâcle in Indochina. Much as the press had enthroned him for earlier apparent successes, Kissinger now finally became the villain of the seeming failures. Yet if many of the blunders were his and the revelations long overdue, the still shallow public imagery ironically misrepresented the man who once had benefited so much from it. In some cases it exaggerated his responsibility for failure; in others it obscured his most promising reforms as Secretary of State. And as the 1976 election approached, bringing with it the prospect of Kissinger's departure, both the Congress and the press had fallen back into the familiar weary cynicism and resignation. He seemed certain to end his tenure largely as he began— his gifts and flaws understood only dimly through the larger public malaise that hung over American foreign policy.

The disenchantment traced to the Cyprus crisis of July and August 1974 just as Nixon fell from office. In an exception to the superficial, cartoon criticism that commonly followed major events, much of the story of U.S. policy in the episode was told a year later in *Foreign Policy* magazine by Laurence Stern, a Washington *Post* journalist who had also investigated the U.S. economic war on Chile in Allende's closing days. It would have been a by then familiar recital of neglected intelligence, shadows of CIA complicity, maladroit diplomacy, and indifference to human costs—had Stern's colleagues not been so long content to report the glossy surface of policy. But what was a worn pattern seemed to most a novelty, and Kissinger's first major public defeat.

The crisis, as Stern recounted, grew out of the inflamed ethnic politics setting Greece and the Greek-Cypriot majority—in favor of union *(enosis)* with the mother country—against Turkey and the 18 percent Turkish minority on the small resort island. Twice since the 1960 independence of Cyprus, in 1964 and again in 1967, Ankara had nearly gone to war in defense of the minority, only to be stopped by heavy pressure from the United States to prevent fighting be-

tween two NATO allies. Under an ostensibly nonaligned régime of
the imperious and protean Archbishop Makarios, Cyprus trod a precarious balance between incessant Greek plots for *enosis,* Turkish
ambitions to dismember the island, and great powers watching anxiously the potential instability on the old volatile frontier of the Bal-
kans and the Mideast. Washington's relations with both Greece and
Turkey had mortgaged the influence that would be needed in 1974.
The Johnson administration stood by in easy acceptance (if not with
a little CIA encouragement) as a Greek junta in April 1967 destroyed
the constitutional democracy that might have put unwieldy leftists
in power in Athens. When the U.S. Embassy the night of the coup
flashed to Washington a report on "tanks in Constitution Square,"
Dean Rusk was quietly expressive of the policy. Given the telegram
by an aide, he poured a bourbon and water, watched another television program on his large Secretarial set, as he completed his routine,
and went home as usual around nine o'clock. Johnson did eventually
impose a partial arms embargo on the torturing tyranny of the Colonels. But Nixon reopened the full flow of weapons in 1970, and until
1974 Washington shamelessly supported the junta in customary and
rising kickback payments in arms aid for the sake of its major naval
and intelligence bases.

With the Turks, policy was somewhat sterner but similarly con-
strained. Though Johnson's envoys had threatened the Ankara oligarchy with an arms cut off to deter intervention in 1964 and 1967,
Turkey housed equally vital U.S. bases and sophisticated electronic
listening posts along the Soviet border, installations that made possible, for example, intelligence on Russian military moves of the kind
that spurred the October alert. If anything, Nixon and Kissinger
were more cordial to Turkey than to Greece, except for the overriding embarrassment of an American domestic issue. As part of its
popular campaign against unprecedented drug traffic, the administration found itself politically compelled in 1970–71 to pressure the
Turks for some agreement to limit their legal and lucrative growth
of opium poppies. Whatever its impact on crime and drug addiction
and votes for Nixon in American cities, the negotiation yielded only
a temporary ban and added to Turkey's sense of being diplomatically
bullied by the United States.

This was the setting when intelligence warnings of a Greek-insti-
gated coup in Cyprus streamed into Foggy Bottom beginning in

February 1974. Those warnings, in Stern's recreation of the sequence, led the Cyprus desk to suggest a formal U.S. approach to the Greek junta to discourage further plotting. But in both Athens and Nicosia the intelligence came as little more than the latest in a ceaseless cycle of conspiracies. Ominous predictions of assassination and overthrow had been almost commonplace since 1970, and though there were actual attempts to kill Makarios—some by elements known well by and to the CIA—the reports early in 1974 were broadly discounted both in Washington and the Mediterranean. At the same time, the U.S. ambassador in Athens, Henry J. Tasca, a State Department economist who was at the climax of three routine decades in the bureaucracy, had, after five years in Greece, noticeably cooled his earlier ardor toward the junta. He had been instructed by Kissinger in March to avoid any admonition to the régime. But when more alarming intelligence gathered in June and Kissinger told the envoy to warn off the head of the junta, General Ioannides, the secret police chief, Tasca simply passed the message to lesser officials and refused to see the general, whom he personally disliked and regarded as "a cop" beneath a diplomat's station. In early July, Cypriot newspapers published what proved to be incredibly accurate predictions of the forthcoming coup attempt, though afterward Kissinger, Tasca, and the CIA would all argue that intelligence on a coup was difficult to get. The plotters struck on July 15, driving Makarios into exile after failing to kill him, installing a fanatic conspirator as the new president pledged to *enosis*, frightening the Turkish minority, provoking the Turkish government, and taking Washington by muddled surprise.

Inside the State Department, the first reaction to the ousting of Makarios was a sense of relief at being rid of a recalcitrant politician. As the gravity of the crisis became apparent, there persisted a bland official refusal to condemn the violent overthrow of a government, and the provocative character of the radical new Cypriot régime, or even to acknowledge external Greek complicity, on which secret State and CIA reports were unanimous. The policy was due in part to Kissinger's distracted failure to see the magnitude of the crisis, and in large measure to the State Department's reluctance to offend the client junta in Athens. On July 17, Kissinger sent Sisco to conduct a second-echelon shuttle between Greece and Turkey to forestall a clash as in 1964 and 1967. Yet this time the U.S. envoy did not even carry the threat of an arms suspension, and the advent of repression by a régime of militant Greek Cypriots gave the Turks a long-sought opportunity they would not forego. On July 20, Turkish forces landed on Cyprus and strove to secure an enclave. While Sisco was in Athens the next day, pressing for a cease-fire, the Greek junta literally disintegrated under the strain of its divisions over the coup and the prospect of a war with Turkey. In an extraordinary sequel, the officers deposed Ioannides and handed over power to a moderate civilian régime whose leaders were variously summoned from house arrest or foreign exile. Meanwhile, a cease-fire went into effect on Cyprus and the radicals abdicated. Kissinger welcomed the new Greek régime with effusive phone calls to its politicians. With a peaceable régime installed in Greece, and Turkish pride supposedly appeased by the intervention, at this point the crisis seemed quelled. For the moment, American's Cyprus policy appeared to have been rescued from its initial blunders by sheer good luck.

But no one, least of all Kissinger, reckoned with the force of Turkish irredenta. Talks in Geneva dragged on as the Turks slowly devoured land in Cyprus by means of low-level violence. Once again, Kissinger refused to brand the aggressors publicly, and privately told aides he would not oppose Ankara's territorial ambitions. He believed the country was otherwise more important to U.S. security in the Mediterranean than the new civilian government in Greece. On August 14, the Turkish army of 40,000 swept past token resistance to annex nearly half the island. A flood of refugees poured from the 200,000 Greek Cypriots caught in the seizure. Among the debris was not only a terrible human cost on Cyprus but also American prestige and interests in the region. Relations with the new Athens régime began with bitterness, for which the United States would eventually pay dearly in base rights and aid. On Cyprus the Turkish invasion left still wider and deeper hatreds, festering toward some new eruption in an uncertain future. U.S. policy, wrote Stern, "was one of vacillation, impotence, and indifference to legal and constitutional principle."

But the failure lay not alone in "Henry's" preference for the Greek Colonels and then for the Turks, or in insouciant ambassadors and ignored intelligence. Its cold-bloodedness and folly were made possible too—as in Pakistan, Chile, Burundi, and a host of other cases —by the quiet acquiescence of so many junior men in State. The failure of U.S. policy was also made possible because Kissinger was so solitary at the top of the government, his biases unchallenged, as one U.S. President collapsed and another took over in customary ignorance and awe of foreign policy. Moreover, it was in some respects another of the dubious legacies of the Johnson years. However impotent his mandate, Sisco went to Athens and Ankara against a history of too many Democratic "troubleshooters" (including Cyrus Vance, Kissinger's successor) who had discreetly blackmailed Turkey with weapons. Neither Kissinger nor his predecessors had been able to deal openly with the threat to peace and human rights on the island; neither had paid attention to Cyprus until it became a crisis; neither stayed to try to help heal the problem once the explosion seemed over.

Kissinger's ultimate false step in the Cyprus crisis was on Capitol Hill rather than in the Mediterranean. With the Turks illegally using U.S.-supplied NATO weapons on Cyprus, with a remarkably strong pro-Greek lobby formed after the advent of the civilian government in Athens, with the obvious diplomatic mess on Cyprus adding to Nixon's disgrace, in the face of fresh revelations about Chile and wiretaps, Congress rose up and cut off military aid to Turkey. Though Kissinger and his aides would argue passionately the damage to national security, they badly misjudged—for the moment anyway— how much the very success of détente and Mideast diplomacy had undermined the old resort to fear of the Russians, how much the increasingly visible willfulness of the administration's foreign policies had undermined the old mystique. The congressional rebuke took away the one positive remnant of the crisis, Kissinger's standing with the triumphant Turks. Embittered by the arms embargo, the Ankara régime joined the Greeks and Cypriots in rancor and distrust toward the United States.

Though the first of its kind in nearly five years, the congressional reproof to Kissinger on the Cyprus issue was formidable. Defeat was sharpest in the roll call of the House of Representatives, always less an object of his ardent courtship than the Senate and usually more star-struck and heedless in its abdication to him. On September 24, 1974, the House voted by 307 to 90 to stop military aid to Turkey until "substantial progress" was made toward a Cyprus settlement. In both the Senate and the House, the episode emboldened gathering opposition to the quiet scandal of the arms trade. By the end of

1974, the United States had become far and away the world's biggest weapons merchant. Its $86 billion in military sales and aid since 1950 was twice the Soviet arms exports. And though roughly half that figure went to NATO, even the Congress began to see that too many weapons went to arm internal forces of repression and wars in which both the recipient countries were ostensibly allies or friends of the United States. There had been a halting effort made to moderate the arms traffic after the spectacle of seeing American tanks fighting on both sides of the 1967 Indo-Pakistan war. But the bureaucracy swiftly evaded the legislation; Congress discreetly ignored the defiance; and with the approval of the Johnson régime, the Pentagon, trying to hide the cost of the war in a balance of payments promotion, raised arms sales to a bipartisan art.

Both Nixon and Kissinger saw conventional arms shipments as the simplest expedient to forestall a feared dwindling U.S. influence following the retreat from Vietnam. Behind them, as Johnson, was an enormous and powerful arms industry interlocked throughout the American corporate structure, further encouraged by the insatiable Pentagon hunger for client nations throughout the world. In 1973–74, U.S. foreign arms sales reached a high of $10.8 billion; $9.4 billion sales were made in 1974–75, much of it to tyrannical régimes such as Korea and Indonesia, Iran and Ethiopia, Brazil and Chile. "What a contribution," a retiring FSO bitterly remarked to a congressman on his three decades in the State Department since World War II: "From the arsenal of democracy to the arsenal of dictatorship in one career." To stem that trade in the aftermath of the Cyprus fighting, the Congress finally passed the International Security Assistance Act of 1976 providing a formal Capitol Hill veto over commercial or government sales worth more than $25 million. How the legislation would affect control of the arms traffic, if at all, would depend as always on the seldom sustained courage and attention of congressional oversight, though it was at least a start toward lessening the foreign policy travesties symbolized by Greece and Turkey in the Cyprus crisis.

But the congressional disillusion was also more than a scolding over Cyprus or military sales. In the two weeks in September before the representatives voted the Turkish aid suspension, there appeared the first leaks of CIA testimony on the policy in Chile. In December, revelations of CIA spying against Vietnam war protestors and other dissidents became public, and both houses set up select committees to investigate the intelligence agencies. The Senate committee eventually exposed the details of the Chile story. It was the House committee under New York Democrat Otis Pike, however, that rehearsed the longer, unbroken history of intelligence blunders, emerging with a damning picture of American foreign policy under Kissinger and his predecessors. After probing the CIA's spectral $10 billion budget (including thousands for liquor, procurement of "female companions" for client heads of state, and pornographic movies for similar diplomatic purposes), the committee conducted six case studies. In the matter of the Tet offensive, they uncovered the tragically distorted reports that had prefaced the disaster and then had later covered it up. As for the Soviet invasion of Czechoslovakia in August 1968, the CIA and Pentagon had simply " 'lost' the Russian army for two weeks." It was located at last when Dobrynin officially told Johnson and Rostow of the strike. Poor intelligence had also obscured the beginning of the Arab-Israeli October war, and then hampered Washington's view of the fighting—including, the committee concluded, vague information on the Israeli encirclement of Egyptian troops that set off the U.S.-Soviet confrontation and the October alert.

Part of the story too revealed the now conscious, now senseless mistakes in predicting the coup in Cyprus. The previous spring, in April and May 1974, the CIA had similarly failed to analyze the military coup in Portugal which plunged the country into uncertainty. The Indian explosion of a nuclear bomb, the first in the Third World, also came as a surprise to our vaunted intelligence gatherers. Added to these cases, the committee touched on characteristic episodes in Italy and Iraq. In Rome the 40 Committee and yet another enthusiastic U.S. ambassador *cum* campaign manager, yet another career viceroy named Graham Martin, covertly spent $10 million to swing the 1972 elections to the Christian Democratic party. It was a replica of the Chile scenario down to Martin threatening to have the embassy marine guards carry off the CIA station chief over the issue of controlling the black money. In Iraq, Kissinger and the CIA had recommended for Nixon's approval, in 1972, some $16 million in covert support for the rebellious Kurds fighting for autonomy against a leftist dictatorship in Baghdad. The support was requested at the behest of their client, the shah of Iran, who was then locked in a border squabble with Iraq and wanted to use the Kurds against the Iraquis. In the tangle of oil politics and Middle East maneuvering, the American intervention was only designed to weaken and distract the Iraquis—*not* as the CIA assured the Kurds, to sustain their struggle for independence. Holding the purse strings for their arms and ammunition, Kissinger had personally ordered the Kurds to refrain from attacking the Iraquis at a vulnerable moment during the October war.

When the shah and Iraq concluded a border agreement early in 1975 (the day after Kissinger announced a U.S.-Iranian trade pact calling for $22 billion of purchases in the United States), CIA support of the Kurds abruptly stopped, again at the whim of the shah. The Iraquis then moved on the Kurds, knowing the covert aid was gone, in a military offensive that nearly wiped out the rebels, including innocent civilians. As if to deliver the final blow, Washington refused humanitarian aid to the refugees from the slaughter. The Pike Committee footnoted the final, pathetic message from General Barzini, the Kurdish rebel leader, to the American government that had so generously, so cynically supported him. "Your Excellency," he wrote Henry Kissinger in a letter arriving March 10, 1975, ". . . our hearts bleed to see . . . the destruction of our defenceless people in an unprecedented manner. . . . We feel, Your Excellency, that the United States has a moral and political responsibility towards our people who have committed themselves to your country's policy." Months before, after his appointment as Secretary of State, Kissinger had charmed the press at San Clemente. "Do you prefer to be called Mr. Secretary or Dr. Secretary?" asked one of the claque. "I won't stand on protocol," he had answered them. "If you will just call me Excellency, it will be O.K." There were laughs all around in California in 1973; in 1975 there was no reply to Barzini's letter.

Of the several subjects investigated by the Pike Committee, however, one above all became the focus of the broader political discontent with Kissinger in Congress—the handling of the famous SALT negotiations. His "passion for secrecy" had plagued the accords, the committee found, and verification of the treaty was "hindered by arbitrary and inconsistent attempts to prevent leaks of SALT data." The congressional and public agitation over Kissinger's SALT policy grew with mounting emotion during 1975, soon to be encrusted with issues of trade, human rights, and a general devil theory of détente which fed political ambitions among the Democrats and revived comfortable old phobias in the Republican right. As Congress never quite seemed to understand in that debauchery of the debate, what Kissinger had achieved or surrendered with the Soviets was not so simple.

However controversial the SALT agreements, however hard to quantify what détente had provided or sacrificed in strategic weaponry, however limited or lax the first Moscow Treaty of May 1972, even its ardent critics like Senator Henry Jackson agreed that the agreement had saved a generation of weapons unbuilt and billions unspent. Under attack in 1976, Kissinger warned that if a new arms limitation were not concluded with the Soviets soon, Congress would be asked for an added $20 billion in strategic weapons. Probably conservative, his figure stood impressively against the Ford administration proposals to increase military spending by billions apart from the outcome of SALT II, or next to the "major savings" of $5 billion in the Pentagon budget loudly trumpeted by Democratic candidate Jimmy Carter.

In any event, most in Congress overlooked that the more important long-run advantage of SALT transcended specific dollar figures. In the course of those often tortuous negotiations, Washington (and the Politburo) had conducted the first systematic examination of the costs and benefits of the vast nuclear arsenals both nations had piled up since 1945. The bargaining for SALT—between the delegations in Helsinki and between Kissinger and the joint chiefs in the West Basement of the White House—had thrown desperately needed light on the bureaucratic inertia of the Pentagon, and in some sense changed how the United States was governed in matters of national security. Ironically, it was Kissinger's own new inertia, spawned by his vested interest in détente, that threatened to become the fatal flaw of SALT. A reformer for arms control in 1969–72, Kissinger by 1976 had become the beleaguered defender of his own record and orthodoxy in strategic issues. To gain the Moscow accords, he had used hard facts to battle the generals and admirals with their slanted intelligence and stubborn rationalizations. Now he was loath to reexamine, on the basis of other, equally hard facts, either his own misjudgments or his methods.

Three questions of possible Soviet violations came to torment the treaty, and Kissinger's response to each was evasive at best. Though

280]   UNCERTAIN GREATNESS

the treaty explicitly prohibited new land-based missile launchers, the Soviets in 1972–75 had built some 200 new III-X concrete silos. To congressional critics Kissinger accounted for the new silos as "command and control centers," though he did not explain why they should then have "blow-away" lids, the sort used to cap missile silos. Similarly, the 1972 ABM treaty provided that new test facilities would be located within existing ranges. Yet the Soviets proceeded in the following months to build a new ABM radar complex in Kamchatka, more than 3,000 miles from their own test range in Central Asia. By secret satellite reconnaissance intelligence, it was revealed that the Kamchatka radar was readily convertible into a full-fledged ABM site of the sort that SALT was precisely designed to rule out. Like the peculiar "command" silos, it was a breach of the spirit of the treaty, if not, as Kissinger argued, of its technical letter. Finally, and perhaps most seriously, since 1972 the Russians had steadily deployed the new SS-19 missile, which, according to CIA analysts, could carry more than double the payload SALT I was supposed to have frozen in limiting the number of "heavy" SS-9 missiles. But since the Soviets had never themselves defined "light" and "heavy" in the 1971–72 negotiations and afterward claimed the SS-19 was "light," Kissinger was forced to term the SS-19 an issue of "interpretation." The American position was to accept the deployment and try to limit the new missiles in SALT II. By the summer of 1976 the effort would be unavailing.

Added to those questions of Soviet compliance, related doubts about the singular Kissinger style in arms negotiations began to arise. Retired from the joint chiefs to run for the Senate in Virginia, Admiral Elmo Zumwalt complained to congressional committees that one-man diplomacy put Kissinger alone at the table with Soviet experts at critical moments in SALT I when the U.S. side needed its own technical specialists to judge the give and take. Kissinger's legendary secretiveness (matched, Zumwalt neglected to note, by Nixon's) had blinded U.S. intelligence analysts to important data flowing in the personal negotiations in SALT and put Kissinger himself in an "interesting position." "He had to review intelligence estimates prepared without access to data he had withheld," Zumwalt testified to the Senate Select Committee on Intelligence. "He then had to judge, if he could without being an expert intelligence analyst, how to compensate for these flaws, having in mind the information he had with-

held." Even allowing for the admiral's own biases and political ambitions, as well as Kissinger's intellectual virtuosity, the charge exposed
inherent weaknesses in the 1972 statesmanship. It was not only Kissinger's arrogance, of course, but also the style of the Nixon government of which Zumwalt, among others, was a part and even a central
beneficiary. (Chosen by Laird over several senior admirals to be chief
of Naval Operations, he had been approved by the White House as
a young officer unlikely to be Laird's lackey.) In a régime where the
White House frequently saw the Pentagon or State Department as
a more devious, dangerous adversary than either Moscow or Hanoi,
the compulsive secrecy that plugged leaks and gave Kissinger negotiating freedom also placed the SALT bargaining on a precariously
narrow base.

As SALT turned from bureaucratic revision to reality and became
very much Kissinger's personal achievement, the instruments and
techniques that had made it possible began to atrophy. By 1975, the
Verification Panel had become a rubber stamp for the Secretary of
State. The once independent systems analysis staff was a largely
forgotten appendage. It was the result of much the same bureaucratic seduction that had overtaken Kissinger in the war policy. With
a rising stake in the outcome of a policy, he had ceased to ask the
demanding questions. Willing believer in the military briefings from
Saigon because it had suited his purposes, he now became, no less
than any of the civil servants he despised, a chronic skeptic about any
military intelligence on SALT that threatened to sabotage further
agreement either in or out of the administration. Yet his motives
were certainly more than the mere vanity his worst critics saw in his
evasions. In 1975, as over the previous six years, he had calculated
that some Soviet shiftiness was minor compared to the larger goal of
keeping the talks going. It was the expedience of a man who saw the
insanity of the arms race clearer than any of the other lesser mad-
nesses of foreign policy, and it was the indelible mark of his statesmanship. His political mistake, as in the Cyprus crisis, was ultimately a domestic one. Amid the residue of public fear, suspicion, and
ignorance on strategic issues, any apparent "weakness" or laxity
would imperil the negotiations as surely as an insistence on harsh enforcement.

At the center of the SALT criticism, as of that of the nuclear arms
race, remained the old irrationality—that any of the imagined advan-

tages or disadvantages was little more than marginal when both the United States and the USSR possessed the capacity to incinerate one another, and poison most of the rest of mankind, many times over. In fact, in the willingness to adjust the two nations' nuclear arsenals, SALT had reduced tensions, perhaps lessened the chance of accident and miscalculation by giving each side a clearer strategic picture of the other, and encouraged those always fragile bureaucratic and political forces on both sides working to control the arms rivalry. At Vladivostok in November 1974—another, albeit smaller summit made possible by Kissinger's feverish back channel diplomacy—Ford and Brezhnev went further to agree tentatively to numerical ceilings both on strategic delivery vehicles and on MIRV missiles, setting the agenda for future negotiations.

But the basic fact of the mad rivalry remained unaffected by the SALT talks. No agreement, no item on the agenda, had threatened the U.S. forward-based nuclear forces in Europe and the Mediterranean that held the Russians within minutes of devastation. No treaty had yet halted the Pentagon's study of a new mobile M-X missile, twice as powerful as the Minuteman, or the development of the destabilizing cruise missile able to fly under radar and missile defenses to any target in the Soviet Union. No diplomacy by Henry Kissinger had affected the secret U.S. research on a wave of weaponry in the 1980s that would probably render SALT and its modest sanity obsolete. Research continued on future super submarines with more and much larger missiles than ever before; lasers were being developed to destroy the defenses and reconnaissance capabilities on which so much of the Moscow agreements rested; remotely piloted vehicles were being planned which would patrol constantly, elude radar, but which might also malfunction, launching an unintended attack. Research on electronic clouds went ahead, offering a new promise of defense, and thus reopening the old temptation for a preemptive strike. What no congressional critic dared charge in the successive celebration and inquisition of SALT was that it had achieved so very little. A decade late because of the political and bureaucratic paralysis of the Kennedy and Johnson administrations, limited and fitful even when Nixon and Kissinger applied extraordinary energy, intelligence, deception, and commitment to the task, the strategic arms negotiations left untouched the root balance of terror.

The criticisms which pounded Kissinger because of other aspects of détente—most notably, on the Soviet wheat deal of 1972–73 and on human rights in the Soviet Union—were similarly shallow and twisted. When the wheat sale aggravated an international grain shortage and drove up already inflated prices in the United States, many critics saw it all as another result of Soviet ruthlessness and American surrender. Although it may have been true that Kissinger was anxious to conclude the trade agreements of détente, the politics of food were not that simple, least of all inside the United States. Months before Kissinger went to Moscow in the summer of 1972, the Agriculture Department had considerable intelligence pointing to a worldwide decline in food reserves and a resulting unprecedented demand for American grain. Nevertheless, the Department decided to withhold from production some 62 million acres of farmland (about equal to the total acreage of the United Kingdom). After Kissinger's negotiations encouraging expanded trade, the Russians purchased 18 million tons of U.S. grain for $1.2 billion. The deal set off a buying panic in Europe and Japan. When it was over, U.S. agricultural reserves were exhausted and exports rose by nearly $5 billion. U.S. taxpayers subsidized one-third of the purchases and consumers paid an incalculable cost in grocery stores.

Why had the administration ignored the intelligence of foreign grain shortages and the likely effect of the Russian sale? "Butz didn't want to be known as a cheap-food man in an election year," an official said of the Secretary of Agriculture. Perhaps the telltale intelligence was buried in the Agriculture Department by a combination of bureaucratic incompetence and inertia. Obviously, neither explanation had much to do with Soviet scheming. In a system where intelligence was so easily bungled and the Agriculture Secretary saw himself as a champion of high prices for his constituency of client agribusinesses who profited from a tight market, bureaucratic advocacy had the same disastrous consequences as the imagined Communist conspiracy. Nor did détente account for the disarray of the American domestic food market and skyrocketing grocery prices. There the governing powers were the huge American grain companies that commanded the food industry from seed to shipping. Dominating the commodity exchanges in Chicago, New York, and other cities, only lightly policed by public regulation, the food barons largely shaped American agricultural policy toward consumers both abroad and at home. The system was attacked periodically, both by Congress and private groups, but it went on, and it was there, waiting for Kissinger's negotiation of the Soviet wheat deal. But many critics of détente—cherishing their simpler myth of shrewd Russians stealthily robbing our granaries—seldom appreciated how much the problem had been created by the exploitation of Americans by Americans.

Détente exposed with stark clarity a number of problems in American foreign policy, but it did not create them. Next to the food scandal, there was no more depressing evidence of that than the debate over human rights in the Soviet Union. U.S. pressure on the Russians through private diplomacy by Kissinger, as well as through congressional riders to various trade agreements, did bring some progress on Jewish emigration and caused occasional Kremlin restraint in the persecution of dissidents. More responsive to world opinion than ever before, the Soviets allowed the historic emigration of 130,000 Jews between 1972 and 1975. At the same time, Washington indulged in a notorious reticence on the subject, as well as in petty acts like the symbolic snub of Aleksandr Solzhenitsyn by President Ford in the summer of 1975—all obvious and self-defeating gestures to preserve the diplomatic niceties of détente. Again, however, it was more relevant to recognize that the record of U.S. diplomacy on behalf of human rights had been almost uniformly miserable, with no particular obeisance to the tyrants in Moscow. Many of the same critics and groups who ardently took up the cause of Soviet Jews and dissidents had seemed ignorant (or at least silent) when Kissinger and Nixon managed to overlook the genocide of a quarter million in Burundi, the ethnic slaughters in Iraq, Ethiopia, and Uganda, torture in Chile and Indonesia, not to mention South Vietnam and several other cases. If anything, official U.S. regard for human rights in the USSR, by dint of powerful public pressure, was generally greater than in similar outrages elsewhere after 1972. Such a comparison scarcely vindicated that on-again, off-again concern of the Nixon and Ford administrations with the human costs of the Soviet system. But few critics seemed to recognize that the surrender of principle or responsibility in foreign policy went well beyond détente.

In a larger sense, the critics were right for the wrong reasons. The visible strains caused by détente lay not in the principle of negotiation or relaxation of tension, but deep in the structure of American foreign policy. The fault lay with uncontrolled, unreformed institutions in American society: the military-industrial establishment with its vast stake in fat weapons budgets; public fear and apathy and cowed politicians; the domestic food market run with government complicity by a pervasive cartel of corporate giants; foreign policy bureaucracies in Washington whose status and survival and isolation from democracy bred a reflexive cynical disregard of ideals and human rights in international relations. Nixon and Kissinger had simply manipulated that system; they were part of it. Accepting the potency if not the letter of the strategic mythology, their ceaseless maneuver and deceit delivered the agreements only to make them suspect. In the end they so dominated the process, and so used the domination to personalize their power, that détente became hostage to their political fate. When the President destroyed himself, when the capricious media worm slowly turned for Kissinger, beginning with Cyprus and the Chile revelations, détente was bound to suffer, whatever the reality behind the politics. To a press and public long blinded to their real diplomacy and still largely oblivious to the issues dredged to the surface in détente, the problems suddenly seemed sinister, even a betrayal. What had been betrayed so directly, though, was the critics' own earlier fatuousness and naïveté. The congressional tempest over SALT and the other issues raged for a time, then faded away into ritual campaign rhetoric about "staying number one" and being "tougher" with the Russians. The policy of détente was generally no better understood, the flaws it had exposed no closer to reform, than before the disillusion set in. Though it was to endure in this half-light—no politician could reasonably dispense with its diplomatic and political rewards—détente was yet another casualty of Kissinger's furtiveness, the public ignorance it perpetuated, the nativist distrust it provoked.

The congressional revolt against Kissinger reached its high tide in the spring of 1975, during the final collapse in Indochina. Having earlier restricted U.S. bombing after the 1973 settlement, the Congress now refused to vote the emergency supplemental appropriations requested by Ford in a last vain, guilt-ridden effort to purchase a nation-state that did not exist in South Vietnam. The episode was sadly symbolic of so much of the past, and probably of the future, of

American foreign policy. Privately, Kissinger had assured Congress and the press that the 1973 accords, fortified by the Christmas bombing and the massive arms deliveries before the truce, had given Thieu the "decent interval" required by the original "honor" of the American commitment. The presence of the North Vietnamese troops in the South was, of course, the dominant reality. Weak and increasingly repressive in its rule, still shored up by a large U.S. official establishment in contravention of the agreement, the Thieu régime refused to negotiate a political settlement and matched Hanoi's military violations. When the 1975 spring offensive struck in the Central Highlands, neither Washington nor Saigon saw the shape of the threat or the final extremity of the South Vietnamese situation.

The daily conjunction of events in March and April told a story of the small country's agony and the great power's now plain indifference to what it had wrought. On March 8, Kissinger was in Aswan with Sadat; the next day, Hanoi opened the new front in the Highlands. On the twenty-fifth, Hue was abandoned; the next day, bitter at his failure with the Israelis, Kissinger pronounced the Middle East in "potentially grave danger." On April 9, the Ford White House confessed after congressional leaks that Nixon had given Thieu secret assurances in 1973 that the United States would retaliate against Hanoi for cease-fire violations; the next day, Ford asked Congress for almost $1 billion in aid to Thieu. On April 30 Saigon fell, the climax of a spectacle of frenzy and panic nearly unprecedented in modern military history. When Rogers had signed the Paris agreements in 1973, admiring reporters had asked Kissinger's office where the architect of the peace had been at the actual moment of the signing, the early hours of the morning in Washington. The reply sent back was typically fetching: "Making love not war." No one would think to ask where he was now, as Hanoi's tanks broke into the grounds of the presidential palace where he had told General Thieu in October 1972 about those last-minute details.

Still, there would be one last act of the old dash to make everyone feel better. Two weeks later, on a darkening May evening, Kissinger would stand silhouetted in his West Wing office and glance through the tall windows to notice that White House reporters on the driveway outside were watching him. To the amusement of his audience, as Hugh Sidey reported later, the Secretary of State pretended to lunge upward toward the window, shedding his coat in Clark Kent fashion before taking flight. The self-deprecation broke the tension as the Ford administration went through its own trial of force in Southeast Asia. On May 12, the Cambodian Communists had seized thirty-nine crewmen from the freighter *Mayaguez.* Two days later, shielded by fighters from the carrier *Coral Sea,* a company of marines went in, guns blazing, and the hostages came out safe. "Uncle Sam went out of Cambodia and slammed the door," explained James Reston with unconcealed chauvinism in *The New York Times.* A frustrated President had acted forcefully. The Congress, press, and public, all with mixed feelings about Viet Cong flags over Saigon, approved. But like the decade of U.S. intervention it closed, the *Mayaguez* incident was not what it seemed. Washington left Indochina in much the same fashion as it had gone there and stayed—in a policy of muddled, impulsive, and senselessly sacrificial acts.

Diplomatic notes requesting the crew's release had gone to Cambodia through Peking on May 12. Some thirty-six hours later, having written and broadcast a lengthy propaganda-laden rebuke, the Cambodians released the crew not under massive attack by American guns but rather because of a diplomatic decision. Yet the marines were ordered in the same afternoon Ford asked the UN to intercede, their assault beginning less than two hours before the planned release of the crew. Had Cambodia not already released the men, the raid might have backfired disastrously. Lower-level experts were excluded from the decisionmaking as usual, while Washington operated with no diplomatic intelligence on the new Cambodian régime. And for the umpteenth time in Indochina, from the Tonkin Gulf to the Tet offensive, American forces were committed to battle with fatally inaccurate military intelligence. A marine company landed on Tang Island in the Gulf of Siam expecting to rescue the crew, and found instead savage resistance. In Washington, the simplest command and control had failed—or was callously allowed to fail. Between the Pentagon's receipt of the news that the crewmen were returned and the presidential order to stop military action, there was a lapse of twenty-one minutes. During those twenty-one minutes the carrier planes bombed the Cambodian mainland. The bombing was obviously a punitive gesture, unrelated to the release or protection of the marines already mauled and retiring from the island. "The momentum of the operation was too strong," said one high official afterward in words redolent of August 1914.

The American casualties were thirty-eight dead and forty-nine wounded. There had even been thought, Kissinger later confided to reporters on his plane, of using B-52s to make the point. The new régime struck not as a last resort after exhaustive diplomacy, not in some genuinely informed calculus of the enemy's intentions or even the crew's whereabouts, but by a largely intuitive judgment that it had to. But the intended signal to other players in the credibility and prestige game—whether Arabs, Israelis, Koreans, Soviets, or Chinese, all of whom had to take a more precise view of events than the U.S. press and Congress—was not edifying. Washington's crisis diplomacy was seemingly uncoordinated and hypocritical, its military intelligence chronically flawed, its command and control unreliable, its escalation to bombing almost a reflexive resort. The *Mayaguez* incident presented some future adversary with the precedent of a diplomacy they could not trust and a military operation neither side could measure, the ingredients not of credibility but of catastrophe. "It did not help that much," a caustic official would say later, "that this time we had a President who was sober."

Under the waving flag, however, the Congress was suddenly mute and again uninterested in details. The new President had clearly violated the long-fought 1973 War Powers Act, which expressly obligated him to consult Congress "before introducing U.S. armed forces into hostilities. . . ." The *Mayaguez* incident not only laid bare the enduring folly in the executive's foreign policy but also the waning of the congressional rebellion. The majorities that had voted the war powers and anti-bombing legislation of 1973–74, and even the Turkish aid cut-off and CIA investigations, were fugitive. They were never so much anti-militaristic or anti-imperial in the sense of opposing the gunboat heroics of *Mayaguez*. The specter haunting most of the Congress was less arbitrary presidential foreign policy acts than the great *faux pas* committed in Vietnam: land embroilment in Southeast Asia. Once that danger had receded in the spring of 1975, for most congressmen the rest was relatively unimportant. Thus over the first half of the year there would be a quiet reversal of the Turkish aid suspension (though no "progress" had been made toward a Cyprus settlement). Potential Democratic presidential candidates like Senator Walter Mondale defected from support of the Mansfield amendment to cut troops in Europe or from opposition to the new B-1 bomber, and there began the familiar genteel co-opting of the Senate Select Committee on Intelligence. The Congress returned to its customary fear of taking even partial responsibility in foreign affairs. Like a surgeon opening the body to find it gnawed in a dozen dark places by a malignant growth, they would now simply close the wound over in fatigue, fright, and indifference, hoping the dark places would somehow not spread.

As with the congressional estrangement, the critical press clippings on Kissinger also trailed off by the summer of 1975, after *Mayaguez* and a new Arab-Israeli settlement dimmed memories of the winter and spring. But the souring had lasted just long enough to make the failure of the press in dealing with Henry Kissinger very nearly complete. Awash in the new clichés of debunking him, the media missed some of his more constructive initiatives as Secretary of State. One of the worst costs of journalism's six-year separate peace with "Henry" had been the aversion of both to economic issues. Yet in 1975, as the energy crisis and world famine made headlines, and Kissinger began at last to devote serious attention to economics, his new concern was no better reported or understood than his earlier neglect had been. In late May, for example, he gave two major speeches on the subject—one proposing a $1 billion world food reserve, the other delivering to Europeans a diplomatically touchy admonition to reform their domestic economics by developing alternative energy sources independent of Arab oil. The obscurity of the speeches was not just the result of editorial oversight. Stemming from heated bureaucratic battles within the régime to take economic policy away from Treasury and Agriculture, the speeches were a bid to establish Kissinger's political authority in an area he had never bothered to address, let alone control. His interest—and that bid— languished when media attention and the political response was so meager. The process was repeated in late June when, after constant clamoring from his aides for his attention and public commitment, he delivered what the State Department announced as a "very significant" speech to incoming FSOs. The address dealt with administrative reform. The heart of the reform was that State's regional bureaus, the traditional power base of the permanent bureaucracy, were to be divested of the financial resources and authority to make key assignments. That function was to go henceforth to a new task force directly under the Secretary. In a rough analogy to business politics, it was as if the headquarters management of a large chain had suddenly taken from local managers the power to hire, fire, and reassign their local personnel. However, as with the May economic speeches, the bureaucratic reform, its limits and potential significance, was largely ignored by the press. At least to have begun to discuss the enormous behind-the-scenes impact of personnel practices and budget control would have meant making a start to understand the shaping of foreign policy beyond Kissinger's personal drama, and perhaps to have spurred him to greater attention to the subject. But the "news" passed unnoticed, and the Secretary was soon back to the conduct of diplomacy with a handful of aides on the seventh floor, bureaucratic reform remaining a messy, unremarkable excursion.

The restructuring and rejuvenation of the State Department bureaucracy might have been one of his most important accomplishments. No Secretary of State entered office more acutely aware, both by intellect and experience, of the special paralysis of the Department and its foreign missions. No Secretary brought so much power and prestige, such presidential cachet from a Nixon who hated the bureaucrats. No Secretary possessed more freedom than Kissinger under Ford, who was uniquely in bondage to whatever Kissinger might have done to the Department. By any reckoning it was an extraordinary moment. But it was squandered. The unparalleled power was itself an obstacle. It gave him at once a small legion of enemies who had suffered the Department's eclipse under Rogers. It gave him, too, the capacity to run foreign policy from the larger paneled office in Foggy Bottom exactly as he had run it from the West Basement—in disregard and in spite of the bureaucracy. He would make his necessary alliances with the careerists, would bring in his own people at the highest levels, as he did with Eagleburger and Sonnenfeldt; would husband the memoranda and the cables and the meetings as before. It was in that familiar, closed world that his power was most secure, his presence most awesome, his manipulation by bluster, charm, and deception easiest.

His urge to control policy, and his success at it, determined that he would not have the time to reform the bureaucracy, or that he would not need to. But in the end it was also a matter of temperament. Even if he had somehow been given a respite from events, even if he knew the problem better than any of his predecessors, authentic reform would have required a different, wider mode of politics, from the bargaining among disparate groups in the Department to lobbying on Capitol Hill and elsewhere in Washington. It could not be managed by the whispered confidence or small meeting, or least of all by his personal acclaim. So he spurned the chore as he spurned such unruly democratic politics in the nation and world beyond. The century's most thoughtful and practically effective critic of bureaucracy in foreign affairs, Kissinger had no taste or skill to do more than suppress it.

In fact, he left the bureaucracy alive and well to bedevil the next régime. Kissinger had ceded the posts of Assistant Secretaries almost entirely to the career service, and at that often to men whose careers were veritable caricatures of the worst of the private compliance and public irresponsibility of the service. To the East Asian Bureau, and later to a higher post, for example, went Phillip Habib, whose earlier climb was distinguished by his work in charge of public information in Saigon. The African Bureau went to Nathaniel Davis, a stolid, dutiful bureaucrat who as Korry's successor in Chile had followed orders during the overthrow of Allende and the early infatuation with the junta. In the Economic Bureau was Thomas Enders, former deputy chief of the mission in Phnom Penh when it had cooperatively provided targeting for the secret B-52 strikes, as British writer William Shawcross discovered to his horrified disbelief, from an old 1:50,000 scale map that did not show new or relocated villages. To the Latin American job he nominated Harry Schlauderman, deputy to both Korry and Davis in Santiago, who was criticized for his selective congressional testimony on Chile. It was not that these men in particular were evil or incompetent, or should have been denied any responsibility in some new McCarthyesque purge. But their reward with coveted offices embedded in the bureaucracy precisely the values that made it so weak to resist bad policy from elsewhere, and so prone to make its own. While Kissinger—now their "Henry"—came and went in the Secretary's private elevator to the seventh floor, the bureaucracy endured.

His promotion of the bureaucrats in part purchased their neutrality in the new intramural politics he encountered in the Ford régime. Between the State Department and the White House the control was sure enough. The memoranda from Kissinger the Secretary of State went to Kissinger the Presidential Assistant in the guise of General Scowcroft, even after Ford formally divested Kissinger of the White

House title late in 1975. The independent NSC staff that once had challenged the bureaucracy and asked unwanted questions now disappeared, becoming a rubber stamp for whatever flowed by the Secretary's design or neglect from the State Department. Beyond that, the rivalry between cabinet officers was once again fierce. In Schlesinger at the Pentagon he finally faced a cabinet adversary of comparable intellect and deviousness if not ultimate political skill. Through 1975 Schlesinger waged an unremitting bureaucratic attack on SALT, in which he allied himself with the joint chiefs as Laird never had. Inside the government as outside it, the attacks on Kissinger came from the right. Unlike earlier rivals, Schlesinger for a time made skillful use himself of the media, drawing out from the Washington *Post* or *The New York Times* those competitors to "Henry's" reporters or editors who perhaps saw more clearly the perils of the next SALT agreement or the dangers in the "arbitrary" authority of the Secretary of State. By the close of 1975, however, Kissinger would be bureaucratically rescued by Schlesinger's too public squabble with Ford on the Defense budget and in large part by his own sustained relationship with the new President. From the outset his position *vis-à-vis* Ford was unprecedented in modern American politics. Even at its lowest point his stature in the press, public, and Congress far surpassed the President's. Virtually Ford's first act as President had been to assure Kissinger's continuity in the new administration. The inevitable sniping from the Ford White House staff, and the equally inevitable private Kissinger disdain for the other men around the President, began soon in the régime, and reached its peak, along with the public and congressional criticism, midway in 1975. But the political and personal realities never altered. Ford entered the foreign affairs responsibilities of the presidency as the epitome of the uninformed, unprepared, expert-awed American politician, all with the added burden of being the unknown, unelected successor to the most corrupt administration in memory. Without a sense of his own independent position in foreign policy, or the need for a fresh, independent adviser and staff to shape it, Ford found Kissinger indispensable in appearance and fact. Though the quality of their personal relations was very different from Kissinger's with Nixon—with Ford he felt an obvious warmth, candor, and ease—the random concentration of power continued to corrupt American policy.

The old influences in new garb came together vividly in the régime's major blunder in Angola in the last half of 1975. Seeing his own authority and the larger executive prerogative in foreign policy at stake after the congressional assaults earlier in the year, prodded by tests of manliness and Russophobia from Schlesinger and the chiefs, and full too of his *Mayaguez* triumph, Kissinger seized upon the Portuguese departure from Angola and the jockeying for post-independence power. The story would have everything: CIA clients who could not fight; 40 Committee agendas loaded by both the CIA and Kissinger (each, of course, for their own reasons) toward intervention; the dissent and eventual quiet resignation of African Assistant Secretary Davis, who got the job because he was "Henry's" man, was ignored because Kissinger knew he did not know Africa, and resigned to protect his career, as one official put it, from "one Chile too many." The 40 Committee voted the millions. The supine White House staff passed along the recommendation to Ford, who approved it. And "Henry's" men quietly passed on the news to certain senior congressional figures who likewise approved it, without bothering to tell their less deserving colleagues. So the dollars poured into Angola, provoking the Soviets to arm their more capable clients. The war went badly, the covert subsidies finally leaked into *The New York Times* from traveling senators and disgruntled bureaucrats, and the unconsulted majority of the Senate voted in December to prohibit further covert aid to Angola. More than $30 million, more abandoned clients, and a part of the administration's meager prestige was left behind in the bush of southern Africa.

But sordid as it was, revealing the *deus ex machina* of Henry Kissinger and a government-wide system in which policy flowed from impulse and bureaucratic self-interest, Angola was only another untoward interlude. The more telling development was the final atrophy over the following months of the Senate and House Intelligence committees. The Pike Committee Report would be officially suppressed by Congress, to be published only by means of a celebrated leak. The Church Committee drafted its final report, obligingly deleted its most shocking revelations on a point-by-point censorship by the CIA, and disbanded in favor of a permanent oversight committee composed of many of the same senators who accepted the original co-option. By the spring of 1976, there would be no effective public or congressional power to balance Kissinger's continuing dominance of policy, or the similar dominance of his successors.

After nearly eight years in control of foreign policy, there still seemed little sense in Washington or in the nation at large in 1976 of the ingredients of his success or his abuses, little understanding of just how rare were his brilliance and independence in American government, how dangerous his unchecked power given the weakness and mediocrity of the government and presidents he commanded. Perhaps the final irony was that in a sense the survival of his achievements, if not his reputation, would depend upon the rest of his countrymen seeing all these facts clearly at last, knowing the secrets he had tried so hard to keep from them.

Epilogue

It is Washington, at the leaden end of summer 1976, Jimmy Carter, an obscure but ambitious Southern politician, is challenging Gerald Ford in a typically deceitful campaign for the presidency. As part of the ritual hoax, each candidate, by his own fears and calculations of image, tries to pretend that Richard Nixon never existed. More important than this quadrennial sham, however, is the fact that Henry Kissinger is drawing to the close of his historic autocracy in American foreign policy.

Kissinger is practicing his parting diplomacy this summer on unlikely ground—southern Africa. The professor who put "something in it for the jigs," who puzzled over the Ibos of Biafra being both gifted and "more negroid," now shuttles back and forth to Pretoria and Salisbury and Dar Es Salaam to negotiate a peaceful transition to black majority rule in Rhodesia. His new concern is protean but serious enough. In the mounting danger of a full-scale race war he sees the prospect of Soviet gains that will jeopardize détente and have a dangerous, unpredictable impact of white-black violence on U.S. domestic society. Justice is now clearly in the national interest as he defines it. And for a moment the old mystique seems to work. Amid the cynicism and hypocrisy on both sides, the folly of "tar baby" is swiftly forgotten; the morally brazen new American mediation is accepted, as similar diplomacy is accepted in the Middle East, because it serves the purposes of the protagonists. But the diplomacy

soon peters out, sapped by the same forces that have so long marked
Washington's policy in southern Africa. In the client-obsessed State
Department bureaucracy, which has regarded postings in the white-
ruled countries with a cryptic suspicion, there is still no authentic
sensitivity or sophisticated knowledge of the history, fears, and convictions that shape both sides and their relationships with one another. Nor is there a wider readiness in the administration to confront the vast American corporate interests or the cozy CIA liaison
with South Africa that have always quietly mocked the official public
disapproval of the racist régimes. So Kissinger dickers with the cor-
nered whites and the wary blacks, makes acrid jokes about their
common stupidity and manias much as he joked about the Arabs,
Israelis, and Russians, and leaves the parties with an ambiguous formula that seems near acceptance but under closer attention evapo-
rates.

In any case, the effort appears to redeem the earlier débâcle in
Angola. At an earlier stage it serves to remove Kissinger from Washington while he is under savage political attack from the Republican
right in the primary campaigns. Yet the southern African diplomacy
also symbolizes in a larger sense the limits of Kissinger's statesmanship. After one negotiating session in Pretoria, an American aide, a
veteran of Kissinger's shuttles, compares the South African whites
with the Israelis in their profound sense of ethnic vindication and
siege. Yes, remarks another diplomat wistfully, both peoples are a
little like Henry Kissinger himself at this late point—"self-confident,
gifted, everything on their side but history."

Kissinger's magic in the past has been to exploit and knit together
deeper national interests already present: an opening to a fearfully
isolated Peking, détente with the straining Soviets, the final tortuous
ratification of Hanoi's earned victory and Washington's accepted
defeat in Indochina, the marriage of Arab pride and Israeli humility
after the October 1973 war. These were classically tasks of diplomacy, problems of frontiers and sovereignty and military restraint
that lay within the power of governments (if not always their will) to
resolve among themselves. The settlements are incomplete and fragile, but as the diplomat who drew out their possibilities, Kissinger's
place in history seems impressive. The sad and ominous irony is that
just as he has come to grips at last with these realities, other, quite
different crises are already breaking over him. Beyond the ordering

of new boundaries or the military disengagement of new powers, he is suddenly confronted with the equally complex and dangerous problems of resource scarcities, inflation, harsh disparities in wealth and technology and a staggering list of related perils.

It is not only that Kissinger is bored by economics or that all of this has become too much for one man. As the outgrowth of domestic politics of nation-states, such problems are largely out of the reach of conventional diplomacy even to address, let alone remedy. The great power condominium conceived and contrived by Kissinger may be able to settle more traditional disputes between societies, but it has little capacity to affect the crises embedded within those societies.

The forces now threatening international disaster on so many fronts are, in a sense, too basic. The food crisis is not a diplomatic problem, somehow relieved by a bargain in Rome or Geneva. Famine has grown largely out of private market monopolies in the rich countries and land-tenure injustices in the hungry nations—both conditions deeply rooted in local economics and politics, and both changed only by drastic internal reforms no diplomacy can bring. Nor can governments talk away, even if they dared, the rising affluence in western Europe, the Soviet Union and Japan, which also consumes dwindling food production.

Similarly, there are no diplomatically negotiable answers to the intricate industrial needs of Europe and Japan that leave them both mortally hostage to foreign oil suppliers. Only enormous technological and cultural change within those societies can alter that bondage. Foreign policies cannot correct the peculiar disproportions in the British and Italian economies, or modernize uncompetitive American industries, or relieve inflation and unemployment in the wealthy countries, or surmount the profound resistance to population control in poor countries, where the birth rate threatens to swamp mankind. No external force can stay for long the swelling wave of violent change inside Latin American societies riven by privilege and want. For much the same reasons, Kissinger's diplomacy does not now determine the fate of southern Africa, where internal influences of economics and the psychology of race are decisive.

It has become a cliché after Vietnam that America lacks the power to control much of what happens in the world. The more important point now is that the most serious international problems surpass the power of any régime or diplomatic combine of régimes, mainly because the solutions might endanger the existence of the very governments involved. Only after a radical reordering of domestic arrangements will diplomats be able to come together again creatively to certify the new international arrangements based on whatever emerges—much as Kissinger helped the world come to terms with the Russian and Chinese revolutions. It seems unavoidable that Henry Kissinger will be a casualty in this historical turning, and he senses the gathering powerlessness of his art. It was, after all, the pervasive domestic forces of industrialization and nationalism that tore apart the elaborate nineteenth-century European diplomatic condominium he has tried to copy. In the end, the most telling criticism of the Kissinger achievement will not be that it was often inhuman and devious, but rather that it was too largely irrelevant.

As he departs, even the successes of Kissinger's conventional diplomacy seem hostage to the hatreds he has sought to heal. In a final swing through the Middle East, he hears President Assad of Syria confidently predict the eventual abandonment of Israel by an oil-hungry West. "We can wait," Assad says quietly in seeing him out. "We can wait."

Still, his achievements in Peking and Moscow, the tempering of suicidal isolation and hostility among the world's most powerful states, will endure. Whatever its stripe, however inept by comparison, the next administration will strive to emulate and expand that diplomacy. His statesmanship is now as much a part of American foreign policy as was the opposite cold war madness a decade before. So in Washington, even in this last faded summer of his reign, Kissinger stands alone. No American representative since Benjamin Franklin has reached his grasp. No politician surpasses his public stature. No other statesman, no possible successor eclipses his presence. In his apparent brilliance and virtuosity he is the standard by which diplomats are to be measured for years to come. Asked who his heroes are, he has answered Franklin Roosevelt, Churchill, De Gaulle. They are figures of moment to match his lofty vision of himself, men worthy of his service. But the reality has always been harsher than the appearance or the vision. He has not been Roosevelt's Secretary of State or De Gaulle's Foreign Minister; he has been Richard Nixon's.

Pity has come late to Kissinger's view of the fallen President who made possible the glory. Nixon was an "unpleasant" man, Kissinger is overheard telling guests at a Canadian state dinner late in 1975. It is a tame echo of the disgust and contempt he has often felt and expressed. Yet there has always been the other Nixon, the Nixon who heeded him, elevated him, and ultimately spared him by taking the brunt of public responsibility for an evil and malice they shared no less than their success. It is hard to imagine men more bedeviled by political vices and virtues, so capable at once of wisdom and ignorance, of courage and weakness. Journalistic folklore will have it in the hoary cliché of vapid ruler and strong adviser. It was never so simple. Now Kissinger had already begun to fumigate his files, to remove those telling phone transcripts. The aide who was hired to have them ready to leave fast in 1969 should the "Gestapo" force him out, will now assemble them for lucrative memoir-writing. But no erasure of the past can blot out their common outrages, from the Cambodian bombings to the taps to the squalor of later policies in Bangladesh and Chile. No memoir can change the truth that these men were, in historian Christopher Lasch's powerful indictment, "fatally removed from American life."

And yet, for all of Henry Kissinger's compromise and expedience, it is frightening to think of another man, of any of the establishment figures before or after him, facing Nixon and that government. The sodden nights, the numberless humorings and deflections, the curbing of impulse where it might have set in motion some ultimate atrocity—there is no easy balance sheet on the cost or the savings. Equally disturbing is how it all happened to begin with. For Nixon the responsibility is clear; he was elected. That Kissinger was beside him, or at the other end of the phone, was a caprice of history.

We might ask, as Kissinger leaves, what lies ahead for the men who constituted the Nixon régime, who did its daily work in foreign affairs. William Rogers will return to his lucrative Manhattan law practice, Melvin Laird will proceed to a Reader's Digest sinecure of elder Republican statesmanship, Joseph Sisco to the presidency of a Washington, D.C., college. Flexible as always, Elliot Richardson will adorn the new Carter Administration as Ambassador At Large to negotiate law of the sea issues. And back in the uniform he wore so long and so notably, Alexander Haig has been named Supreme Commander of NATO, his dutiful reward from a grateful Ford Administration. But Richardson and Haig will hardly be alone in the continuity of foreign policy officialdom. Of the old 1969 NSC Staff, many will return in the "new" Carter régime: Harold Saunders as a senior aide in the State Department, Richard Moose as Eagleburger's successor as Deputy Under Secretary for Administration, Anthony Lake as Director of Policy Planning at State, Fred Bergston as an Assistant Secretary of the Treasury. And throughout prestigious positions in State and the Pentagon remain bureaucrats who watched, and served, in silence. Don McHenry, once one of Rogers's close aides drawn from the UN group at State, will become a Deputy Ambassador to Andrew Young at the United Nations. "I understand you people hire everybody I fire," Kissinger reportedly jested with President-elect Carter and Vice President-elect Mondale at a preinaugural briefing. As usual, for the country at least, it is not the joke it seems.

As Kissinger retires, his paradoxical role recalls what Winston Churchill once said of Lenin and Russia; that the worst misfortune was his coming, the next worse—his leaving. For Kissinger bequeaths power to a provincial, mediocre establishment that has survived its past folly by public amnesia and indifference. The second-rank (and second-rate) men who staffed the folly of the 1960s, the spilling of so much blood, the wasting of money and public honesty, will return in their numbers under Jimmy Carter—survivors, as they hoped and maneuvered, of the disasters blindly blamed on only the handful of Rusks, Rostows, and Bundys at the top. Vance is Secretary of State; another Pentagon alumnus, Harold Brown, runs Defense; Humphrey's old adviser, Zbigniew Brzezinski, is at the White House—and on runs the establishment list. Kissinger was distinct in quality (if not perhaps in kind) from that élite. The distinction is crucial. Moreover, he leaves them confronting the old vexing problem they could never master, the unreformed, ever-unrepentant bureaucracy. Kissinger will be gone, truly replaced by other lesser men. Yet the images of the institution remain, changed by name only: a Korry anguishing over methods of influencing a régime in Chile, a Melady pausing as the corpse-laden trucks roll by his embassy in the night, a Truehart agonizing about the lying in Saigon only to preside over more in Lagos, a Blood meeting with his staff to send one last honest cable to Foggy Bottom, knowing his career may be at stake. Kissinger's dictatorship in foreign policy has been cruel and repressive and wasteful.

It has allowed much of the worst of the system to continue. Unless the foreign policy bureaucracies are genuinely and sweepingly reformed, however, no American statesmanship worth the name will be possible without command and control very like what he has practiced.

In the summer of 1976 that change is still unlikely to come from the usual sources of power and influence. The press and Congress watch the campaign, prepare to greet the soiled, unimaginative men of the new administration, with the same stunning superficiality and co-option they have displayed under Kissinger.

No one would be able to work that change so well, in fact, as Henry Kissinger himself. His command of public respect is still awesome, a formidable political weapon for a former professor with few readers, and nowhere is the proof stronger than in the early record of his successors. In its first months in power, the nervous new Carter government has spoken out uncertainly on human rights while avoiding any tangible action of enforcement, hurrying to negotiate in the Middle East or Moscow without bureaucratic discipline at home or success abroad, straining to show its *ersatz* candor with the Congress and public—all in a self-conscious, sometimes silly effort to exorcise the pudgy, slightly accented ghost whose fame it covets and seems scarcely to understand. His flaws hidden, ignored, misunderstood, excused, Kissinger takes from his celebrated tenure the rare power to educate, to tell the truths behind the phony veil and, most of all, to be heeded. He can, if only he chooses, write the books and make the speeches, embody the opposition which might truly free his countrymen of the myths and misgovernment which he and others before and now after have so long exploited. The opportunity is not academic. If the old foreign policy system persists, as he well knows, it will not only bury the worst but also devour the best of what he has done with his life. For the fatal danger to the achievements of his secret diplomacy is the public distrust and insensibility that flourishes in secrecy, along with the malignant habits of government in foreign affairs. Enlightenment will demand extraordinary gifts and authority, and for the moment at least, he has both. Yet it may be the final irony of his flawed and ironic public service that the model which haunts him here too is still Richard Nixon. For truly to protect and preserve his accomplishments from bureaucratic attrition, establishment incompetence and public prejudice, he must transform and transcend *his* politics much as Nixon turned from Red-baiter to the negotiator of détente.

If Kissinger's statesmanship is to survive for long, the zealot for secrecy must become the advocate of openness, the master of bureaucratic maneuver, the proponent of bureaucratic reform, the seducer of the press and Congress the critic of every such seduction, the practitioner of ruthless *Realpolitik* the champion of a new humanity in American foreign policy. The change is unlikely. But the stakes are awesome. If he can negotiate this final passage, his country's greatness—and his own—will be far less uncertain.

Index